CRISES IN FOREIGN POLICY
A SIMULATION ANALYSIS

AN ADVANCED STUDY IN POLITICAL SCIENCE

Written under the auspices of the
Center of International Studies, Princeton University.

CRISES IN
FOREIGN POLICY

A Simulation Analysis

Charles F. Hermann
Princeton University

The Bobbs-Merrill Company, Inc.
Indianapolis and New York

James A. Robinson
The Ohio State University
Consulting Editor

Published for
Center of International Studies
Princeton University

JX 1417
H46

To the Simulation Staff

Geoffrey Belisle
Tom Dodegge
Dale Dupree
Peter Grazis
Melody Heaps
Juliana Kane
Bob Levin
Roger Majak

Penny Martin
Mike McGuire
Grant McKernie
John Merriman
Thomas Morr
John Olsen
Carol Price
Richard Ramsdell

Ellen Robbins
Mary Dow Robechek
Andrea Schlanger
Allen Sherman
Marilyn Snow
Susan Sullivan
Alan Wyner

ACKNOWLEDGMENTS

These acknowledgments serve two purposes. First, they attempt to express my appreciation to the many people who contributed so greatly to this research undertaking. Second, they give the reader who may be unfamiliar with simulation research some indication of the manpower that such an enterprise may demand. The acknowledgments demonstrate the latter point with greater clarity than could be done by a general statement elsewhere in the text.

Project Michelson at the U. S. Naval Ordnance Test Station, China Lake, California, sponsored this research under Contract N123(60530)-32779A. As head of the project at that time, Thomas W. Milburn not only funded the research but also expressed interest in it and offered ideas. The contract involved two other researchers—James A. Robinson, the principal investigator, and Margaret G. Hermann, my wife.

Authors who are married usually reserve acknowledgment of their spouses until last. Without casting aspersions on the merits of this practice, I want to change the procedure, in this instance, to dramatize better the extent of my indebtedness to her. My wife carried out her own psychological study in the simulation as well as assuming a major portion of the administrative matters, training observers, worrying over the innumerable details of running a simulation, sharing my problems, and helping in countless other ways during the period of writing.

Other than my wife, no person is as deserving of credit and appreciation for assisting in this undertaking as is my co-investigator, James

Robinson. After he conceived the project to study decision making in times of crisis, his activities ranged from working on the research design to directing, for eleven weeks, the simulated nations manned by members of the staff. His constructive criticism and enthusiastic encouragement single him out as a valued personal friend as well as an astute dissertation advisor.

When the project was executed, all three of the investigators were associated with the International Relations Program at Northwestern University. The members of that Program—faculty and students alike—contributed to the development of this research, even to the point of rescheduling their weekly meeting in order not to interfere with our simulation activities. I wish especially to thank two men who, during that period, served as able co-directors of the International Relations Program—Richard C. Snyder and Harold Guetzkow. Richard Snyder is the intellectual mentor for the decision-making approach which this study attempts to pursue, and he pioneered the interest in crisis as an occasion for studying decision. Harold Guetzkow, of course, is responsible for the Inter-Nation Simulation. More than that, however, he captured my imagination with his approach to politics.

This book was written after I came to Princeton University, and here, also, various parts of the University community provided critical services. The Center of International Studies, under the directorship of Klaus Knorr, made research time available and provided secretarial service for the preparation of the manuscript. The Princeton University Computer Center and the Office of Survey Research and Statistical Studies generously provided access to their equipment.

Valuable suggestions were made by those who read an earlier draft of the manuscript. Aside from Harold Guetzkow and James Robinson, this task—so basic to the preparation of any book—was performed by Kenneth Janda at Northwestern, Richard Brody at Stanford, and Stanley Kelley and Walter Murphy at Princeton. Several chapters reflect Harold Sprout's comments, since a number of lively exchanges were conducted with him over various aspects of the manuscript. Although none of these individuals bears responsibility for the quality of the final product, each has influenced the author's thinking on many of the issues presented. A special word of thanks goes to Mrs. Norma Johnson for her skill in typing the final draft and to Robert Cantor, Michael Gehret, and Arthur Holden for their work on the numerous tables and citations.

Next, I would like to acknowledge an essential group, the 325 petty officers in the United States Navy who served as willing and able simulation participants during the period they were stationed at Great Lakes Naval Training Center. Their help in the project was made possible through the generous cooperation of Captain E. G. Sanderson, Mr. J. F. Peterman, Captain S. E. Watson, and our extremely efficient weekly coordinator, Chief David Oliver.

Finally, tribute must be given the simulation staff. These 23 students (all but two of them were students at Northwestern University at the time) either assisted in the operation of the simulation for eleven weeks or coded the data and punched it on cards in the months that followed. Twelve of their number volunteered for the operation as well as the analysis and they have a unique perspective on the total project. Some of the staff work was exciting, much more of it was dull, but all of it demanded commitment and patience. To the staff goes much of the credit for the low between-run variance, for the low rate of missing data, and for the high inter-coder reliabilities. For these contributions and many others which they cheerfully made, this book is dedicated to the simulation staff.

Charles F. Hermann
Princeton, New Jersey

CONTENTS

TABLES

FIGURES

INTRODUCTION

The laboratory setting for the simulation study of crisis this book describes is in striking contrast to the situations in the capitals of the world where policy makers struggle with the critical problems of international politics. Nevertheless, the objective of this research is to increase our systematic knowledge of international crises. How much can simulations increase our understanding of actual international affairs? This question can have no satisfactory answer until a series of studies that use the technique are available for evaluation. The present examination of crisis is one such investigation.

Although the primary data of this study came from a simulation of international politics, the first chapter is devoted to accounts of two crises in foreign policy that involved the United States. One led to the decision to defend South Korea in 1950, and the other led to the decision to force the removal of offensive missiles from Cuba in 1962. These two situations help to define crisis and help to illustrate numerous hypotheses that the research investigates. Before reviewing the Korean and Cuban crises, however, a brief description of the framework that guided the reconstruction of these situations as well as the design of the simulation is required.

That framework, or approach, is decision making. Like any approach to politics, decision making provides a focus or orientation. The decision-making analysis puts order into the disparate elements of politics by advancing organizing concepts and by identifying fundamental processes.

Although many alternative formulations of decision making have been advanced, certain basic properties can be specified for any conscious choice. Fundamental is the individual or aggregation of individuals who are decision makers. The task begins with the individual's awareness that a decision is needed. This is often, but not always, triggered by some recent change in his environment. Before there can be a choice, the individual or group must identify one or more alternative responses. When only one alternative or option is perceived, the choice is between adopting it, searching for further alternatives, or doing nothing. Regardless of the number of options, if the choice between them is not made at random, then the individual or group considers the possible consequences or outcomes that may result from each alternative. When an alternative has more than one possible outcome, the decision maker estimates the likelihood that a given outcome will occur. (Normally, this is not a process involving the calculation of exact probabilities. In a bargaining situation, for example, it may be simply the judgment that a given action is more likely to lead to a concession from another negotiator than it is to increase his resistance to any agreement.) Before choosing, the decision maker must determine which outcome(s) is most desirable with regard to his goals or the goals of those persons he represents. Of course, a complete analysis of the decision-making process cannot end with the selection of an alternative, for the task of executing the decision remains. Finally, the decision maker perceives feedback from his decision which may create a need for a further decision.

A person confronted with a decision will seldom be aware of undertaking the described set of activities. In some instances, the decision is so routine that it requires only a moment between the emergence of the problem and the decision. If a person has faced the same problem repeatedly, he feels he knows the appropriate response without reexamining the bases for his choice. Considerations other than the routine ones may make this description inaccurate in a particular case. In a formal organization some steps will be performed by different organizational units with the result that various groups or agencies will see themselves not as decision makers, but only as advisors, information gatherers, and so forth. Despite these difficulties, the generalized description of the decision-making process introduces some of the basic variables—alternatives, search, outcomes, goals—that are salient for a decision-making analysis of foreign policy.

In examining foreign policy decision making, considerable attention must be given to the conditions which influence the policy makers. For example, we might ask: Is the decision made in the field by the ambassador and embassy staff, or is it considered by the foreign ministry and other departments in the capital? How wide and at what level is the participation in making the decision? Under what conditions are subordinates rewarded or reprimanded for proposing innovations in policy? What individuals and agencies must be consulted in forming the decision? Do the involved individuals view the problem as similar to issues they have previously experienced? If this is true, was their response to solving the earlier problem(s) successful? Moreover, what are the individual characteristics, styles, and values of those persons who will make the decision?

Expressed in more general terms, these questions introduce the organizational roles and relations, the communication and information patterns, the participants' definition of the situation, and the personalities of the decision makers. Frequently these features must be examined in order to explain what alternatives are considered and what outcomes are regarded as desirable. In other words, to apply decision-making analysis to the conduct of foreign policy, the complex setting in which choices are made must be added to the basic properties associated with any choice process. It is unlikely that all these clusters of decision-making variables will be equally important in accounting for a given kind of decision. Certain properties, like organizational characteristics, may be more important under some conditions than others.

In the enlarged conceptualization of the decision-making process, one important element is the occasion for decision, that is, the nature of the situation that the policy maker sees will require a choice. Not only may the nature of the situation have a direct influence on the decision, but also it will influence which other variables in the decision-making framework are important. Of course, almost all decision-making entities confront various kinds of situations. Yet, one of the distinguishing characteristics of organizations that deal with foreign policy is the extremely diverse situations which they continuously face.[1] What impact do variations in the situation have on formulating foreign policy? This question can be cast another way: Can we identify different occasions for decision so that each set of situations makes certain types of decision making more or less likely?

"One can hope to learn from experience," Kenneth Waltz suggests, but he adds, "and yet in international relations, it must be expected that each succeeding experience will be novel."[2] When considered in exhaustive detail, every foreign policy situation is unique. For any analysis such as decision making, however, attempts are made to abstract salient features which a particular situation shares with a number of others. In everyday life this practice is common; otherwise, we would find it painfully difficult to cope with even the simplest event. Based on certain shared features, we establish classes of situations in daily affairs (e.g., baby crying, guests arriving, boss demanding) which call for certain kinds of responses. If we can correctly recognize a new situation as an instance of a general set of situations, we can avoid past mistakes or employ responses that have proven successful. In examining the affairs of nations, the task is similar, although, of course, more complex. We need to identify classes of situations which are associated with different kinds of decision making and policies.

In developing systematic knowledge, not just any classification of foreign policy situations will do. Classification arrangements are required that will allow any competent observer to determine whether a given situation is a member of a specified set. Once the situation has been classified, this information also must enable us to increase our knowledge about the likelihood of various kinds of behavior. In short, the classification must lead to testable hypotheses that relate the type of foreign policy situation to how the decision will be made and what it will be.

Crisis is one potential class of situations. This term has been used to characterize recurrent critical events in international politics. In its present form, however, crisis is loosely applied to describe any "hot

---

[1] R. C. Snyder, H. W. Bruck, and B. Sapin, eds., *Foreign Policy Decision Making* (New York: Free Press, 1962), p. 104.

[2] K. N. Waltz, "Electoral Punishment and Foreign Policy Crises," in J. N. Rosenau, ed., *Domestic Sources of Foreign Policy* (New York: Free Press, 1967), p. 281.

spot" in world affairs. The concept has no accepted meaning. Although crises are generally held to have a major impact on decision making, unless a precise definition is used, we cannot be confident that similar decision processes are the result of similar situations.

The problem of defining crisis introduces one of the two broad objectives of this book. First, the research provides an investigation through simulation of a macro hypothesis. The hypothesis contends that when crisis is defined in a manner to be stipulated, a pattern of decision making occurs which is not found if any of the crisis properties are absent. Second, the book investigates the use of simulation to explore a series of more specific or micro hypotheses about the effects of crisis on the decision process. The first two chapters are concerned with the definition of crisis. Chapter 1 reviews two decisions made by the United States government that have been described as crises. The following chapters make repeated references to both of these decisions—the decision to resist the invasion of South Korea in 1950, and the decision to blockade Cuba after the introduction of long-range missiles in 1962. In Chapter 2, a review of various definitions of crisis and the characteristics of the Korean and Cuban decisions provide the basis for the proposed definition of crisis. After the independent variable of the study has been defined in the second chapter, Chapter 3 presents the simulation and research design. This chapter explains how 325 Navy petty officers acted as national decision makers in eleven separate trials of the simulation with each run containing the same set of crisis situations. A discussion of the reactions of these simulated governments, as they pertain to 26 hypotheses about crisis decision making, constitutes the next three chapters.

Exploration of these individual hypotheses fulfills one of the book's intended purposes. The combined results of all these hypotheses provide information for the other purpose: a definition of crisis. In Chapter 8, the simulation participants' responses to situations that have all the specified characteristics of a crisis are compared to their reactions to situations that have only some of the stipulated properties of a crisis. When these results are accumulated for all 26 hypotheses, the macro hypothesis —the proposed definition of crisis—is evaluated.

Chapter 1

TWO CRISIS DECISIONS

The Cuban Missile Crisis[1]

Shortly before 9:00 Tuesday morning, October 16, 1962, McGeorge Bundy, President Kennedy's Special Advisor on National Security Affairs, entered the living quarters of the White House. He confronted the President with photographic evidence of Soviet missiles discovered in a reconnaissance flight over the San Cristobal area of Cuba which had been made less than 48 hours earlier. On several previous occasions, the President had publicly warned that if offensive missiles were emplaced in Cuba, "the gravest issues would arise."[2] Now he possessed proof of the missiles' existence.

Undoubtedly, the President perceived the Soviet missiles as a major threat to the United States. The Soviet Union would, first of all, achieve(1) an immediate psychological victory by placing offensive weapons so

---

[1] This narrative and the one on the Korean decision are not intended to be exhaustive accounts. Instead they illustrate some of the processes which we will hypothesize occur in crisis situations. In addition to the sources cited, the account of the Cuban decision draws on several interviews which the author had with individuals who participated in that decision. Although these respondents must remain anonymous, their assistance is gratefully acknowledged.

[2] D. L. Larson, *The "Cuban Crisis" of 1962* (Boston: Houghton Mifflin, 1963), p. 3.

close to America and its allies in the Western Hemisphere. Chairman Khrushchev would acquire a lever with which he could engage in political bargaining with the President on Berlin or other East-West issues. Although such relatively unprotected missiles would be unlikely to significantly alter the strategic balance between the Soviet Union and the United States, the military implications could not be dismissed. When combined with those from offshore submarines, the missiles in Cuba would provide the Soviet Union with a first-strike nuclear capability against which there would be extremely short warning. Moreover, John F. Kennedy may very well have felt a sense of betrayal. Repeated assurances that the Soviets had no intention of establishing an offensive base in Cuba were now revealed as deliberate deception. The efforts to bring about a détente were at an end. Acutely aware of the danger to American objectives, the President quickly enumerated the advisors who should join him in the Cabinet Room before noon on Tuesday.

A small number of men assembled in the Cabinet Room that morning. Although a few others joined the original 14 officials in later sessions, the initial meeting established the kind of decision-making unit that would be responsible for the American response. The problem would not be handled by established inter-departmental committees, but rather by a small, ad hoc group of the President's most respected advisors.[3]

In the morning, the discussion was relatively unstructured. Various aspects of the situation were introduced, and individuals offered their immediate reactions to the evidence presented to them. Comments were made about the possible intentions of the Soviet Union. The advisors agreed with the President that some form of action was necessary, and briefly mentioned possible reactions that would receive extensive consideration in later sessions. Cuba could be invaded. The island could be blockaded. During the first day, however, an air strike against the missile bases was suggested repeatedly. The initial alternatives seemed to be either bombing the rocket facilities or a vaguely defined "doing something

---

[3] The group of advisors had no formal status until the National Security Council met a week after the missiles were discovered. When it met, the Council designated the ad hoc group as its own Executive Committee—subsequently shortened to ExCom.

else."[4] Before the advisors left the President to continue their discussions at the State Department, Kennedy issued several immediate orders. First, although a response could not be delayed for long, more information had to be secured from intensified aerial reconnaissance. Second, the United States' action had to occur almost simultaneously with the revelation that America had discovered the missile sites. These two decisions emphasized the need for maximum secrecy. None of America's allies was to be informed of the missile discovery or what the government's response might be. That evening at 6:30 the group rejoined the President at the White House. They proceeded to do this regularly each night for the next few weeks.

During the second day and night (Wednesday, October 17), activity was centered in the conference room of Under Secretary of State George Ball. The participants moved back and forth between these intense but informal discussions and their regular tasks. Alternative courses of action were enumerated and at least six possible responses were discussed.[5] Among the six, however, attention was directed to two— air strike or blockade. A third alternative, a full-scale landing on Cuba, was a contingency plan previously prepared by the Pentagon. To ExCom members it seemed an unlikely first response. Because that option had to be preserved, however, complex operations were prepared to move men and materiel into striking position.

One reason the invasion plan that already existed was not considered as a first response was that time was required for its implementation and the ExCom perceived little time available for action. On Wednesday morning the Intelligence Board reported new photographic evidence. Bases were discovered under construction for two kinds of

---

[4] Early that Tuesday afternoon, the President briefed his Ambassador to the United Nations, Adlai Stevenson. Kennedy is reported to have said, "We'll have to do something quickly . . . I suppose the alternatives are to go in by air and wipe them out, or to take other steps to render the weapons inoperable." E. Abel, *The Missile Crisis* (Philadelphia: Lippincott, 1966), p. 49. At this first meeting, the President's brother, Attorney General Robert F. Kennedy, told the ExCom that they needed more alternatives because "surely there was some course in between bombing and doing nothing." A. M. Schlesinger, Jr., *A Thousand Days* (Boston: Houghton Mifflin, 1965), p. 803.

[5] T. C. Sorensen, *Kennedy* (New York: Harper and Row, 1965), p. 682; Abel, *Missile Crisis*, pp. 60–63.

missiles—1,000 mile medium range ballistic missiles (MRBM) and 2,200 mile intermediate range ballistic missiles (IRBM). The Intelligence Board estimated that between 16 and 32 of the MRBM's would be operational within a week.[6] If the United States policy makers did not act quickly they would be faced with a *fait accompli*. Armed missiles could prove extremely dangerous to remove.

On Thursday, October 18, Soviet Foreign Minister Andrei Gromyko called on President Kennedy. In this meeting, which had been scheduled before the crisis, Mr. Gromyko gave assurances that the armaments furnished Cuba were strictly defensive, not offensive. The President read to the Foreign Minister the statement he had issued at a September press conference that warned of the consequences of placing offensive weapons in Cuba. Unaware that the missiles had been detected, the Soviet diplomat persisted in carrying out the plan to conceal the bases until they were complete. He evidently was under instructions to maintain the critical element of surprise in the new move against the United States. Even though the Soviet Union had not been able to hide the missiles until construction was finished, the attempt to place missiles in Cuba had caught the American policy makers by surprise. Although offensive missiles frequently had been reported over the last several years, careful investigations had established that the information was either false or was related to surface-to-air missiles (SAM's) whose short range constituted no offensive threat to the United States. Moreover, most of the administration's national security leadership considered such a move by the Soviet Union as extremely unlikely. They had been surprised. By providing Mr. Gromyko with no clue as to his knowledge of the bases, President Kennedy elected to incorporate surprise into the countermove.

Even as Kennedy and Gromyko met, debate continued among members of the ExCom over the alternatives of a naval blockade or an air strike. The discussion had quickly narrowed to these two alternatives and the advisors were almost evenly divided. But by late that evening, when nine members of the group drove to the White House, a clear majority favored the blockade. During the consultation the President observed, "Whatever you fellows are recommending today you will be

---

[6] *Hearings on Military Posture and HR 2440* before the Committee on Armed Forces, U.S. House of Representatives (88 Cong., 1 Sess., 1963), p. 241. Also see Abel, *Missile Crisis*, p. 63.

sorry about a week from now."[7] Everyone was profoundly aware of the major risks associated with either move. That evening orders were dispatched to explore the legal grounds and military preparations necessary for a naval blockade. Perhaps it was at the same time that a request was made for an estimate of the number of civilian casualties which might result from air strikes. To avoid arousing public suspicion and apprehension, it was agreed that the President should proceed the next day with his publicly announced campaign tour through the Midwest. He would not break it off until his continuous presence in Washington became absolutely necessary.

The next day (Friday, October 19) the President's departure was delayed half an hour by the Joint Chiefs of Staff, who urged him to adopt the air strike as the initial response. Meanwhile, the ExCom was briefed on the legal aspects of a naval blockade. Renewed hesitation about the blockade developed, only to be countered by strong moral arguments against bombing missile installations and related targets that might produce as many as 25,000 Russian and Cuban casualties.[8] Those who argued that the United States must not be put in the position of committing a "Pearl Harbor" and that the heavy Soviet casualties might force the Russians to expand the conflict, won the renewed support of most of the ExCom for the blockade option. In the afternoon the Caribbean and Atlantic Commands were placed on alert. That evening, in a telephone conversation with some members of the group, the President decided to break off his tour and return to Washington the following day.

Saturday morning, October 20, reporters in Chicago learned that the President was returning to the Capital because he was suffering from a "cold." When he reached Washington, Kennedy received the recommendation for a blockade. The President gave the blockade, or quarantine as he designated it, tentative approval subject to his review and final authorization the next day.

---

[7] Schlesinger, *Thousand Days*, p. 805. On the division between advisors over the appropriate American response, Robert F. Kennedy recalled that the group was "split almost even—perhaps seven one way, five another." *New York Times*, October 14, 1964, p. 1.

[8] Several years after the missile crisis, Robert F. Kennedy reported that this figure had been the estimate of the casualties from an air strike. See *New York Times*, October 14, 1964, p. 1.

From the outset, those officials involved in the Cuban decision had driven themselves at an exhausting pace.[9] As the week wore away, plans crystallized and the intensive activity of more and more people became increasingly difficult to conceal. By the weekend the press had numerous clues—Dean Rusk's cancellation of a speech in Virginia, the request that the Joint Chiefs remain in Washington, sudden inaccessibility of old friends in the State and Defense Departments, lights burning all night in key offices, the military buildup in the southeastern United States, and Kennedy's sudden return. "It didn't seem logical to us, as political as he is and as tough as he is, for him to come waltzing back here because of a little cold," observed the *New York Times*'s James Reston.[10] The administration knew that time was running out. President Kennedy scheduled a nationwide address for Monday evening, October 22, six days after Bundy had delivered the reconnaissance photographs.

On that Monday, Soviet Ambassador Dobrynin received a copy of the President's address and a covering letter an hour before Kennedy spoke to the nation. About the same time, allies and neutrals assembled for briefings in other parts of the State Department. While the diplomatic community learned of America's decision to blockade Cuba, the Defense Department ordered all military forces on alert throughout the world. The Strategic Air Command began the biggest airborne alert in its history, which involved more B-52 bombers on constant airborne status than had ever been used before and much greater dispersal of B-47's.

---

[9] Some feeling for the stress experienced by the policy makers is revealed by Secretary Rusk's comments, "We had to go on a twenty-four hour basis here in the Department of State. My own colleagues, Under Secretary George Ball and Deputy Under Secretary Alex Johnson, took time [*sic*] about staying in the Department at night, so that we had a senior officer on duty at all times. . . . Senior officers did their own typing; some of my own basic papers were done in my own handwriting. . . ." from "Interview of Secretary Rusk by David Schoenbrun of CBS News," reprinted in Larson, *Cuban Crisis*, p. 268. Theodore C. Sorensen, Special Counsel to the President, later wrote, "I saw first-hand, during the long days and nights of the Cuban crisis, how brutally physical and mental fatigue can numb the good sense as well as the senses of normally articulate men." T. C. Sorensen, *Decision-Making in the White House* (New York: Columbia University Press, 1964), p. 76.

[10] Quoted in an interview with R. E. Steele. See Steele's "The Anticipation of History: A Study in Speculative Reporting." (Unpublished master's thesis, Northwestern University, Evanston, Illinois, 1963), p. 11.

All missile crews in the United States and abroad were placed on Maximum Alert. The Navy ordered 180 ships to stand by for the Cuban operation. Two days later the Navy launched an air and sea search for Russian merchant ships and submarines across 3.5 million square miles of ocean. On Monday, twenty-four hours had already elapsed since Kennedy had activated the war plan that would allow the first troops to land on Cuban beaches eight days later if this fateful step was required. This plan called for a force of 100,000 Army troops. The largest invasion force since World War II was rapidly assembling.[11]

Thirteen hours after Kennedy's address (Tuesday morning, October 23), the Soviet Union issued its first reply which Washington interpreted as indicating that "the Kremlin had been caught off guard and was playing for time to think out its next move."[12] During the day, grave signs of Soviet recalcitrance began to appear. The Soviet Union and the other Warsaw Pact countries placed their armed forces on alert. In the Atlantic Ocean, 25 Soviet ships heading toward Cuba continued on course, and a concentration of Russian submarines began to converge in the area around the island.[13] Later, an American industrialist, on a business trip to Moscow, was surprised to receive an urgent request to talk with Chairman Khrushchev. During the conversation the Soviet leader said that if commercial ships of his nation were searched "he would instruct his submarines to sink the American naval vessels."[14]

The United States policy makers had not sought the counsel of other nations in formulating their response, but once the decision was reached every effort was made to gain support from other countries. At the United Nations, the Security Council deadlocked on conflicting Soviet and American resolutions. In contrast to this stalemate, the Organization of American States unanimously adopted a resolution calling for

---

[11] F. Knebel, "Washington Crisis: 154 Hours on the Brink of War," *Look*, 26 (December 18, 1962), 44. W. W. Kaufmann, *The McNamara Strategy* (New York: Harper and Row, 1964), pp. 271–272.

[12] E. W. Kenworthy, A. Lewis, and M. Frankel, "Cuban Crisis: A Step by Step Review," *New York Times*, November 3, 1962, pp. 1, 6–7. Reprinted in Larson, *Cuban Crisis*, p. 235.

[13] H. W. Baldwin, "The Soviet Submarine Threat," *The Reporter*, 31 (September 1964), 39.

[14] W. E. Knox, "Close-up of Khrushchev During a Crisis," *New York Times Magazine*, November 18, 1962, p. 32.

the instigation of all steps required to remove the offensive weapons. The unanimity of the vote came as a surprise to American diplomats— as did the strong indications of support for the American action from NATO members. Shortly after the OAS vote, late in the afternoon, the President issued the "Proclamation of the Interdiction of Offensive Weapons" that ordered the blockade to begin at 10:00 the next morning, Wednesday, October 24.

On Wednesday, Acting Secretary General U Thant skirted the dispute in the United Nations by addressing identical letters to Chairman Khrushchev and President Kennedy in which he proposed a temporary suspension of arms shipments and of the blockade to allow for negotiations. Also on Wednesday the Defense Department reported that some of the ships approaching Cuba were slowing down or altering their courses. Apparently, the Soviet Union wanted more time before the first confrontation at sea. (Late on the previous evening, the President also had acted to give the Soviets more decision time. At the suggestion of the British Ambassador, David Ormsby Gore, he reduced the perimeter of the blockade so that Moscow would have more time to communicate with ship captains before their vessels were intercepted.) [15]

The Soviet tanker *Bucharest* was intercepted early Thursday morning, October 25, but on instruction from the President the ship was not boarded when its captain responded to telegraphic communication and the Navy satisfied itself that petroleum was the only cargo. Minutes later an East German passenger ship was allowed to pass through the blockade. Diplomatic efforts continued as the possibility of a showdown in the Atlantic increased. Khrushchev accepted U Thant's proposal, but Kennedy indicated that although the United States would negotiate, the blockade would continue until the missiles were removed.

Another anxious twenty-four hours passed before another ship encountered the blockade. On Friday, October 26, search parties boarded, without incident, a ship of Lebanese registry under Soviet charter. When no contraband was found, the vessel was permitted to continue toward Cuba. But further reconnaissance confirmed that construction of the launching facilities and other support installations continued at an

---

[15] Schlesinger, *Thousand Days*, p. 818.

accelerated pace. At this point, members of the ExCom began to doubt whether the blockade alone would accomplish the American objective. Intelligence now estimated that the MRBM's would be operational in a matter of hours. Members of the ExCom began to believe that although the blockade might prevent further shipment of missiles, it was not sufficient to achieve the American objective—the removal of all offensive weapons from Cuba. ExCom discussions returned to plans for a series of air strikes followed by an invasion. Millions of leaflets to be printed in Spanish warning civilians to evacuate target areas were authorized. Robert Kennedy informed Soviet Ambassador Dobrynin that unless the missiles were dismantled the President would take stronger measures within the next several days.

In Moscow, as the weekend approached, the inescapable time of decision drew near.[16] Several alternative courses of action may have been considered by the Soviets. "(1) They could submit to the quarantine . . . (2) they could avoid a showdown by keeping their ships out of the quarantine area . . . or (3) they could precipitate the use of violence by attempting to violate the quarantine, perhaps with the aid of submarines."[17] So far, the Soviets were keeping ships with contraband away from the blockade. At any moment they might take counteraction elsewhere, for example in Berlin, or they could elect to postpone a decision in the belief that the United States would be unwilling to risk further steps. In the Soviet Union on Friday, October 26, two revealing editorials appeared. One entitled "Reason Must Triumph," was in *Pravda*, the Party's major newspaper:

---

[16] Various evidence suggests that the Soviet policy makers also worked under severe stress. On Monday, October 22, Gromyko made the exhausting flight from New York to Moscow only to find on his arrival that the missiles had been discovered and that a blockade of Cuba was about to begin. When he saw Premier Khrushchev later in the week, American businessman William Knox observed that Khrushchev "did appear very tired." Knox, "Close-up of Khrushchev," p. 32ff. From the timing of messages received in Washington, Soviet officials must have worked through the night on at least several occasions. Khrushchev recently commented, "I must confess that I slept one night in my studio fully dressed on the sofa." *New York Times*, June 27, 1967, p. 15.

[17] A. L. Horelick, "The Cuban Missile Crisis: An Analysis of Soviet Calculations and Behavior," *World Politics*, 16 (April 1964), 386.

The Soviet Union, loyal to its peaceloving policy, is itself prepared to do everything possible in order to prevent the outbreak of war and to prevent a military catastrophe.[18]

Quite a different note was struck on the same day by the news organ of the Ministry of Defense, *Krasnaia Zvezda:*

History teaches that one must not give in to pirates. A policy of appeasement of an aggressor has always led to tragic consequences for countries. A decisive demand grows in all countries: destroy the criminal intentions of the warmongers.[19]

Regardless of how many different alternatives were recognized by the Soviet decision makers, evidence such as these conflicting editorials suggests a basic division between the alternatives favored by the military representatives and those advanced by the Party leadership.

Meanwhile in Washington on Friday, October 26, a member of the Soviet embassy contacted a network television correspondent known to have access to State Department officials. Through this informal channel of communication—whose authority could be denied if unsuccessful—the Soviet Union advanced a possible solution: The missiles would be withdrawn and verification by the United Nations permitted, if the United States publicly guaranteed not to invade Cuba.[20] Hope that the crisis would not escalate to nuclear war grew when a cable from Premier Khrushchev arrived in Washington about 9:00 Friday evening. It was one of ten direct communications between Khrushchev and Kennedy during the crisis. The message "contained no specific proposal or conditions, but showed throughout an appreciation of the risk of nuclear war and the need for reaching an agreement."[21]

By the time the ExCom assembled Saturday morning, October 27, the easement hoped for was replaced by confusion and rapidly mounting

---

[18] R. Kolkowicz, *Conflicts in Soviet Party-Military Relations: 1962–1963*, Memorandum RM-3760-PR, Rand Corporation, Santa Monica, California, 1963, p. 14.

[19] *Ibid.*, p. 14.

[20] R. Hilsman, "The Cuban Crisis: How Close We Were to War," *Look*, 28 (August 25, 1964), 17–21.

[21] *Ibid.*, p. 20. This letter has never been made public, but a paraphrase of it appears in Abel, *Missile Crisis*, pp. 178–181.

tension. A second note from Premier Khrushchev made the missile withdrawal conditional on a similar move by the United States in Turkey. Word also reached the White House that a U-2 had been destroyed over Cuba—an action that Cuban military personnel likely could not perform without assistance from those more skilled in operating the complex antiaircraft system required for intercepting a high-altitude airplane. Shooting had started. The ExCom authorized a stern press release that no negotiation could be initiated until the missile buildup in Cuba stopped. The President resolved to accelerate both the blockade and reconnaissance. The Pentagon called up 14,000 air reservists and announced that steps would be taken to protect its photographic flights over Cuba. Robert Kennedy called upon Soviet Ambassador Dobrynin and warned that unless the missiles were withdrawn, America would take military action in the next several days.

Abruptly the situation became even worse. An American U-2, presumably on an air-sampling mission north of Alaska, lost its bearings and strayed over the territory of the Soviet Union. To the Russians it might appear that the United States was collecting final intelligence data for a nuclear attack. Both Soviet and American interceptor aircraft pursued the reconnaissance plane, whose pilot used open radio channels to call for help.

When they met at the White House again that Saturday afternoon, ExCom members considered a further response. They proposed to ignore the most recent Soviet message and to indicate that if the Soviet Union was suggesting it would dismantle its Cuban missile bases under international verification in exchange for guarantees against the invasion of Cuba, the United States would agree. This proposal Kennedy sent in a letter to Khrushchev early Saturday evening. More than ever the ExCom members felt that they were on the brink of greater violence, that failure of this letter to elicit a favorable reply would force them to take stronger military measures. "The President gravely remarked that evening that it seemed to him to be touch and go, that it could now go 'either way.' "[22]

On Sunday morning, October 28, the Moscow radio announced that Premier Khrushchev was sending another letter to the President. In it Khrushchev said that he was ordering the missiles returned to the Soviet

---

[22] Kenworthy et al., "Cuban Crisis," p. 242.

Union and that he would permit some means of verification. In return, he expected the United States to give assurances that there would be no invasion of Cuba. Without waiting for the official text, President Kennedy sent a reply welcoming the Premier's "statesmanlike decision." Two weeks of acute crisis were at an end.

The Cuban missile crisis is the kind of decision-making situation with which the simulation research is concerned. Yet it is inappropriate to offer the attempt to establish missile bases in Cuba as the exclusive illustration of a crisis. In the simulation we do not wish to model a particular historical situation, but rather a class of events with which the Cuban crisis shares common characteristics. In order to distinguish properties which are unique to the 1962 Cuban situation from those found in a broader set of crises, one could review a number of other situations judged to be crises. For our purposes an entire series of case studies does not need to be examined. However, the consideration of one additional crisis will be valuable in identifying what may be recurrent features of such situations. What follows is a somewhat briefer account of a crisis experienced by American policy makers twelve years and four months before long range missiles were detected in Cuba.

The Invasion of South Korea[23]

Saturday evening, June 24, 1950, President Harry S. Truman received a telephone call from Secretary of State Dean Acheson. The President was at his home in Independence, Missouri, and the Secretary of State was on his farm in Maryland. The Secretary said, "Mr. President, I have very serious news. The North Koreans have invaded South Korea."[24] President Truman thought he should return to the capital at once, for he shared his Secretary's view that the situation could have grave consequences for the United States. Although the President talked

---

[23] This account relies extensively on the detailed research concerning the Korean decision conducted by Glenn D. Paige. See his *The Korean Decision* (New York: Free Press, 1968). From a different perspective, Paige has compared the Korean and Cuban cases for the forthcoming volume, C. F. Hermann, ed., *Contemporary Research on International Crises* (New York: Free Press, in preparation).

[24] Harry S. Truman, *Years of Trial and Hope: 1946–1952* (Garden City: Doubleday, 1956), p. 332.

later about the possibility that the Korean invasion could trigger the outbreak of World War III and the problem of defending Japan if Korea were lost, the situation was not immediately recognized by Truman or Acheson as a direct threat to American survival. The American government had publicly announced that Korea was not vital to its defense in the event of a major conflict with the Soviet Union. In the hours and days to come, Truman and his advisors spoke not of a military threat to the United States, but of the danger to the effective operation of collective security and to the peacekeeping function of the United Nations. "The attack on Korea," Secretary Acheson later testified, "was a blow at the foundation of this whole program. It was a challenge to the whole system of collective security, not only in the Far East, but everywhere in the world."[25]

In that first long-distance conversation, the President authorized the necessary preparations for requesting an emergency meeting of the United Nations Security Council. After accepting Acheson's advice that he need not return to Washington until further information was available, Truman requested that he be informed when the plans for calling a meeting of the Security Council were completed. At the State Department, high level officials and their staffs worked through the night to draft a resolution and to devise a strategy for its introduction. No contingency plans regarding Korea existed to guide their work. The attack had come as a surprise to the American government. "The same situation that existed in Korea existed in a number of other places, where the possibility of attack existed, but it was not believed that the attack would take place at that time."[26] At 2:00 Sunday morning Acheson described to

---

[25] *Military Situation in the Far East*, Hearings Before the Committee on Armed Services and the Committee on Foreign Relations, U.S. Senate (82 Cong., 1 Sess., 1951), To Conduct an Inquiry into the Military Situation in the Far East and the Facts Surrounding the Relief of General of the Army Douglas MacArthur from His Assignment to that Area, Part 3, p. 1715.

[26] *Ibid.*, Part 3, p. 1991. In developing this point in his testimony, Dean Acheson stated, "Intelligence was available to the Department prior to the 25th of June, made available by the Far East Command, the CIA, the Department of the Army, and by the State Department representatives here and overseas, and shows that all these agencies were in agreement that the possibility for an attack on the Korean Republic existed at that time, but they were all in agreement that its launching in the summer of 1950 did not appear imminent."

President Truman the proposed resolution. In this second telephone conversation, the President gave final approval to call an emergency meeting of the Security Council.

The third long-distance exchange between the President and his Secretary of State occurred shortly before 3:00 Sunday afternoon, June 25. Several developments had transpired by that time. Acheson had rushed back to Washington to join the Secretary of the Army, the Army Chief of Staff, and officials from the State Department to review the Korean problem. With the information available by noon on Sunday, the Army-State conferees agreed that it looked like a major invasion was being launched against South Korea. The early reports of military action indicated ineffective resistance on the part of the South Koreans. Meanwhile, at 2:00 Sunday afternoon, the United Nations Security Council had begun its emergency session. By the end of the afternoon, the Council passed the resolution that called for the North Koreans to withdraw to the 38th parallel. As the Soviet Union was boycotting the Security Council, Acheson had been able to tell the President during their afternoon telephone conversation that the resolution would probably be passed later in the day. However, neither man thought that the invaders would comply with the United Nations request. Since the reports from Korea were grim, the President decided to return to Washington immediately.

During his flight to Washington, President Truman sent word to his Secretary of State to arrange a dinner meeting between himself and specified advisors. Thirteen men, including the Joint Chiefs of Staff and officials from the State and Defense Departments, awaited the President when he arrived at Blair House. After dinner Secretary Acheson made a series of proposals: (1) to give additional military supplies to the South Koreans; (2) to use American aircraft to cover the evacuation of United States civilians from Inchon; (3) to grant the Air Force the authority to attack North Korean forces that interfered with the evacuation; (4) to move the Seventh Fleet between Formosa and the Chinese mainland to prevent hostilities between the Communist and Nationalist Chinese; and (5) to consider what further assistance might be given South Korea. In the ensuing discussion, the participants agreed that the invasion was engineered by the Soviet Union. Barring direct military intervention by Russia or another Communist state, however, the Army of the Republic of Korea was judged able to turn the attack if given sufficient equipment. No advisor dissented from Acheson's proposals;

no one offered alternative courses of action. The President asked that
General MacArthur send a reconnaissance party to Korea. He authorized
the arms shipments and the steps to insure the safe evacuation of American civilians. Although the Seventh Fleet was directed to sail from the
Philippines toward Japan, Truman said he was not ready to decide if
the Fleet should be used to neutralize Formosa. Finally, the President
made it clear that future steps must be taken in cooperation with the
United Nations.

At 11:45 on Monday morning, June 26, the White House released
the President's first public statement on Korea. It supported the United
Nations resolution and announced the shipment of certain military supplies to Korea. In the middle of the afternoon, the Secretary of State
joined the President to hear the pleas of the South Korean Ambassador,
John M. Chang. Afterwards Acheson returned to his office to consider
what further steps the Korean situation required. The information that
reached Washington that afternoon was that the defensive forces were
deteriorating. At 7:30 that evening, the Secretary recommended that the
President call another conference. The time available for preventive
action was short. Later, in describing this day, Truman wrote, "There was
now no doubt! The Republic of Korea needed help at once if it was not to
be overrun."[27] Truman scheduled the meeting for 9:00 that same evening.

The group that assembled at Blair House consisted of almost the
same advisors who had gathered there twenty-five hours earlier. The
President opened the meeting with a request for an assessment of the
combat situation. From this information, the conferees shared the view
that the South Korean army was collapsing. Acheson offered the recommendations he had prepared during the afternoon. He repeated the plan
to insulate Formosa with the Seventh Fleet. He proposed that the Navy
and Air Force be authorized to give full support to the Korean forces
south of the 38th parallel. He suggested that increased military assistance
be given to the Philippines and to Indochina. In addition, Acheson
recommended that these actions be reported to the United Nations and
that they consider introducing a second Security Council resolution
specifically calling for United Nations members to aid the South Koreans. Finally, the Secretary of State urged a review of all Soviet activities
elsewhere in the world.

In the subsequent discussion, some speculations were made about

---

[27] Truman, *Years of Trial*, p. 337.

Soviet intentions. It was agreed that American actions should be as nonprovocative as possible in order to indicate the desire of the United States to limit the hostilities. Several Army representatives observed that if the Korean armed forces were too mauled, only the commitment of American ground troops could halt the invasion. Despite the risk, "during the discussion of Secretary Acheson's recommendations, not one of the President's advisors took the position that the United States should not undertake military intervention to save South Korea."[28] In the end, the President and his advisors approved all Acheson's proposals.

Next came two days primarily devoted to implementing the measures and seeking support for them. By midday on Tuesday, June 27, Congressional leaders and allied nations had been briefed on the new actions taken by the American government. Shortly thereafter, a White House press release made the President's decisions public knowledge. On Tuesday afternoon the only known direct exchange between the two major powers during the crisis week occurred when the United States Ambassador to the Soviet Union delivered a note to the Soviet Foreign Ministry. The message did not charge the Soviet Union with responsibility for the invasion; instead, it requested that the Soviet leadership use its influence to urge the North Koreans to withdraw. In other words, the communiqué gave "Russia an opportunity to retire gracefully from the chessboard in case it was sufficiently moved by the show of American determination."[29]

Although the United States maintained that the commitment to aid South Korea had been made under the original United Nations resolution, the American representative introduced a new proposal at a second discussion of Korea held by the Security Council on Tuesday afternoon. At 10:30 that evening, with the Soviet Union still absent, the Security Council approved a resolution recommending that "Members of the United Nations furnish such assistance to the Republic of Korea as may be necessary to repel the armed attack and to restore international peace and security in the area."[30] During the same hour, halfway around the world, the North Korean People's Army was capturing Seoul, the capital of the Republic of Korea.

In the United States and throughout the capitals of Europe, there

---

[28] Paige, *Korean Decision*, p. 174.

[29] A. L. Warner, "How the Korea Decision Was Made," *Harpers*, 202 (June 1951), 104.

[30] U. N. Document S/1508, Rev. 1 (June 27, 1950).

had been expressions that Korea would probably be another example of appeasement. On Wednesday, June 28, the public reaction to the President's announcement began to appear in the United States as well as throughout the rest of the non-Communist world. It was overwhelmingly positive.[31] In Britain, Prime Minister Attlee announced that his nation was committing its naval forces in the Far East to the United Nations' action. Amidst these expressions of approval and the discouraging news from Seoul, the President met for the first time during the crisis with the National Security Council—the formal interagency organ that consults with the President on international problems. The situation was reviewed, but no important decisions were reported. While American leaders awaited developments, General Douglas MacArthur flew from Japan to inspect the Korean situation.

On Thursday morning, June 29, it was evident that the South Korean situation continued to deteriorate. Even before MacArthur returned from Korea, his "headquarters [in Tokyo] reported by telecon to the Pentagon that the ROK's [army of the Republic of Korea] had already suffered casualties of about 50 per cent."[32] As the grim statements continued through the morning, Secretary of Defense Johnson urged Truman to have another meeting with his advisors. The President called a meeting of the National Security Council for 5:00 that afternoon.

At the fourth major session between Truman and his top officials, the Defense Secretary advanced some proposals in the form of a directive to General MacArthur. Johnson suggested that (1) air and naval forces be used against military targets in North Korea (2) army signal and transportation units be introduced to improve ground to air communications and speed the supply of materiel to the front, and (3) United States infantry be deployed in limited numbers in the area below the combat zone to protect the evacuation. The discussion revealed concern about broadening the conflict, about introducing American soldiers even in noncombat areas, and anxiety lest the Soviet Union enter the fighting. However, the President approved an order that closely approximated the original suggestions of his Secretary of Defense. During the

---

[31] For a review of the widespread fear that the United States and the United Nations would not aid Korea and the reaction to the broad support that resulted from the presidential announcements on Tuesday, June 27, see Paige, *Korean Decision*, pp. 193–201, 218–221.

[32] Beverly Smith, "The White House Story: Why We Went to War in Korea," *Saturday Evening Post*, 224, No. 19 (November 10, 1951), 86.

meeting Acheson announced that the Soviet Union, in response to the note earlier in the week, had denied responsibility for the North Korean invasion. He also reported that the United Nations had received new offers of air and naval support from Australia, New Zealand, Canada, and the Netherlands. That evening, in a further conversation with President Truman, Acheson indicated that Chiang Kai-shek had made a direct offer of Nationalist Chinese ground forces to the United States for use in Korea.

General MacArthur's assessment of the Korean situation reached the Pentagon Friday morning, June 30:

> The only assurance for the holding of the present line, and the ability to regain later the lost ground, is through the introduction of U.S. ground combat forces into the Korean battle area. To continue to utilize the forces of our Air and Navy without an effective ground element cannot be decisive.[33]

Upon learning MacArthur's recommendations, the Army Chief of Staff began a telecon discussion with the field commander. MacArthur wanted to commit a U. S. regimental combat team at once with a subsequent buildup of as much as two divisions. He felt that any delay would have drastic consequences. At 4:57 A.M. the request was telephoned to President Truman by the Secretary of the Army. The President immediately authorized the combat team and requested a meeting of his advisors for 9:30 A.M. to consider the question of a further commitment of ground forces.

The same small group of advisors assembled at the White House to decide whether to adopt MacArthur's additional suggestion and extensively commit American ground forces. Initially, the President was attracted to the offer by Nationalist China, but his advisors convinced him of the problems in accepting such a force. However, the difficulties created by committing American forces did not lead any of the advisors to oppose General MacArthur's urgent request. The meeting lasted half an hour; at the end of it the President ordered that MacArthur be authorized to use not just two divisions but all the troops under his command. Thus, less than a week after learning of the invasion of Korea,

---

[33] Message quoted in R. A. Appleman, *South to the Naktong, North to the Yalu: June–November 1950* (Washington, D. C.: Office of the Chief of Military History, Department of the Army, 1961), p. 47.

the United States committed the full array of its air, sea, and land forces to implement United Nations' resolutions which America itself had introduced.

Cuba and Korea Compared

At first glance, the results of the two crises led to opposite outcomes: the Korean decision led to war; the Cuban decision did not. Of course, the international setting in which these two events occurred might partially explain this difference. Truman was faced with overt military aggression against a friendly nation, whereas Kennedy was threatened by the potential use of force, not its immediate use, against his country. In 1950, the United States still enjoyed a monopoly in nuclear capability. In 1962, both the United States and the Soviet Union were thermonuclear powers and were rapidly developing missile systems capable of devastating retaliation even if a nuclear-armed enemy struck first. Although the United States' leadership was convinced that the Soviets engineered the Korean invasion, the initial military engagement was against the forces of a small Communist country. By contrast, the Cuban crisis brought the Soviet Union and the United States into direct conflict.

However, these differences cannot hide the similarities that exist between the responses made to Korea and Cuba. In both crises, the decision makers felt some action by the United States was required. They rejected the option of doing nothing at all or of postponing a decision until more external events unfolded. Furthermore, each administration responded to a threatening situation by engaging the military capability of the United States. Not only were military means of achieving objectives used in both instances, but each time the level of intensity of force applied to the situation gradually increased. Every response in the series of decisions reached in the last week of June, 1950, extended the use of force. First air and sea forces were employed to protect the evacuation of American citizens. Then, aircraft were used against enemy military targets. Finally, army combat forces were committed. In Cuba, the crisis was over before the application of force evolved very far. Nevertheless, the pattern is evident—initially, the United States Navy only intercepted ships, then a ship was boarded, and by the last few days of the crisis, preparations were underway for an air strike against the missile bases. This probably would have been followed by a full scale invasion.

There are also contrasts and similarities between the decision processes in the two situations. In the Korean crisis the goals that Truman and his advisors perceived to be endangered were the collective security mechanism of the United Nations as well as the security of many countries, for it was feared that failure to stop the invasion of South Korea would lead to further aggression by Communist nations elsewhere. The relevant objectives perceived by the participants in the Cuban missile crisis concerned the strategic position of the United States vis-à-vis the Soviet Union. Regardless of whether Soviet offensive missiles in Cuba altered objective military relationships, the ExCom members considered them capable of generating a powerful psychological impact on friends and foes alike with respect to the relative position of the Soviet Union and the United States. In summary, the policy makers in both situations arrived at a consensus that the crises affected vital national interests.

In his critical meetings, Truman and his advisors consistently recognized only one general course of action as the appropriate response. By contrast, the ExCom considered a wide range of possible options for eliminating the missile bases. In the early meetings, several individuals made deliberate efforts to search for more alternatives. It should be noted, however, that the range of alternatives considered as possible initial responses for combating the problem quickly narrowed to two. The decision-making units that examined the possible courses of action were remarkably similar in nature. In both instances, the primary decisional unit was a small, ad hoc group rather than the formal organizational machinery normally used to conduct foreign policy. President Truman and his advisors reached their decision without consulting Congress or American allies, but once a decision was reached extensive efforts were made to win both domestic and foreign support for their action. In the Cuban crisis, the Kennedy administration followed a similar pattern of communication.

As hypotheses about crises are introduced in the simulation research, we will be able to compare further the decision-making processes and outcomes in Korea and Cuba. Another area of comparison concerns the properties of these two incidents that identify them as members of a class of situations called crises. This issue is part of a larger question which concerns a possible definition of that concept.

Chapter 2

THE CONCEPT
OF CRISIS

Definitions of Crisis

The word crisis comes from the Greek *krinein*, to separate. In traditional medical terms a crisis denotes that change in a disease which indicates whether the outcome is to be recovery or death.[1]

Crises as Turning Points. Some investigators of social behavior define crisis as the critical turning or branching point in some human activity. Their definition is analogous to the one in common medical usage. As in a medical crisis, the turning point—or "hinge of fate" as one diplomat describes it[2]—contains indeterminancy; thus, human control is limited. When understood as a turning point, crisis is associated with rapid or sudden change. The *Encyclopedia of the Social Sciences,* which discusses the concept in an economic context, defines crisis as "a grave and sudden disturbance of economic equilibrium."[3] Change

---

[1] R. C. North, O. R. Holsti, M. G. Zaninovich, and D. A. Zinnes, *Content Analysis* (Evanston: Northwestern University Press, 1963), p. 4.

[2] E. A. Gullion, "Crisis Management: Lessons from the Congo," in *Crises and Concepts in International Affairs,* The International Studies Association Proceedings, Sixth Annual Meeting (April 1965), p. 49.

[3] J. Lescure, "Crisis," in E. R. A. Seligman, ed., *Encyclopedia of the Social Sciences,* 4 (New York: Macmillan, 1937), 595. In an article on crisis prepared for the new *International Encyclopedia of the Social Sciences,* James A. Robinson advances several alternative definitions of the concept and examines it more from the perspective of politics. The broader treatment in the latter article suggests the increased interest in the study of crises.

also is indicated when crisis is stipulated as a fluctuation in the energy applied by nations to a situation. "When there is evidence of a striking increase in the expenditure of physical energy in a particular geographical location, then and there an acute international crisis can be said to exist."[4]

Some definitions emphasize not the speed of change or the quantity of energy invested in it, but rather the degree of change. Wolfenstein, for example, conceives of a crisis as a situation which threatens to transform "an existing political and social order."[5] Still others view crisis as the agent of change. To account for the lack of governmental reorganization in Syracuse, New York, one study concluded that the absence of crises contributed to the failure to reform. "If Onondaga County faced crisis, more incentive for change might be found."[6] This interpretation identifies crisis as the situation that triggers change rather than that which constitutes the change itself.

In international politics, the use of crisis as a critical turning point often refers to a specific kind of change—sudden variations in the level of conflict or in the intensity of hostilities which could lead to conflict. Thus, Wiener and Kahn describe a crisis as "a situation involving significant actual or potential international conflict in either a novel form or at an abruptly changing level."[7] "An international crisis," according to Young, "is a set of rapidly unfolding events which raises the impact of destabilizing forces in the general international system or any of its subsystems substantially above 'normal' (i.e., average) levels and increases the likelihood of violence occurring in the system."[8] Richardson comments that "an international crisis may be viewed as the decisive moment in a conflict, the turning point opening the way to an outcome

[4] C. A. McClelland, ed., *Quemoy: An Acute International Crisis*, San Francisco International Studies Project, VIII (San Francisco State College, San Francisco, California, 1959), 39.

[5] E. V. Wolfenstein, "Some Psychological Aspects of Crisis Leaders," in L. J. Edinger, ed., *Political Leadership in Industrialized Societies* (New York: Wiley, 1967), p. 156.

[6] R. C. Martin, F. J. Munger, J. Burkhead, G. S. Birkead, H. Herman, H. M. Kagi, L. P. Welch, and C. J. Wingfield, *Decisions in Syracuse* (Bloomington: Indiana University Press, 1961), p. 331.

[7] A. J. Wiener and H. Kahn, *Crisis and Arms Control* (Hudson Institute, 1962), p. 12.

[8] O. R. Young, *The Intermediaries: Third Parties in International Crises* (Princeton: Princeton University Press, 1967), p. 10.

normally involving some redistribution of gains and costs among the participants."[9] A similar position is taken in a study of the Saar conflict.[10] Occasionally, crises may be defined as the critical moments when the conflicting parties either plunge into war or curtail their dispute. Quincy Wright has estimated the likelihood of war in terms of the frequency and severity of crises.[11] From a comparison of the boom-depression business cycle and the diplomacy-war international cycle, Boulding concludes that although both systems proceed "to some kind of boundary or turning point," the absence of countercyclical instruments in the international system "frequently leads to a crisis in the form of war."[12] In other words, one of the distinctive characteristics of international political crises, according to this economist, is their association with war.

Crisis seen as a turning-point is illustrated in the Soviet Union's installation of missiles in Cuba. Members of the Stanford University Conflict and Integration Project divided the crisis into four time periods— U. S. debates response, U. S. establishes blockade, bargaining transpires, and agreements take place.[13] Their analysis of the content of Soviet and American documents revealed that a critical change occurred in the decision makers' perceptions of each other between the second and third stages. The perceptions became less charged with negative affect; statements of intense activity subsided. Other analysts, as well as the policy makers themselves, have viewed the settlement of the Cuban crisis as a point of demarcation for East-West negotiations. When the confrontation was over, Kennedy wrote to Khrushchev, "Perhaps now, as we step back from danger, we can together make real progress in this vital field [of disarmament]."[14] The Korean decision and the subsequent conflict can be viewed as a turning point in the Cold War, albeit in the

[9] J. L. Richardson, "International Crises: A Research Project" (mimeo, University of Sydney, Sydney, Australia, no date), p. 6.

[10] J. Freymond, *The Saar Conflict* (New York: Praeger, 1960), p. xiv.

[11] Q. Wright, *A Study of War*, 2nd ed. (Chicago: University of Chicago Press, 1965), p. 1272.

[12] K. E. Boulding, *Conflict and Defense* (New York: Harper and Row, 1963), p. 250.

[13] O. R. Holsti, R. A. Brody, and R. C. North, "Measuring Affect and Action in International Reaction Models," *Journal of Peace Research*, 3–4 (July 1964), 170–190.

[14] D. L. Larson, *The "Cuban Crisis" of 1962* (Boston: Houghton Mifflin, 1963), p. 167.

opposite direction from the Cuban missile crisis. For example, the Korean War led to a sharp rise in the proportion of the Gross National Product which the United States and the countries of Western Europe allocated to national defense—an increase in defense expenditures which continued even after the Korean hostilities had subsided.

Crises as Traits or Characteristics. Another way to define crisis is to identify certain traits that a situation has, or traits of the entity (such as a nation) that experiences the situation. This approach is called trait or characteristic listing. Occasionally, trait definitions of crisis rest on a single characteristic. Schelling defines an international crisis as a situation characterized by great uncertainty and risk of violence. "The essence of the crisis is its unpredictability."[15] More often, however, a number of crisis traits are mentioned. For example, in his study of Soviet foreign policy making, Triska mentions features of crisis that are of concern to decision makers (threat, reduced time for decision, stress) and others that affect international systems (increase in international tension and instability).[16] Two reviews of crisis listing multiple characteristics will be examined in some detail.

Miller and Iscoe extract five crisis traits from definitions of crisis used in studies of individual and small group activity:[17]

1. Time factor: The crisis situation is "acute rather than chronic and ranges from very brief periods of time to longer periods which are not yet clearly defined."
2. Marked changes in behavior: Behavior under crisis is characterized by inefficiency, frustration, and scapegoating.

---

[15] T. C. Schelling, *Arms and Influence* (New Haven: Yale University Press, 1966), p. 96. Examples of crisis defined in terms of a single trait outside international politics are found in R. L. Hamblin, "Group Integration During a Crisis," *Human Relations,* 11 (1958), 67, and H. B. Williams, "Some Functions of Communication in Crisis Behavior," *Human Organization,* 16 (Summer 1957), 15.

[16] J. F. Triska, *Studies in Deterrence XIII: Pattern and Level of Risk in Soviet Foreign Policy-Making, 1945–1963, NOTS TP* 3880, U. S. Naval Ordnance Test Station, China Lake, California (October 1966), p. 7.

[17] E. Miller and I. Iscoe, "The Concept of Crisis: Current Status and Mental Health Implications," *Human Organization,* 22 (Fall 1963), 196. Reprinted with permission of the publisher.

3. Subjective aspects: "There is a perception of threat or danger to important life goals . . . accompanied frequently by anxiety, fear, guilt, or defensive reactions."
4. Relativistic aspects: "What constitutes a crisis to one individual or group does not constitute it for another group."
5. Organismic tension: "The person in crisis will experience generalized physical tension which may be expressed in a variety of symptoms including those commonly associated with anxiety."

Wiener and Kahn have made a more extensive compilation of characteristics of international crises:[18]

1. Turning points are perceived by the decision makers.
2. Decisions and actions are required: Action decisions are defined to include explicit judgments to postpone action and decisions not to take action.
3. Threats, warnings, or promises are seen by the decision makers: " 'Threat seen' is a relatively powerful factor in forcing recognition of a situation as a crisis, while 'promise seen' is ordinarily less likely to be judged a critical situation [except as] . . . a loss of some unique or irretrievable opportunity is threatened."
4. The outcome will shape the future: "The outcome of the crisis will be important; . . . moreover, the decision may be determinative of the future course of events."
5. Events converge: "Crises frequently have the aspect of seeming to result from a convergence, confluence, or concurrence of events."
6. Uncertainties increase: "In most crises, relative to normal uncertainties about the immediate future, there is a large range of outcomes possible."
7. Control of events by the decision makers is decreased.
8. Urgency increases: "The situation is felt as urgent, demanding, and exigent. For many actors this results in feelings of great stress and anxiety."
9. Information may become more inadequate.
10. Time pressures increase.
11. Interrelations among actors are changed: "Bargaining positions and

---

[18] Wiener and Kahn, *Crisis and Arms Control*, pp. 8–11. Reprinted with permission of the authors.

other elements of power are altered by changes in time pressures, urgency, uncertainty, etc."

12. International tensions increase: "Tension increase might best be viewed as a hypothetical construct, somewhat metaphorical, referring to attributes of the international system during crises."

Wiener and Kahn note that these twelve traits are not mutually exclusive, nor does this list constitute the necessary and sufficient conditions for crisis to occur. Although the authors do not list the characteristics according to importance, some traits are held as salient to any crisis, whereas others are considered marginal.

Of particular interest are the characteristics of crisis that appear on both lists because the fields summarized by the two compilations are diverse. A reduction in available time is mentioned (Miller-Iscoe, item 1, and Wiener-Kahn, item 10). Threats are included in both (Miller-Iscoe, item 3, and Wiener-Kahn, item 3), as are the symptoms of stress and anxiety (Miller-Iscoe, items 3 and 5; Wiener-Kahn, item 8). Although tension is also a shared trait (Miller-Iscoe, item 5, and Wiener-Kahn, item 12), the term is used differently.[19]

Evaluation of Definitions. The various definitions of crisis have been grouped into two categories. Some identify crisis as a critical turning point, that is, as an abrupt change in some variable. Other definitions emphasize certain characteristics or traits as common to those situations specified as crises. These alternative approaches to defining crisis can be evaluated against two requirements for concepts that are scientifically useful. First, the concept must be involved in the construction of theory—in this instance, theoretical connections between a class of situations and foreign policies. Second, the concept must be able to be represented by empirical operations that will permit predictive state-

---

[19] A clear distinction is rarely made between the concept of crisis and a number of seemingly related terms (e.g., anxiety, disaster, panic, stress, tension, threat). Some authors identify crisis as a stimulus to which certain kinds of behavior—like anxiety or panic—are frequent responses. Several of these terms are often found in a particular area of academic study. For example, some fields of psychology study threat, anxiety, and stress, whereas disaster and panic become the focus of certain areas of sociology. Vague differentiations will continue, in all likelihood, until distinguishable empirical phenomena can be identified with the terms.

ments.[20] In a strict sense, the first criterion can be applied only after the crisis propositions are interrelated in a partial theory. However, we can consider the explanatory role of a particular formulation of crisis as well as examine the second criterion concerning prediction.

Both groups of definitions of crisis encounter some limitations when applied against the explanation criterion. Crisis has been specified as the turning point in a number of variables—a sharp move away from economic equilibrium, a sudden change in exertion of physical energy, a rapid variation in the conflict pattern, or the specific point in a conflict when further hostilities lead to war. This diversity suggests that crises are encountered in a variety of human activities. It also reveals that by itself the notion of turning point does not explain *what* constitutes a crisis, but only *where*, in a temporal or spatial dimension, it takes place. Even when we specify in which variable an abrupt change becomes a crisis, our definition does not suggest *why* the turning point transpires.

The traits or characteristics approach to defining crisis also encounters limitations. In the two lists offered as illustrations, some traits appeared to be consequences or effects of other characteristics incorporated in the same definition. The result may be a definition not merely of a single situation, but rather of a sequence of related situations. Each situation is defined by a separate characteristic which varies with a trait in the preceding situation. In effect, the definition hides a series of hypotheses. For example, is crisis a situation characterized by inadequate information, anxiety, and a feeling of losing control over events; or is there an unspecified situation which results in inadequate information, which in turn increases anxiety, which in turn produces a feeling of losing control over events?

It is of great benefit to identify the corollaries and effects of a variable, just as it is helpful to recognize the symptoms of a disease manifested in the patient. In most cases, however, successful treatment

---

[20] In his "Fundamentals of Concept Formation in Empirical Science," *International Encyclopedia of Unified Science*, 7, 2 (1952), 39ff, Carl Hempel states that concepts should have "theoretical or systematic import" and "empirical import." Similar criteria can be derived from G. Bergmann, *Philosophy of Science* (Madison: University of Wisconsin Press, 1957), p. 50, and A. Kaplan, *The Conduct of Inquiry* (San Francisco: Chandler, 1964), p. 79.

is dependent upon isolating the virus or other source of the ailment that produces the symptoms. Measles is not the appearance of red blotches on the skin, but these spots are indicators that the measles virus is present. By analogy, we can distinguish between properties of a crisis situation and its symptoms. Once the situation and its effects are empirically established, explanation and prediction will be improved.

From the standpoint of prediction, the turning point conceptualizations can be particularly troublesome. To define crisis as a critical turning point is something like telling a poisonous from a nonpoisonous snake by whether or not the person bitten dies. Not until some time after the bite can the diagnosis be made—too late, of course, for prediction. Analogously, the turning point construction cannot identify the crisis until after the "turn" or change occurs. This difficulty with the predictive criterion has been recognized by several authors who have defined the concept in that manner. "But how were we to choose the 'turning points' . . . if we did not have beforehand an over-all view of the succession of events?"[21] Wiener and Kahn[22] reason that a crisis exists when those policy makers involved *perceive* it to be a critical turning point regardless of whether a sharp change actually occurs or not. This position reduces the dependency upon post-hoc analysis only if those individuals able to test predictions can readily determine the perceptions of policy makers. A similar problem faces trait definitions which depend on the perceptions of decision makers.

In addition to their theoretical and empirical import, these two conceptualizations of crisis present somewhat different perspectives on the study of international politics. Understood as a turning point, crisis readily becomes a concept in the systemic analysis of international affairs. In this form of analysis, attention is drawn to various patterns of interaction among the relevant actors in the world. When the nation is the basic unit of analysis, the systems approach examines the relationships between nations rather than the processes within nations. Crisis lends itself to the systems perspective particularly when it is defined as an abrupt change or turning point in a pattern of interaction between nations that increases instability or possibly transforms an actor or the entire system.

---

[21] Freymond, *Saar Conflict*, p. xiv.
[22] Wiener and Kahn, *Crisis and Arms Control*, pp. 8–9.

Although the trait definition of crisis could be used in a systems approach, such a definition is especially valuable when studying internal processes by which policies are formed. If the characteristics of a crisis are interpreted as what the individual policy makers perceive, then the concept becomes quite relevant to the decision-making approach. Crisis becomes an occasion for decision. Attention is directed to the way in which the perception of the situation affects the decision process.

In summary, various formulations of crisis can be associated with different approaches to international politics. The manner in which the concept is formed depends, in part, upon the questions raised and the problems examined. Regardless of the approach, crisis must still be evaluated against such criteria as theoretical and empirical import. Since this study is concerned with decision making, crisis will be defined as a series of situational characteristics that are hypothesized to produce certain effects on making foreign policy decisions. By examining the validity of such hypotheses we can further evaluate the concept against the prediction and explanation criteria.

High Threat, Short Time, and Surprise

This section explores the empirical and theoretical worth of the concept of crisis defined in terms of three situational attributes: Crisis is a situation that (1) threatens the high-priority goals of the decision-making unit; (2) restricts the amount of time available for response before the situation is transformed; and (3) surprises the members of the decision-making unit when it occurs.

High threat is defined as a potential hindrance or obstruction to some object or state of affairs that a decision-making unit is motivated to achieve. For threat to occur, the decision makers must recognize that achievement of their goal or objective can be impeded or entirely obstructed.[23] *Short decision time* requires that in a restricted period of time the situation will be altered in some major way. After the situation is modified, a decision is either no longer possible or must be made under

---

[23] For a development of this definition of threat, see Margaret G. Hermann, "Testing a Model of Psychological Stress," *Journal of Personality*, 34 (1966), 381–396.

less favorable circumstances. Decision time can be shortened by reducing actual recorded time or by increasing the complexity of the task while the amount of actual time remains constant. Thus, if one of two tasks involves more coordination and subtasks than the other, it will induce greater time pressures than the simpler situation. *Surprise* is the third characteristic of crisis and should not be confused with the distinction between programmed and unprogrammed decision making.[24] Programmed decisions are made by applying procedures and rules established by handling problems previous to the one confronting the decision-making unit at the time. No routinized procedures exist for unprogrammed decisions. The absence of established procedures is often associated with a situation that has the unexpected or unanticipated qualities of surprise, but this relationship is not necessary. Surprise is defined, not as the lack of a programmed routine, but as the absence of awareness on the part of policy makers that the situation is likely to occur.

Several features of this definition of crisis require emphasis. First, all three attributes are necessary if a situation is to be called a crisis. Our contention is that a situation characterized by high threat, short decision time, and surprise will have different effects on decision making than a situation that possesses only one or two of these traits. The interaction of all three characteristics is hypothesized to have a unique influence on the formulation of policy. Certainly other variables such as who the policy makers are or what nations are involved will influence the outcome, but the argument is that the combination of these three situational variables also plays a significant role.

The second point is that this definition makes no attempt to be consistent with all the meanings various people have attached to the word crisis. We have already demonstrated that there is no generally accepted meaning of the concept. Ours is a stipulated definition which sacrifices some of the rich nuances and broad applicability found in the everyday use of the term in the hope of developing a concept with some predictive and explanatory power.

Although the proposed definition is not a deliberate effort to distill the common core of meaning found in the various uses of the word

---

[24] H. A. Simon, "The Role of Expectations in an Adaptive or Behavioristic Model," in Mary J. Bowman, ed., *Expectations, Uncertainty, and Business Behavior* (New York: Social Science Research Council, 1958).

crisis, enough similarity exists to warrant designating these three attributes as crisis characteristics rather than introducing some new situational term. The characteristics of high threat, short time, and surprise are present in a number of international situations that are frequently labeled crises. For the United States, all three crisis traits were present in the 1962 Soviet buildup of missiles in Cuba. President Kennedy referred to threat in his address to the nation on October 22: "This urgent transformation of Cuba into an important strategic base . . . constitutes an explicit threat to the peace and security of all the Americas. . . ."[25] Our earlier account of the missile crisis pointed out the short decision time and that since even the more complex sites were nearly completed, the United States would soon be confronted with a *fait accompli* if an immediate response were not made. America's desire to keep the discovery of the bases secret until the response plans were complete augmented the need for speed. Regarding the unanticipated nature of the situation, "there is no doubt that by deploying offensive nuclear missiles in Cuba, the Soviet Union did surprise Washington, including its intelligence bureaucracy."[26]

The United States, by its response, precipitated a crisis for the Soviet Union. As planned, the American policy makers caught their counterparts in the Soviet Union by surprise with the blockade. Evidence that Soviet leaders were surprised was indicated by their efforts to gain more time (for example, attempting to slow down merchant ships, and initially sending out vague messages). Khrushchev alluded to the threat and time pressures confronting the Soviet decision makers in his address before the Supreme Soviet: "We viewed the received telegrams as signs of extreme alarm. And it was indeed [a state] of alarm. . . . Immediate action was necessary to prevent an attack on Cuba and to preserve the peace."[27]

These three crisis traits were also present in the Korean decision. The United States devoted considerable effort in the early period following World War II to develop a collective security system and to establish the United Nations as an institution for keeping the peace. The

---

[25] Larson, *Cuban Crisis*, p. 41.

[26] K. Knorr, "Failures in Rational Intelligence Estimates: The Case of the Cuban Missiles," *World Politics*, 16 (April 1964), 457.

[27] R. Kolkowicz, *Conflicts in Soviet Party-Military Relations: 1962–1963*, Memorandum RM-3760-PR, RAND Corporation, Santa Monica, California, 1963, p. 10.

invasion of the Republic of Korea threatened to undermine these objectives. Time was short. Once the North Koreans seized the southern half of the peninsula, any move to displace them would be extremely difficult. Moreover, although American leaders judged invasion to be a possibility, they thought it very unlikely. "The surprise in Washington on Sunday, 25 June 1950, according to some observers, resembled that of another, earlier Sunday—Pearl Harbor, 7 December 1941."[28] From their systematic study of the Korean decision, Snyder and Paige conclude, "This was a major crucial decision in view of the cost in money and lives. . . . The decision time was unusually short. . . . The occasion for decision was one of surprise."[29]

Not all situations commonly described as crises fit the proposed definition, but the number of international situations bearing the characteristics is relatively large, and they are by no means limited to events in the Cold War. The outbreak of World War I is another illustration. Between the assassination of the Austro-Hungarian Archduke and the start of the war six weeks later, events characterized as "sudden surprise" and "point of no return" (high threat) have been identified for each of the major European powers.[30] The time lapse between the point of surprise and the point of no return was a maximum of six days for each of the principal nations. The time pressures are supported by the short lapse of time between the ultimatum to Serbia and the declaration of general war. The acceleration of verbal hostility between the major powers is further evidence of the extensive threat.[31]

Other investigators who use the trait approach to define crisis have specified one or more of the hypothesized characteristics. We have already noted that Miller and Iscoe include both the threat to high

---

[28] R. E. Appleman, *South to the Naktong, North to the Yalu: June–November 1950* (Washington, D.C.: Office of the Chief of Military History, Dept. of the Army, 1961), p. 37.

[29] R. C. Snyder and G. D. Paige, "The United States Decision to Resist Aggression in Korea: The Application of an Analytical Scheme," *Administrative Science Quarterly*, 3 (December 1958), 366.

[30] B. M. Russett, "Cause, Surprise, and No Escape," *Journal of Politics*, 24 (February 1962), 12.

[31] See D. A. Zinnes, R. C. North, and H. E. Koch, Jr., "Capability, Threat, and the Outbreak of War," in J. N. Rosenau, ed., *International Politics and Foreign Policy* (New York: Free Press, 1961), pp. 469–482; also D. A. Zinnes, "The Expression and Perception of Hostility in Prewar Crisis: 1914," in J. D. Singer, ed., *Quantitative International Politics* (New York: Free Press, 1968), pp. 85–119.

priority goals (item 3) and short decision time (item 1), as do Wiener and Kahn (items 3 and 10). In addition to other studies previously mentioned, both the threat and time attributes are incorporated in definitions by Milburn, Robinson, and Snyder.[32] Several other formulations of the concept cite the threat characteristic, and another emphasizes the importance of limited time.[33] R. T. LaPiere, who pioneered the use of crisis as a technical concept, asserts that only when phenomena are unpredictable can they be defined as crises.[34] Lasswell also suggests the unanticipated quality of crisis when he says that "the structure of expectation is the dominant feature of crisis."[35] A policy planner in the State Department concludes that the element of surprise in crisis places substantial constraints upon his task. "The number of theoretically possible crises in the years ahead is virtually infinite. Even to try to plan systematically for all that are moderately likely would be a questionable expenditure of resources."[36]

We have called attention to the interactive nature of the three crisis traits and to their appearance both in international situations and in other definitions of the concept. A third point is that the proposed definition is formulated from the perspective of the decision makers who ex-

---

[32] See T. W. Milburn, "What Constitutes Effective Deterrence?" in D. J. Hekhuis, A. L. Burns, and C. McClintock, eds., *International Stability* (New York: Wiley, 1964), p. 180; J. A. Robinson, "The Concept of Crisis in Decision-Making," in *Series Studies in Social and Economic Sciences*, National Institute of Social and Behavioral Science, Symposia Studies Series No. 11, Washington, D. C. (1962), p. 6; and R. C. Snyder, "The Korean Decision (1950) and the Analysis of Crisis Decision-Making," *Working Group Reports, Military Operations Research Society*, 1963, pp. 244, 246.

[33] Attention to the threat characteristic appears in H. D. Lasswell and associates, *Language of Politics* (New York: George Stewart, 1949), p. 23; also in Williams, "Functions of Communication," p. 15. Limited decision time is stressed in Hamblin, "Group Integration," p. 67.

[34] R. T. LaPiere, *Collective Behavior* (New York: McGraw-Hill, 1938), pp. 438–439.

[35] Lasswell *et al.*, *Language of Politics*, p. 23.

[36] G. A. Morgan, "Planning in Foreign Affairs: The State of the Art," *Foreign Affairs*, 39 (January 1961), 278. Without denying the element of surprise in crisis, a number of crisis management studies disagree with Morgan's conclusion that planning is not an effective way to cope with crises. One of the most frequent policy recommendations is for more planning to meet potential crises. For example, see J. C. Ausland and H. F. Richardson, "Crisis Management: Berlin, Cyprus, Laos," *Foreign Affairs*, 44, 2 (January 1966), 291–303; also Wiener and Kahn, *Crisis and Arms Control*, p. 183ff.

perience the crisis; that is, the situation threatens *their* goals, it surprises *them*, and it is *they* who are faced with short decision time. In other words, a crisis is identified in terms of the policy makers' "definition of the situation."[37] Defining crisis in this manner produces the relativistic aspects of the concept identified by Miller and Iscoe (item 4). Whereas the installation of rockets in Cuba by the Soviet Union was a crisis for American decision makers as soon as the missiles were detected, the situation was not a crisis for the U. S. S. R. until the United States made its response.

A crisis might more adequately be conceived not as a single situation, but as a succession of situations, continuing through time, which requires policy makers to redefine their image of the situation on the basis of additional information and past experience.[38] Thus, for American policy makers, the Korean crisis at first consisted of a situation defined as an invasion which could be repelled by the South Korean Army if they were given military supplies. The situation was repeatedly redefined as it became more apparent that only the intervention of United States, forces could prevent the seizure of the Republic of Korea. A series of evolving situations becomes a crisis for a nation when its decision makers define the situation as an unanticipated threat to national goals, the solution to which involves a short time for decision.

A final feature of the proposed definition of crisis involves the location of each trait on a continuum or dimension. International situations vary in the amount of threat, decision time, and awareness they present to a given group of policy makers. Therefore, we can conceive of the threat recognized in a particular international situation as falling, at some point, along a scale whose extremes might be "no threat" and

---

[37] R. C. Snyder, H. W. Bruck, and B. Sapin, eds., *Foreign Policy Decision Making* (New York: Free Press, 1962), pp. 75–85.

[38] W. Riker, "Events and Situations," *Journal of Philosophy*, 54 (January 1957), 60–61, describes situations as, "The boundaries, the stops and starts, that humans impose on continuous reality. . . ." or more formally, "A situation is an arrangement and condition of movers and actors in a specified, instantaneous, and spatially extended location." This definition, which is similar to that found in Snyder *et al.*, eds., *Foreign Policy Decision Making*, pp. 80–81, suggests the analogy of a single frame in a continuous motion picture. The antecedent conditions that precede the initial situation of any arbitrary sequence are important to the present definition of crisis. It is the failure of the decision makers to foresee the possible threat to their objectives that creates the unanticipated dimension.

"the greatest threat imaginable." A similar continuum could be constructed for time and awareness. For example, although both the Korean and Cuban decisions would be located toward the short decision time end of that continuum, Korea would be somewhat closer to the extreme point on the scale than the missile decision would be. In available physical time as well as in the perceptions of the decision makers, the former situation appears to have involved more acute time constraints. Thus, each of the three crisis characteristics can be conceptualized as near the extreme on their respective dimensions. We designate the three dimensions corresponding to the crisis characteristics as threat, decision time, and awareness. Any international situation can be identified according to its position on the three dimensions.

The cube represented in Figure 1 provides a three-dimensional display of the manner in which situations can be located by their threat, decision time, and awareness properties. The intersections of the dimensions, which form the corners of the cube, are the eight extreme combinations of these situational qualities. Each point of intersection can be described as an "ideal type" of situation, in that it is the analytical extreme "with which the real situation or action is compared and surveyed for the explication of certain of its significant components."[39] In Figure 1, several illustrative situations—plotted from the perspective of American decision makers—are shown to approach the corners of the cube, although they fall short of being ideal types.

Further situational analysis might reveal that various combinations of the three dimensions have differing impacts on the process of foreign policy decision making. In the present study, however, the analysis will be confined to the study of crisis situations. Though all but one of the corners forming the cube in Figure 1 could be described as "non-crisis" extremes, we will use that designation only for situations which cluster around the end of the diagonal opposite crisis (point A), that is, the end designated low threat, extended time, and anticipation (point G).[40]

---

[39] M. Weber, *The Methodology of the Social Sciences* (Glencoe: Free Press, 1949), p. 93.

[40] The ideal-type situations, represented by the eight corners of Figure 1, and their hypothesized decision processes are presented in C. F. Hermann, "International Crises as a Situational Variable," in J. N. Rosenau, ed., *International Politics and Foreign Policy*, second edition (New York: Free Press, in press).

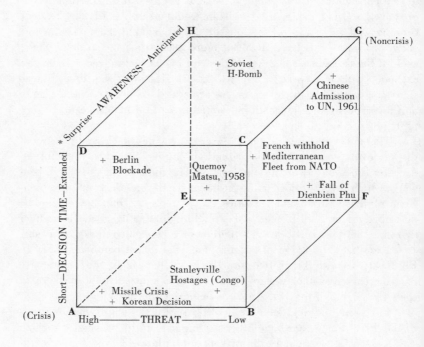

FIGURE 1   **A Representation of the Three Dimensions of Threat, Decision Time, and Awareness with Illustrative Situations from the Perspective of American Decision Makers**

A. High Threat/Short
   Time/Surprise
B. Low Threat/Short
   Time/Surprise
C. Low Threat/Extended
   Time/Surprise
D. High Threat/Extended
   Time/Surprise

E. High Threat/Short
   Time/Anticipated
F. Low Threat/Short
   Time/Anticipated
G. Low Threat/Extended
   Time/Anticipated
H. High Threat/Extended
   Time/Anticipated

Chapter 3

INTRODUCING CRISES
IN FOREIGN POLICY
ORGANIZATIONS

A Simulation Research Design

Simulation as a Research Method

Selection of Simulation. Simulation was used as the technique for studying crisis. Situations involving high threat, short time, and surprise were produced in a simulation of international politics. Like all models, simulations are means of representing properties of one system, A, through some other independent system, A'. Used in this general manner, the term "model" includes political games and simulations as well as such devices as geographical maps, chemical equations, and aerodynamic windtunnels. Compared to other models, a distinctive element of simulations is their ability to represent changes that may occur in a complex system even though these changes cannot be accurately forecast by humans who know only the initial properties of the system. Simulations are operating models that can represent the dynamic, nonlinear qualities that so often characterize human behavior. For this reason simulations recently have become of considerable interest to social scientists. In political science, for example, both computer and noncomputer operating models have been used to study national elections, public opinion, legislative behavior, developing societies, disarmament problems, judicial decisions, and international politics.[1]

---

[1] For a survey of simulation activity throughout the social sciences, see H. Guetzkow, ed., *Simulation in Social Science: Readings* (Englewood Cliffs: Prentice-Hall, 1962); also R. P. Abelson, "Simulation of Social Be-

Crises can be studied by interviewing those who participate in the formulation and conduct of foreign policy. Detailed case studies of previous crises, such as the two described in Chapter 1, can be compiled. Alternatively, crises can be analyzed by content analysis which uses written documents and quantifiable records of past events.[2] Given these and other methods for direct analysis, why were political crises investigated in a simulation of world politics?

Access, control, and replication are three words that signify the merits of a laboratory technique like simulation. These advantages are important in the construction of empirical theories of politics. The crowded lives of policy makers make them virtually inaccessible to systematic observation during periods of emergency. This was illustrated by the problems of reporting the news that the press faced in situations like the Korean and Cuban crises. Personal reflections and interviews must be deferred until later when memory lapses and intervening events might bias and hinder accurate reconstruction of earlier situations. Furthermore, in the press of his activity, a policy maker may not be aware of significant influences upon his actions. The sensitivity of written documents about crises often precludes public access to them for a number of years. By contrast, a researcher has almost complete access to the participants, the events, and the histories of a simulated world.

Ernest Nagel, a philosopher of science, contends that to make scientific headway "either *controlled* experimentation . . . or *controlled* investigation . . . appears to be indispensable."[3] Unfortunately, students of political behavior seldom have the control of human affairs necessary for the critical tests required to confirm or reject hypotheses. In the real world,[4] a recurrent series of events may be confounded with major

---

havior," in G. Lindzey and E. Aronson, eds., *Handbook of Social Psychology*. Revised edition (Reading, Mass.: Addison-Wesley, 1968). The various uses of this technique in political science are described in C. F. Hermann, "Simulation: Political Processes," in the *International Encyclopedia of the Social Sciences*, 14 (New York: Macmillan, 1968), 274–281.

[2] These alternative methods for studying crisis are used in the contributions to Hermann, ed., *Contemporary Research on International Crises*.

[3] E. Nagel, *The Structure of Science* (New York: Harcourt, Brace & World, 1961), p. 453.

[4] The terms "reality" and "real" are used here to contrast what occurs in simulations with the actual worlds they are intended to represent. Sidney Verba in "Simulation, Reality, and Theory in International Relations,"

uncontrolled elements capable of producing untested—and occasionally, untestable—rival explanations. Although political scientists eventually want to be able to interpret international politics in all its richness and complexity, the capacity to hold some features of a political process relatively constant, or to eliminate them entirely, makes it possible to determine what changes in one variable are associated with changes in some other identifiable variables.

"Repeatability is a key element in all controlled experimentation."[5] As this comment suggests, simulation makes possible the repeated observations necessary to verify hypotheses. A simulation can be assigned the same set of initial conditions and can be played through a set of circumstances over and over again. In actual international affairs, however, the natural occurrence of comparable events may be sharply separated in time and space. In some instances a situation may happen only once, as in the case of the proliferation of nuclear weapons.[6]

These qualities of access, control, and replication identify simulation as a method of experimentation under laboratory conditions. We already have noted a distinguishing feature of simulations that makes them particularly valuable for the study of political problems. This is their ability to "operate," that is, to represent the complex, dynamic processes that may occur as a political system continues over a period of time.

Despite the assets of simulation, there are notable liabilities.

World Politics, 16 (April 1964), 495*n.,* has observed that these terms may be misleading because in simulations "there are real people interacting or real computers computing." He might have added that it is often difficult to establish what is the "reality" to be modeled. A better designation for the phenomena to be represented by a simulation might be "referent system."

[5] R. C. Snyder, "Some Perspectives on the Use of Experimental Techniques in the Study of International Relations," in H. Guetzkow, C. F. Alger, R. A. Brody, R. C. Noel, and R. C. Snyder, *Simulation in International Relations* (Englewood Cliffs: Prentice-Hall, 1963), p. 7.

[6] Several simulations have explored historical, nonrecurrent events. One study involved seventeen replications of the spread of nuclear weapons. See R. A. Brody, "Some Systemic Effects of the Spread of Nuclear Weapons Technology: A Study Through Simulation of a Multi-Nuclear Future," *Journal of Conflict Resolution,* 7 (December 1963), 665–753. Another study simulated twice the political crisis prior to World War I. See C. F. Hermann and M. G. Hermann, "An Attempt to Simulate the Outbreak of World War I," *American Political Science Review,* 61 (June 1967), 400–416.

Validity is a critical problem. That is, does the simulation replicate the features of the reality it is intended to portray? It is easy to be incredulous about a method for studying international politics in which variables are ignored, simplified, or transformed. It is easy to have strong reservations about a method that either involves no humans or involves human participants who frequently lack relevant political experience and who seldom are exposed to the actual consequences of their decisions. Might it not be appropriate to be cautious about a method which, as one observer has noted, can produce "war without pain"?[7]

Similar difficulties can be found in a vast array of other models used to increase our understanding of the world. Consider as an illustration the Mercator projection of the world. A spheroid more than 7,930 miles in diameter is represented on a flat piece of paper, usually small enough to hold. Almost all the known features of our earth are excluded from such models. Mercator maps do attempt to represent the location and relative size of major land masses and bodies of water, although in the upper latitudes even these properties are badly distorted. Despite the limitations, models of this type serve a valuable purpose.

The comparison of simulations to maps should not be construed as an argument for the quick acceptance of simulations. On the contrary, we wish to emphasize the need for more validity assessments of most of the models used to interpret reality—whether they be verbal, pictorial, or mathematical. One advantage of simulations may be that most people are unwilling to accept their results in an uncritical manner; therefore, simulation findings are likely to be more carefully scrutinized than are those derived from some other models.

Elsewhere, a proposal was made to tackle the problems of simulation validation with a multiple strategy in which research moves back and forth between simulation data and data collected from the political world it represents.[8] The relative newness of simulation requires that research topics be investigated with this method and the results compared with parallel studies that check the same hypotheses with materials drawn from actual foreign policy and world politics. If models of selected

---

[7] T. C. Schelling, "War Without Pain," *World Politics*, 15 (April 1963), 465–485.

[8] C. F. Hermann, "Validation Problems in Games and Simulations with Special Reference to Models of International Politics," *Behavioral Science*, 12 (May 1967), 216–231.

features of international politics can be devised with a high degree of correspondence, their use as an additional research tool can help offset the limitations of other methods.

Inter-Nation Simulation Description. The particular operating model, or representation of international politics, used in this research is the Inter-Nation Simulation. Because detailed descriptions of the selected simulation are found elsewhere,[9] this description outlines only the basic model and features relevant to our research.

The Inter-Nation Simulation combines the activity of human participants with a programmed set of relationships designed to represent aspects of international affairs. The relationships contained in the programmed calculations operate in the same manner in every simulation trial (or run) and provide continuity in the model.[10] The participants are usually different in each run and assume foreign policy roles for one of several nations. The Inter-Nation Simulation operates in cycles or periods, each 50 to 70 minutes long. In every period the human and programmed aspects of the simulation interact when the participants report how they have allocated their nation's resources. On the basis of that information, the established programs are used to compute the resources available to the nation in the subsequent period and to determine whether the governmental decision makers maintained themselves in office.

---

[9] Brody, "Systemic Effects of Spread of Nuclear Weapons"; W. J. Crow, "A Study of Strategic Doctrines Using the Inter-Nation Simulation," *Journal of Conflict Resolution*, 7 (September 1963), 580–589; Guetzkow *et al.*, *Simulation in International Relations*; H. Guetzkow, "Some Correspondences Between Simulations and 'Realities' in International Relations," in M. Kaplan, ed., *New Approaches to International Relations* (New York: St. Martin's, 1968). Also see the *Inter-Nation Simulation Kit* prepared by H. Guetzkow and C. H. Cherryholmes, and distributed by Science Research Associates, Inc.

[10] The programmed calculations can either be conducted on a computer or with a staff of four or five trained persons using desk calculators and other special aids. Although the Inter-Nation Simulation calculations have been modified from time to time, the basic model was written in a FORTRAN program called INSCAL by Robert Pendley at Northwestern University. Lack of access to a computer at our field location dictated that our calculations be done manually.

One prominent characteristic of the Inter-Nation Simulation is its abstract quality; that is, it does not attempt to represent specific nations in the contemporary world. Heads of government are not identified as premiers, chairmen, or presidents, but as Central Decision Makers. Real world political titles are similarly avoided for the other roles. Nor are nations identified as France, the Soviet Union, or the United States, but they are assigned fictional names like Algo, Bega, or Colo. The intent is to encourage the participants in the simulation to respond with their own predispositions toward events in the simulated world rather than to play the role of contemporary world leaders. Unless the individuals in the simulation are analysts of a particular nation and its policy makers, their expectations of how the role should be played are likely to lead to substantial distortions of reality. To avert these difficulties, the Inter-Nation Simulation is constructed for the operation of behaviors that both professional decision makers and those not normally engaged in public policy share when acting under the constraints imposed upon them by a real or simulated political environment.

The number of nations in the game is determined by the needs of the particular study. In each nation, two or more individuals assume the role of decision makers. The head of government, the Central Decision Maker (CDM), has ultimate authority for all governmental policies. Further specification of roles depends upon the number of other individuals assigned to the nation, but at various times provisions have been made for an Internal Decision Maker (IDM) who is in charge of budgetary allocations, an External Decision Maker (EDM) who is responsible for foreign affairs, and a Force Decision Maker (FDM) who controls military matters. Unlike these four individuals, the Aspiring Decision Maker (ADM) is not a government member, but the representative of rival national elites who attempts to gain the office of CDM. With the exception of the ADM, role-occupants hold office at the pleasure of the Central Decision Maker, who tries to further his policies and remain as head of the government.

The participants in each nation make decisions about how to utilize various kinds of resources. The natural, human, and industrial resources of a nation are compressed into a single prototypic variable designated Basic Capability. This simulation unit approximates the Gross National Product. Basic Capabilities can be used to produce additional Basic Capabilities or three other types of resources: (1) Consumption Satisfaction units, which represent the totality of goods and services available to the population and the quantity of which reflects the nation's standard of living; (2) Nuclear Force Capabilities, which are equivalent to nuclear military devices; and (3) Conventional Force Capabilities, which constitute all non-nuclear military elements. Every nation has a Generation Rate for each type of unit. These rates represent the state of development and efficiency in the industries necessary for producing one of the simulation units. The higher the Generation Rate, the more new resources are developed for each Basic Capability unit assigned to that type of production. In each period every nation must allocate for its population enough of its Basic Capabilities to maintain a subsistence standard of living. After meeting this Consumption Satisfaction Minimum, decision makers allocate their resources according to their own objectives.

Decisions regarding the allocation of resources are recorded on the Decision Form which is completed once, by each nation, during every 50 to 70 minute period. This statement of allocations parallels a government's annual budget; thus, a simulation period is roughly equivalent to a year. Simulation staff members, or a computer program, calculate the consequences of the Decision Form according to the programmed relationships in the operating model. These computations determine the government's likelihood of remaining in office and the new distribution of its available resources. Results are quickly supplied to the national decision makers, who use them as the basis for their next period's decisions. In summary, the Decision Form is the major connection between the free activity of the participants and the structured program in the simulation.

The Central Decision Maker and his government are dependent for their continuance in office on the Validators, who are a symbolic representation of politically effective groups in the society such as military juntas, political parties, or pressure groups. Each government is assumed to require the support of the dominant validating groups in its country. Governments differ, however, in sensitivity to the demands of their Validators. This ideological factor—the degree to which governments must be responsive to the Validators' desires—is represented as Decision Latitude. The greater the Decision Latitude, the less attentive the government need be to dissatisfactions of the critical elites without risking loss of office. Even the most dictatorial government, however, will fall if the wants of its needed political supporters are neglected for too long. When the Validators become too dissatisfied with the policies of their government, they may vote the incumbents out of office, or in a nation that does not permit elections, they may overthrow the regime and allow the Aspiring Decision Maker to establish a new government.

The Validators' level of satisfaction is based primarily on two components. One is the number of Consumption Satisfaction units beyond the minimal subsistence level with which the Validators are supplied. The second is the nation's relative security, that is, how the nation's military strength plus that of any allied government compares with the armaments of any potentially hostile nation or alliance. A new level of Validator Satisfaction is calculated by the computer or staff when it determines the new resources produced by the nation. At the beginning of a period this information is reported to each simulated nation on a new Decision Form. If a government discovers that the overall level of satisfaction among its Validators is falling and its Decision Latitude is so low that it cannot ignore the discontented elites, then some efforts must be made to meet their demands. When revolution seems likely, a government can order a portion of its existing conventional military forces to Internal Control, thereby increasing the probability that the regime can defeat with force any attempt to overthrow it.

Complementing the more structured internal aspects of the Inter-Nation Simulation are the less programmed arrangements for interaction between nations. Written messages may be exchanged between any participants whether or not they are members of the same nation. Bilateral or multilateral conferences can be arranged for face to face communication. A World Newspaper, issued at regular intervals, and an International Organization provide further channels for communication.

The substantive interactions between nations are quite diverse. Trades and aids are encouraged both by differing sets of Generation Rates and by the differing amounts of resources available to the nations at the beginning of the game. The possibility of forming economic or political alliances fosters political aid and development programs. Both limited and total wars can be executed according to any one of a variety of strategies. A counterforce strategy is achieved by attacking enemy Force Capabilities, a countervalue strategy by attacking Basic Capabilities, and a massive retaliation strategy by a nuclear response against all types of targets. Governments may be subverted; nations may combine or disappear; disarmament programs may be adopted; radical changes in the relative economic or military position of nations or alliances may occur. The particular course of events in the simulated international sphere is a function of the decision makers and the internal constraints under which they operate.

Summary. In this section we have offered three reasons—access, control, and replication—for studying crisis decision making through a laboratory technique like simulation. The merit of simulation as a model capable of representing dynamic, nonlinear processes has been noted. Finally, the particular operating model, the Inter-Nation Simulation, has been described as involving individuals assigned to foreign policy roles who (1) interact with other nations and (2) make periodic allocations of their national resources to satisfy their nation's elites and to obtain other objectives. From the interactions between nations and the allocation of resources, the future of each nation is computed with programmed calculations.

Adapting the Simulation: Organizational Context

Foreign Policy Organizations. Previous research with the Inter-Nation Simulation concerned the actions and interactions of nations as units or, alternatively, it concentrated on individual personalities and behaviors.[11] By contrast, the present research explores the decision-

---

[11] Studies with the Inter-Nation Simulation that have focused on national interaction include Brody, "Systemic Effects of Spread of Nuclear Weapons"; W. J. Crow and L. N. Solomon, "A Simulation Study of Strategic Doctrines" (mimeo, Western Behavioral Sciences Institute, La Jolla, California, 1962); J. R. Raser and W. J. Crow, "Winsafe II: An Inter-Nation Simulation Study of Deterrence Postures Embodying Capacity to Delay Response" (mimeo, Western Behavioral Sciences Institute, La Jolla, California, 1964); G. D. Wright, "Inter-Group Communication and Attraction in Inter-Nation Simulation" (unpublished doctoral dissertation, Washington University, St. Louis, Missouri, 1963). Among those examining individual behavior are: Margaret G. Hermann, "Stress, Self-Esteem, and Defensiveness in an Inter-Nation Simulation" (unpublished doctoral dissertation, Northwestern University, Evanston, Illinois, 1965); M. J. Driver, "Conceptual Structure and Group Processes in an Inter-Nation Simulation." Research Bulletin RB–62–15, Educational Testing Service and Princeton University, Princeton, New Jersey, 1962; Hermann and Hermann, "An Attempt to Simulate"; A. W. Sherman, "The Social Psychology of Bilateral Negotiations" (unpublished master's thesis, Northwestern University, Evanston, Illinois, 1963).

making process within nations, and therefore, the simulation must represent the organizational environment in which actual policy makers operate.

The intricate network of communication and coordination necessary for a State Department decision, the interagency bargaining involved in building strategic policy, and the discussions of foreign policy machinery presented in comparative foreign policy texts alert us to the organizational context in which foreign policy is conducted.[12] Although they recognize some differences between governmental foreign policy organizations and other types of organizations, Snyder, Bruck, and Sapin observe that "foreign policy-making is most fruitfully analyzed as decision-making in an organizational context."[13] The basic Inter-Nation Simulation model contains some elements of an organizational environment; however, in research whose primary substantive focus is the process by which nations handle crises, the representation of organizational features is of particular importance. The resulting task involved two questions. First, what are the critical features of any organization?[14] Second, how can these features be incorporated into the Inter-Nation Simulation?

Zelditch and Hopkins list four major elements necessary to establish

---

[12] Examples of literature emphasizing the organizational aspects of foreign policy formation are J. E. Black and K. W. Thompson, *Foreign Policies in a World of Change* (New York: Harper and Row, 1963); S. P. Huntington, *The Common Defense* (New York: Columbia University Press, 1961); R. C. Macridis, ed., *Foreign Policy in World Politics*, 3rd ed. (Englewood Cliffs: Prentice-Hall, 1967); C. Ogburn, Jr., "The Flow of Policy-Making in the Department of State," in J. N. Rosenau, ed., *International Politics and Foreign Policy* (New York: Free Press, 1961), pp. 229–233.

[13] Snyder *et al.*, eds., *Foreign Policy Decision Making*, p. 103.

[14] How many different bureaucratic organizations are normally engaged in the conduct of a major nation's foreign policy? The answer depends on how organizational boundaries are defined. In the United States, for example, one could identify the Departments of State and Defense, the White House, CIA, USIA, and, on numerous policy issues, many other organizations. Alternatively, they can be collapsed under a single heading like "the Executive Branch." For the present, whether the simulated nation should represent one or several organizations is subordinate to establishing organizational features that distinguish it from other human collectivities such as small groups or communities.

an organization in a laboratory setting.[15] Their criteria for an organization are that it be (1) formalized with explicitly established policies and rules; (2) differentiated through both distinct subunits and separated statuses within the subunits; (3) integrated through rigorously defined subordination; and (4) complicated structurally with at least three subunits involving various levels of authority. For the crisis research, an effort was made to represent these features in the simulation through the detailed specification of roles, the creation of special-task subunits, the introduction of mediated communication, and the establishment of a hierarchy of authority.

Role Specification. To promote the first two criteria (formalized rules, differentiated statuses) of Zelditch and Hopkins, one property introduced in the simulation was the separation and definition of roles. A total of five different roles was used in each simulated nation (CDM, IDM, EDM, FDM, and ADM). To define and separate each position, every participant was furnished with a written description of his role before the simulation began. Further explanations were made in the oral instructions. During the simulation, role distinctions were encouraged by limiting the distribution of some forms and information to those positions with primary responsibility for particular tasks. Reports on these tasks, periodically required from each participant, acted to reinforce their role assignments.

Special-Task Subgroups. The creation of subgroups within the simulated governments attempted to fulfill the criteria of "distinct subgroups" and "structural complexity" advanced by Zelditch and Hopkins. Several steps were taken to establish two policy groups in each govern-

---

[15] M. Zelditch, Jr., and T. K. Hopkins, "Laboratory Experiments with Organizations," in A. Etzioni, ed., *Complex Organizations: A Sociological Reader* (New York: Holt, Rinehart and Winston, 1961), pp. 472–473. Although differing in their emphasis, other references which lend support to one or more of these characteristics as the distinguishing properties of organizations include P. M. Blau and W. R. Scott, *Formal Organizations* (San Francisco: Chandler, 1962), p. 14; R. M. Cyert and J. G. March, *A Behavioral Theory of the Firm* (Englewood Cliffs: Prentice-Hall, 1963), p. 27; R. H. Hall, "The Concept of Bureaucracy: An Empirical Assessment," *American Journal of Sociology,* 69 (July 1963), 33; and J. G. March and H. A. Simon with H. Guetzkow, *Organizations* (New York: Wiley, 1958), pp. 2–4.

ment—one consisting of the Central (CDM) and Internal (IDM) Decision Makers, the other composed of the External (EDM) and Force (FDM) Decision Makers. In addition to these two-man groups within each government, the Aspiring Decision Maker (ADM) acted as the representative of another, nongovernmental group. Part of the training session before each simulation was conducted with the EDMs and FDMs meeting separately from the other three role occupants. Furthermore, the *Participants' Manual,* circulated before the simulation, emphasized the need for the CDM and IDM to work closely together, and it alerted the ADM that, should he become head of the government, his IDM would be the person in whom he should have the greatest confidence. During the simulation, regular meetings between the CDM and IDM and between the EDM and FDM were incorporated into the schedule. In their meetings, the CDM and IDM made official allocation of the nation's resources, whereas the EDM-FDM meetings were devoted to surveying the current world situation and designing policies to meet it.

The written communications of the participants provided a partial check on how much the two subgroups emerged in the simulated foreign policy organizations. A variable called a two-way message channel was introduced to measure the development of the subgroup. A message channel is a connection between any two simulation participants that is established by the exchange of written communications. Channels with some *mutual* initiation of messages were assumed to constitute a better indicator of shared interests and need to interact than those in which all the messages were sent by one individual and largely ignored by the other. Two-way message channels are those in which at least 25 per cent of the total number of messages were initiated by one participant and no more than 75 per cent by the other. By definition the measure is limited to groups composed of only two individuals. If the proposed subgroups materialize, then frequent and active two-way communication should occur between the decision makers in the specified groups.

The results revealed by the data in Table 1 are somewhat unexpected. The most frequent two-way channels, which also contain the highest average volume of messages across all eleven runs, were between the Central Decision Maker and each of the three individuals in his government. The single largest message volume was between the CDM and his IDM, which suggests considerable collaboration and the probability that in most runs they became a subgroup. The attempt, however,

TABLE 1 **Two-Way Message Channels Based on Written Communications in 66 Simulated Nations**

	Within Government						Between Government Member & ADM			
	CDM IDM	CDM FDM	CDM EDM	EDM IDM	EDM FDM	IDM FDM	ADM CDM	ADM FDM	ADM IDM	ADM EDM
Number of 2-Way Channels[a]	43	44	45	38	19	2	34	7	4	14
Total Messages in 2-Way Channels	524	461	411	300	86	9	209	33	16	46
Average Number of Messages in 2-Way Channels	12.19	10.48	9.13	7.89	4.53	4.50	6.15	4.71	4.00	3.29

[a] In each nation one channel could be established between any two positions. Therefore, the highest possible number of two-way message channels in each combination of positions for the entire study was 66.

to establish the EDM and FDM as a secondary policy group was not very successful according to these data. Exchanges between these two positions ranked sixth in the frequency with which two-way channels were formed and seventh in the average number of messages exchanged. An unexpectedly strong interaction appears to have emerged between the Internal and External Decision Makers. That interaction constituted the fourth most frequently used channel. Because the indicator was designed to identify two-man groups, it is not clear whether these two officials formed a three-man unit involving the CDM, as suggested by the

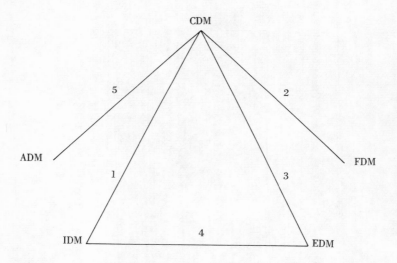

FIGURE 2   **Most Frequently Used Two-Way Message Channels Within the 66 Simulated Nations**

NOTE: Each line represents a two-way channel. Numbers correspond to the rank order of the volume of written messages exchanged in the channel.

triangle in Figure 2. If each of the lines in Figure 2 is assumed to represent a subgroup, then the nations tended to separate into five such divisions. On the other hand, the figure can be interpreted as containing a three-man group (CDM-EDM-IDM) with the CDM also participating in two additional groups—one with the FDM and the other with the ADM. Either way Figure 2 is examined, it suggests that the simulated nations frequently contained subunits, although not necessarily those intended by the experimenters.

Mediated Communication. In addition to the formation of subgroups, the Zelditch and Hopkins criterion of structural complexity was introduced in the simulation by the use of mediated communication. Guetzkow and Bowes wrote, "Organizations are groups which seem distinguishable from 'small' groups by virtue of the indirect, mediated interaction which occurs among their members."[16] The implication here is that a relatively small group of individuals can produce behavior that resembles an organization if the primary means of interaction is not carried out in face to face exchanges. In the present study, each participant worked by himself in a separate cubicle. Although conference time was available, its use was regulated. This forced participants to do much of their communication through written messages.

Authority Hierarchy. A final organizational attribute introduced in the simulation was a hierarchy of authority. The development of an authority structure can be related to the Zelditch and Hopkins's criteria of formalized rules and defined subordination. As in previous simulation exercises, the Central Decision Maker was given the ultimate authority in the nation. To lengthen the chain of authority, the Internal Decision Maker was designated second-in-command with the External and Force Decision Makers responsible to him. The IDM regulated the conference time available to the men in these two positions. His authorization was required before the FDM could complete military trades or grants and before the EDM could arrange comparable nonmilitary exchanges.

Data collected in the simulation provide several means of estimating the amount of recognition the participants gave to the designated authority structure. A partial indicator of the effectiveness of this arrangement is displayed in Table 2 by the pattern of written communications initiated by the EDM and FDM. In both roles, the largest volume of messages was addressed to the CDM. The next largest number of messages was addressed to the IDM.

---

[16] H. Guetzkow and A. E. Bowes, "The Development of Organizations in a Laboratory," *Management Science*, 3 (July 1957), 380.

TABLE 2 **Volume of Written Messages Initiated by EDMs and FDMs to Other Roles in Their Nations ($N = 66$ nations)**

		Addressee				
		CDM	IDM	EDM	FDM	ADM
Initiator	EDM	305	174	—	76	26
	FDM	311	116	71	—	28

Assuming that authority is associated with the number of communication channels in which a role occupant actively participates, Figure 2 also provides information on the pattern of authority. In that figure, all four of the potential channels connecting the Central Decision Maker to the other participants in his nation are among the five most frequently used two-way message channels. The authority of the IDM is less clear. The common channel between the Internal and External Decision Makers results in their involvement in an equal number of communication channels.

Additional information about the authority structure comes from ratings made by observers during conferences between the simulation participants. Trained observers judged each participant on his success in influencing the group's decision.[17] For each of the five roles, the observers' ratings were totaled for all the conferences held by the 66 nations in the study. The difference in successful influence between the various roles was subjected to statistical analysis.[18] The influence scores

---

[17] The instructions and ten-point rating scale used by the observers were as follows:

How successful was each participant in influencing the decisions of the group? Place the symbol for each participant (C, I, E, F, A) somewhere on the following line.

```
:     :     :     :     :     :     :     :     :     :     :
1     2     3     4     5     6     7     8     9     10
Successful                                          Unsuccessful
```

To determine to what extent our coders could agree on how to rate the influence of the participants, a sample of 169 conference participants was rated by two different observers. A rank-order correlation indicated that the inter-coder reliability between trained observers was .70.

[18] Two statistical tests were involved in establishing whether there were significant differences between the observer ratings of influence for the five simulation positions. First, a Kruskal-Wallis one-way analysis of vari-

of heads of government (CDMs) were greater than those of the other roles ($p < .01$).[19] The Internal Decision Makers, who were designated second-in-command, were judged to exercise significantly greater influence than either the roles of the military (FDM) or those of the opposition (ADM) ($p < .05$). However, the role of the IDM did not exert significantly more influence than did the role of the foreign minister (EDM). For their part, the External Decision Makers exercised significantly more influence than did the Aspiring Decision Makers ($p < .01$), but the EDMs did not differ from the Force Decision Makers. Finally, the influence rating of the FDMs was higher than that of the ADMs ($p < .01$). The ADMs (the representatives of the opposition) were judged least successful in influencing group decisions. These various indicators of the authority structure suggest the CDMs were recognized as being the highest authority. The IDMs were second-in-command but were closely challenged by the EDMs.

Summary. To summarize, a study of decision making in foreign policy crises requires that attention be directed to the organizational context in which real world policy makers work. Four criteria proposed

---

ance was performed to ascertain whether any significant difference existed among the five roles examined collectively. See S. Siegel, *Nonparametric Statistics for the Behavioral Sciences* (New York: McGraw-Hill, 1956), pp. 184–193. When a significant result was obtained, the roles were compared in pairs using Mann-Whitney U tests to determine between which particular roles a significant difference appeared (see Appendix III).

[19] The parenthetical remark refers to the probability (p) that no statistically significant difference exists between the influence scores of CDMs and those of any other position. In other words, there is a certain probability that the influence differences found in our sample of 66 simulated nations are only chance differences and would disappear if we had conducted more simulations. Similarly, one sample of 10 tosses of a coin might result in 10 heads and 0 tails, even though a larger series of coin tosses could be expected to more closely approximate a 50-50 split between heads and tails. A test of significance for a given statistic tells us with what degree of confidence we can reject the null hypothesis. (A null hypothesis states that there is no difference in the population from which the two samples are drawn.) The significance test reported at this point in the text ($p < .01$) is read, "The probability (that the observed difference results only from chance) is less than 1 in 100." The null hypothesis will be rejected in this study when p is equal to or less than .05.

by Zelditch and Hopkins were used as guide lines for employing a small group of people in a laboratory setting to represent a complex organization. The procedures introduced in the simulation and the criteria they were intended to fulfill are as follows: (1) specification of roles (criteria—formalized rules, differentiated statuses and subgroups); (2) special-task subgroups (criteria—differentiated statuses and subgroups, structural complexity); (3) mediated communication (criterion—structural complexity); and (4) hierarchy of authority (criteria—formalized rules, defined subordination).

Adapting the Simulation: Goals, Confederates, and Other Modifications

Assigning National Goals. In the few previous simulations that have specified objectives for national leaders to pursue, these goals have been broad in scope (e.g., security, domination, or internal growth) and without programmed incentives for their achievement.[20] To include threat to goals as a crisis characteristic required that national objectives be clearly specified and that inducements be designed to motivate the participants. To increase similarity between runs, the same nation should experience comparable threats to the same set of goals in every trial or replication.

All the governments shared two common goals: (1) preserving their nations as separate units; and (2) maintaining their governments in office. Each nation received three of six other designated objectives. Although each of these six goals was shared by three nations, every nation had a unique combination of three goals. Several considerations entered the decision to give nations multiple goals. First, the correspondence to reality seemed increased, inasmuch as a "nation with but a single goal is a dangerous fiction."[21] Second, each nation should experience a series of situations differing in the degree of threat. It was

---

[20] See Guetzkow *et al.*, *Simulation in International Politics*, pp. 29, 32; and D. L. Meier, "Progress Report: Event Simulation Project." Unpublished manuscript, Northwestern University, Evanston, Illinois, 1963, ditto, p. 2.

[21] T. W. Milburn, "What Constitutes Effective Deterrence?" in D. J. Hekhuis, A. L. Burns, and C. McClintock, eds., *International Stability* (New York: Wiley, 1964), p. 176.

easier to create distinctive threat conditions when the same goal did not have to be repeatedly endangered. The third consideration for establishing a range of objectives was to permit a test of the hypothesis that decision makers tend to reorder the priorities of their goals under crisis.

A variety of techniques was used to encourage goal achievement in the simulation. Several weeks before the experiment began, the simulation participants were given a list of goals that actual countries might pursue in international relations. The list included the six goals that were assigned later to the various simulated nations. The decision makers were asked to rate all the listed goals on a four-point scale ranging from "not at all important" to "considerably important." Subsequently, an individual was placed in a nation only if he had rated all three of its objectives on the upper half of the scale. The *Participants' Manual* also stressed the necessity of working toward the assigned national goals if one was to excel as a decision maker. In the real world, policy makers are seldom presented with an exclusive and clearly specified method for moving toward a broad national objective; but in the simulation, goals were arranged for the participants so that their progress or retrogression on each one could be measured. The goals and their simulation specifications for development were:

1. Promote democracy in your own country and in the rest of the world. (Determined by reductions in Decision Latitude initiated by the decision makers.)
2. Strengthen the national defense system of your nation against external attack. (Determined by the proportion of Basic Capabilities allocated to the defense of other Basic Capabilities and of Nuclear Force Capabilities.)
3. Improve the strength of your original military alliance in relation to that of its rival. (Determined by calculations made on the total relative strength of military alliances.)
4. Increase the proportion of consumer goods available to the population of your nation. (Determined by the proportion of Consumption Satisfaction units produced above the minimum required.)
5. Develop and expand your nation's nuclear capability. (Determined by the increase in Nuclear Force Capabilities.)
6. Expand the resources of the economic development bank. (Determined by the total Basic Capability assets of the World Bank.)

At the end of each period, when the consequences were calculated for a nation's use of its resources, the simulation staff also checked on one of the three specific, national goals. In any period a government's progress was measured on only one objective—to expedite the quick reporting of results. This selective checking also emphasized that at any particular time it was possible that the Validators were not equally concerned with all their goals. Participants did not know which goal would be computed. Nations that ignored the calculated goal experienced a reduction in overall Validator Satisfaction, thus increasing the probability of the government losing office. If the examination revealed advances toward the objective, the level of Validator Satisfaction was increased, and in addition, the nation was given a bonus in Basic Capability units. The rationale given to the decision makers for the increase in resources was that the Validators expand production when they recognize that the government is fulfilling a desired objective. Finally, the decision makers were reminded of their goals in two ways. A list of national goals was posted in every office, and they were required to rate the importance of their goals every period.

Confederate Participants. To insure comparable crises in each replication (run) of the simulation, a group of staff members posed as participants and initiated the experimental situations, that is, they deliberately "staged" crisis and noncrisis situations. Each experimental situation was introduced as a message from one of the staff participants or confederates. A number of different positions were manned by these agents. Two of the eight nations were operated by two-man confederate teams. The permanent International Organization chairman, the newspaper editor, and one of the simulation directors also used their positions to plant crisis and noncrisis messages.

Although staff participants were male college students and the other participants were Navy personnel, a ploy was developed to conceal their experimental function. At the beginning of the training session, the directors noted that there was an insufficient number of men to represent the scheduled number of nations. Before the assembled participants the directors stated that they would use university students familiar with the simulation for the remaining positions. In an hour (during which time the Navy participants received further instruction) the staff members arrived and were assigned roles even though it was announced that their number prevented a full contingent of decision makers in the remaining two nations. At the end of the simulation, most of the Navy participants completed a questionnaire in which one-third of the respondents (105 out of 315) identified correctly at least one of the positions assumed by confederates. Of this one-third, 25 per cent (26 out of 105) also believed that one or more of the nations operated by Navy personnel were confederates. In other words, by the end of the experiment, 79 of the 315 participants (25 per cent) who completed the questionnaire identified one or more confederate roles without erroneously including nonconfederates.[22]

World Bank. Several other modifications were made in the Inter-Nation Simulation. A World Development Bank was created at the beginning of each run with authority to invest the Basic Capabilities of its member nations in the production of new Basic Capabilities. For the less developed countries, the return on their bank investments was greater than they could obtain through their internal Generation Rates. The World Development Bank was introduced to provide the necessary structure for the related goal assigned to some nations.

Blockade, and Propaganda and Subversion. As part of the research design, threats were classified according to their intensity. The kind of hostile measures short of war that one nation might direct against another was augmented to facilitate the creation of different levels of threat. Two actions were introduced—Blockade, and Propaganda and Subversion. If a nation had the required number of Conventional Force Capabilities, its leaders could assign them to blockade another country. A partially blockaded nation could arrange a limited number of trades or aids, but there was a probability that any such

---

[22] The question asked was, "Would you say there could have been any participants in the simulation acting under instruction from the simulation directors? (Yes, No) If you answered yes, indicate who these participants are by position and nation." The identical question was also asked after an Inter-Nation Simulation conducted at Princeton University. Seven of 31 undergraduate participants (23 per cent) suspected confederates, although none was actually involved. Therefore, given the nature of the question and the simulation, the proportion of Navy personnel who believed confederates were present may not be unusually high.

exchange would be intercepted by the blockading forces. If it was intercepted, the trade was not allowed. With a larger allocation of Force
Capabilities, a complete Blockade could be established that prevented
the target nation from engaging in any trades or grants. Blockades
continued until the Force Capabilities were allocated for other purposes
or until they were attacked and destroyed. Propaganda and Subversion,
first developed for Inter-Nation Simulation at the Western Behavioral
Sciences Institute, permitted any nation to invest a limited number of
Basic Capabilities, throughout each period, in an attempt to raise or
lower the overall Validator Satisfaction of another nation. The probability that the propaganda would be effective increased somewhat as
the size of the investment increased.

Aspiring Decision Makers. Because the role of Aspiring Decision Maker (the representative of the opposition elites) has seldom been
used, the activities associated with that role required considerable explication. An ADM could, through negotiations with the Central Decision
Maker, abdicate his function as a representative of rival elites and join
the government. An ADM who elected to oppose the government was
encouraged (1) to submit competing Decision Forms in an appeal to
the Validators; (2) to challenge the CDM to policy debates in the World
Newspaper; (3) to seek the support of foreign nations who could invest
in Propaganda and Subversion favoring the ADM; and (4) to attend
sessions of his nation's conferences, the World Bank, and the International Organization to make his position known.

Observers and Forms. Several of the means of collecting data
influenced the way the simulation operated. One staff member was assigned to each country, as an observer, with responsibility for arranging
and tape recording conferences between that nation's decision makers.
Although observers were not permitted to engage in the deliberations
of the nation, they were permitted to answer factual questions about
simulation procedures.

The participants themselves completed two questionnaires. At the
beginning of the periods, the decision makers were given a brief form
on which they rated the importance of their goals, the friendliness of
other nations, and the amount of world tension. Immediately after an
experimental situation, they completed a longer questionnaire indicating

their reaction to that incident. The participants filled out the latter forms for both crisis and noncrisis situations. They were told that the situations were selected at random to provide material for a history of events which would be written after the simulation.

The Experimental Design

Participants and Schedule. The crisis study was conducted at the Great Lakes Naval Training Center during the fall of 1963. It involved eleven replications of the Inter-Nation Simulation. The nonstaff participants were career men in the United States Navy and served as test examiners or technical instructors in such subjects as electronics and fire control. Each run involved 30 different men of petty officer rank. They were drawn from an available population of 414 men of whom 325 eventually participated.[23] Selection was based on previously collected information regarding age, intelligence, education, and the personality trait of self-esteem. In order to keep the simulation runs as parallel as possible, individuals of comparable age, education, intelligence, and self-esteem were randomly assigned to different runs. In each run the 30 Navy participants were given one of the five roles in one of the six experimental nations. When combined with the two staff-operated nations, each simulation world consisted of eight nations plus an International Organization chairman and a two-man newspaper team.

A run was conducted on a single day for ten hours, not including one hour for lunch. During the first three hours of instruction, the experimenters explained and extended the material in the *Participants'*

---

[23] Five absences occurred during the 11 runs. In each instance, the individual who was initially designated as the Aspiring Decision Maker, assumed the vacant position in the government, and the nation operated without an ADM. For the 325 men the median age was 33; the median intelligence score was 113; and the predominant education level was completion of high school. All the men had received advanced technical training in the Navy. Because of the skills demanded by the simulation, no individual who received an intelligence score of less than 97 was selected. Those who scored higher were used whenever possible. A companion investigation, that was conducted along with the present one, examined the individual's ability to cope with stress, and determined how this varied with self-esteem and defensiveness (Hermann, "Stress, Self-Esteem, and Defensiveness").

Manual which had been distributed several days before the simulation. During the following half-hour, participants read a document describing the assumed history of the simulated world, became acquainted with the starting values of the core variables (number of resources, Decision Latitude level, etc.), and organized their first national conferences. The next six hours were divided equally into six periods of playing time in which all but one of the experimental situations were introduced. At the beginning of what the participants assumed would be the seventh period, each nation received an urgent warning that it was about to experience a major attack from an unidentified source. After the nations had issued their responses to this announcement, the simulation was terminated and the balance of that half-hour was used for debriefing through a final questionnaire.

Measuring the Dimensions of Crisis.

To ascertain the impact of the proposed definition of crisis on decision making, each nation's reactions to a series of high threat, short time, surprise situations were compared with its responses to situations characterized by low threat, extended time, and anticipation (noncrisis). In order to assure that all the nations would experience situations varying in the three crisis dimensions, each government operated by Navy personnel was confronted with seven experimental situations introduced by the confederate participants. The set of experimental situations experienced by a nation remained constant across the eleven replications, as did the time available for responding to any given situation. Immediately after the deadline for handling the situation, the target nation's decision makers completed a questionnaire containing items on the amount of threat, decision time, and awareness they perceived. The values obtained from these ratings were used as a measure of the extent to which each dimension of crisis was present in the induced situations.

Threat.

To measure perceived threat in an experimental situation, the participants rated three adjective phrases (Appendix I, item B6). Each of the three phrases—"dangerous," "threatening," and "injurious to nation"—was rated on a four-point scale ranging from "not applicable" (scale value = 0) to "considerably applicable" (scale value = 3). If, as intended, all three scales were actually measures of threat, then in a given situation a participant should mark them all in a similar manner. Using the coefficient alpha,[24] the average reliability for the threat adjectives for all experimental situations was .77. Because of the consistency among the three scales, a single estimate of the perceived threat was formed for each participant by summing his rating of all three adjectives. On the combined scale, threat scores ranged from a minimum value of zero (low threat) to a maximum value of nine (high threat).

Decision Time. The procedure for measuring perceived decision time was similar to that for measuring threat. Two phrases were rated after each experimental situation on a four-point scale (from 0 to 3). The phrases were "creating a deadline for response" and "putting me under time pressures" (Appendix I, item B6). The average reliability for the two items as determined by the coefficient alpha was .65. As with threat, each participant's ratings of the two decision time adjectives were combined on a single scale with a theoretical range of zero (extended time) to six (short time).

Awareness. In the two previous dimensions of crisis several indicators were combined to form a single measure of the dimension; however, only one indicator was available for awareness. The participants reported how much they had anticipated the experimental situation by choosing one of four alternative descriptions listed in the questionnaire (Appendix I, item B4) which they completed after the situation had terminated. The four alternatives were: (a) plans formed before situation occurred; (b) discussions held before situation, but no plans formed; (c) no plans or discussions developed before situation, but it was not a complete surprise; or (d) no plans or discussions developed before situation, and it was a complete surprise. Each alternative was assumed to reflect more awareness than those following it. With only one measure of awareness, the theoretical range of scores was from a minimum of zero (anticipated) to a maximum of three (surprise).

The data collected by these procedures described the perceptions of individual decision makers. Although we recognized the problems in using aggregated individual data to represent the findings of larger

---

[24] L. J. Cronbach, "Coefficient Alpha and the Internal Structure of Tests," *Psychometrika*, 16 (September 1951), 297–334.

social entities, we calculated a mean for each of the three dimensions based on the perceptions of the five decision makers. Thus, for all the experimental situations a national score was determined which represented the degree to which each of the three crisis dimensions was perceived to be present.

Experimenters' Ratings of Dimensions. Whether a situation was judged a crisis or noncrisis depended on the perceptions of the decision makers as measured by the procedure just described. However, in an attempt to insure that all participants experienced events which varied in the amount of threat, time, and awareness, the experimental situations were deliberately constructed to represent empirically distinguishable levels of the dimensions. To emphasize threat, each of the experimental messages was designed to block one of the nation's specified goals. Using four criteria, the three researchers (named in Acknowledgments) rated each situation as high, moderate, or low threat. Decision time was defined as the amount of time between the dispatch of an experimental message and the point at which the threat was executed or the situation was altered by the confederates. Either 15 or 50 minutes (short and extended time respectively) was allowed for the recipient nation's decision makers to respond to the messages. Short time was set so that participants would be rushed, but probably would be able to finish certain minimal simulation activities. The awareness dimension also was dichotomized. Anticipated situations were preceded by warning communications to alert the target nation's decision makers that certain events were about to occur. For surprise situations, no warnings were issued.

Several examples reveal the differences between levels of threat, time, and anticipation that were used in constructing the experimental messages. In the Fenu nation, manned by Navy personnel, one goal of the decision makers was to strengthen their alliance which was called the FEB Bloc. The following message was dispatched by the confederate nation of Amra to threaten the alliance goal:

We've completed special R & D [research and development] project vastly increasing our FCn's [nuclear capability]. We'll soon be able to destroy opposing nations. But we've no desire for domination. As demonstration of our power and peace, attached is carbon of 50 FCn's granted IO [International Organization]. Request you provide evidence (to be confirmed by IO Chairman) of intention to reduce military capability and that the FEB alliance will no longer serve military purpose. If evidence received in 15 minutes, we'll offer assurances that our FCn's will never be used. If no acceptable reply, we have no choice but to treat you as military enemy.

The message was rated as high threat by the experimenters; its reference to a 15-minute deadline indicated that the message provided short decision time. If the message was issued without warning, it was categorized as a surprise. In half the runs, 30 minutes before this message was dispatched, the World Newspaper reported the following story:

SPECIAL R & D PROJECT RUMORED IN AMRA

Reports reaching this newspaper are that Amra is completing a special R & D project that will greatly increase her nuclear capability.

In those runs in which the newspaper release appeared, the situation was classified as anticipated.

Another experimental situation, addressed to the Heon nation, concerned its goal to increase nuclear capability. With regard to that goal, the following newspaper editorial was introduced as a low threat involving extended decision time:

HEON, ASSESS YOUR LEADERSHIP FOR NUCLEAR DISARMAMENT
(An Editorial)

Has Heon done all that a nation in her position—which has unique advantages—could do for the cause of nuclear disarmament? That nation should set aside its dangerous goal regarding nuclear capability and work for peace. If it does not do so within the period, nations in less favorable positions to influence the big powers should enact trade boycotts against Heon. [NOTE: *Fifty minutes remained in the period when this message was issued.*]

When this message was designated as anticipated, one of the confederate nations reported a rumor to Heon, 30 minutes before the editorial appeared:

Hear newspaper editors are unhappy that you have not taken more of a role in starting disarmament.

Other messages were rated as moderate threats by the experimenters. Summaries of all the experimental situations introduced in the simulation and the goals they were intended to obstruct are presented in Appendix II.

For every simulated nation to encounter all possible combinations of threat, time, and awareness—as these dimensions were rated by the experimenters—12 experimental situations per country would have to be introduced (that is, 3 levels of threat $\times$ 2 levels of decision time $\times$ 2 levels of awareness $=$ 12 possible combinations). The time available for each simulation run prevented such an extensive arrangement. Therefore, the six experimental situations especially designed for particular nations included all combinations of threat and time $(3 \times 2 = 6)$.[25] In any given run, half of these six situations were anticipated and half were surprises. In the following run the situations that previously had been anticipated were made surprises and vice versa. All 12 possible types of situations were obtained by combining the results of two runs.

These procedures represent an alternative way of operationalizing the three crisis dimensions. Instead of using the participants' reports of when they experienced a high threat and so on, we could employ the designations given each situation by the experimenters who used measurement criteria that could be reproduced by others. Using the experimenter ratings has several advantages. If this method is used the character of each situation is known in advance, and the order in which crisis and noncrisis events are presented can be controlled. Under these conditions, a more rigorous research design and a more sophisticated statistical analysis can be utilized. Although the simulation runs were designed and executed using the experimenter ratings, the crisis dimen-

---

[25] Each nation received a total of seven experimental situations. The seventh was identical for all six countries in every run and involved notifying the participants of an imminent, large attack on their nations. This was an extra crisis situation. Readers also may note a conflict between the reference to a total of 11 replications or runs and statements which imply that the design involved an even number of runs. The first of the 11 runs was intended as a second pretest of the experiment. Much of these pretest data, however, were of a quality that permitted them to be added to data from the other ten runs when appropriate.

sions are defined in terms of the participants' perceptions in this study.[26] Given the decision-making orientation of the research, we judged that the basic test of the proposed definition of crisis required that the simulation participants be cognizant of the situational characteristics assumed to influence their behavior.

Measuring the crisis dimensions from the perspective of the participants rather than from the specifications of the experimenters involves issues that go beyond the laboratory. In international politics the question becomes one of whether the presence of crisis can be ascertained only by the actors themselves, or whether independent observers can measure the presence of these characteristics without reliance on the actors' reports. It may be that both means of determining crisis will yield similar results or that both means will produce important but different results.[27] This exploration lies beyond the bounds of the present inquiry. For this research, we must indicate how experimental situations perceived as differing in threat, time, and awareness were organized into the necessary samples.

Determining Crisis-Noncrisis Samples. The analysis in the rest of this book is based upon selected samples drawn from the 462 ex-

---

[26] Another report on this same simulation project uses the experimenters' ratings to identify the levels of the three dimensions. In that presentation, the experiment is described as a nested-factorial design with the order of presentation controlled by a partial Latin Square. Five crisis hypotheses are explored using analysis of variance. See C. F. Hermann, "High Threat, Short Time, and Surprise," in Hermann, ed., *Contemporary Research.*

[27] In general the experimenters and participants agreed on the classification of the experimental situations according to the amount of threat, time, and awareness. A t-test based on the data from all the runs established a significant difference in the degree of *perceived* awareness between the situations that had been classified by the experimenters as anticipated and those classified as surprise ($p = .04$). A similar perceptual difference was found between the experimenters' definition of short and extended time ($p = .007$). An analysis of variance on the three levels of threat indicated that a significant difference was perceived between the levels of threat ($p < .001$). Tests on the individual components of variance revealed the significant differences were between high and moderate threat ($p < .01$), and high and low threat ($p < .01$), but not between moderate and low threat.

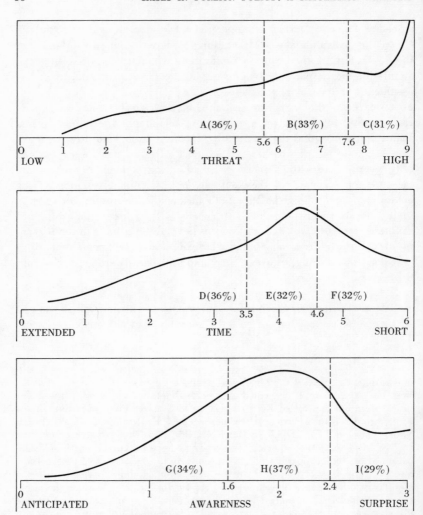

FIGURE 3   **Three Distributions of the 462 Experimental Situations on Perceived Threat, Time, and Awareness Scales**

NOTE: Broken vertical lines mark the scale points on each dimension which divide the distribution into thirds. For all three dimensions, the distribution of scores was separated within six percentage points of equal thirds of the total *N*.

perimental situations that were introduced in the 11 runs. For the samples, the researchers selected situations that the participants perceived as the two extremes of crisis and noncrisis. In other words, decision-making processes and policies in those situations that the decision makers felt had involved the highest degree of threat, time pressure, and surprise were compared with decisions in which all three components of crisis were assessed by the participants as the lowest they had experienced in the simulation. To construct the crisis and noncrisis samples, all the experimental situations were divided into approximately thirds, according to the participants' ratings on each of the three crisis dimensions. Those situations that were in the highest third of the distribution on *all three* of the dimensions were defined as crises. All those in the bottom third of *all three* distributions were designated as noncrises. Figure 3 shows the distribution of the 462 national responses on the three dimensions. The vertical dotted lines in the Figure represent the points on each scale where the distributions were divided into nearly equal thirds. To be included in the crisis sample, a situation must appear in the third of the threat distribution labeled C and reappear in time section F and awareness section I. The noncrisis sample consists of those situations that appear in all three of the sections labeled A, D, and G in the Figure. This procedure produced 24 crises and 24 noncrises with each sample independent of the other, that is, with none of the same situations included in both samples.

To demonstrate that there is a difference between crisis and noncrisis samples on each of the three dimensions, a series of Mann-Whitney *U* tests were performed.[28] The results appear in section A of Table 3. As indicated by the table, the crisis sample differs significantly from the noncrisis sample in the national decision makers' ratings of threat, time, and awareness. When crisis is compared to noncrisis, threat is greater and decision time and awareness are less.

Samples Controlling One or Two Dimensions. Each of the three traits that comprise the proposed definition of crisis can be conceptualized as being located at one extreme of a continuum or dimension. Are the three dimensions on which the traits appear really independent of

---

[28] For a description of this statistic and the form of tabular presentation used to summarize it, see Appendix III. The Appendix also describes the other principal statistics used in this analysis.

TABLE 3 **Results of Mann-Whitney *U* Tests Used to Determine if Differences in Each Set of Paired Samples Occur Only for Uncontrolled Crisis Dimensions**

Paired Samples	Normalized U	p Values when p ≤ .10	Reject Null Hypothesis? (p ≤ .05)
A. Crisis vs. Noncrisis			
Threat	5.94	< .001	yes
Time	5.94	< .001	yes
Awareness	5.94	< .001	yes
B. High vs. Low Threat			
Threat	5.94	< .001	yes
Time (controlled)	0.75	———	no
Awareness (controlled)	0.13	———	no
C. Short vs. Extended Time			
Threat (controlled)	0.33	———	no
Time	5.94	< .001	yes
Awareness (controlled)	0.07	———	no
D. Surprise vs. Anticipation			
Threat (controlled)	0.38	———	no
Time (controlled)	0.07	———	no
Awareness	5.94	< .001	yes
E. High Threat-Short Time vs. Low Threat-Extended Time			
Threat	5.94	< .001	yes
Time	5.94	< .001	yes
Awareness (controlled)	0.57	———	no
F. High Threat-Surprise vs. Low Threat-Anticipation			
Threat	5.94	< .001	yes
Time (controlled)	0.52	———	no
Awareness	5.94	< .001	yes
G. Short Time-Surprise vs. Extended Time-Anticipation			
Threat (controlled)	0.25	———	no
Time	5.94	< .001	yes
Awareness	5.94	< .001	yes

NOTE: All samples have N of 24 experimental situations. For the range of raw scores found in each dimension, see Figure 3. The Mann-Whitney U statistic is described in Appendix III. All p values are 2-tailed.

one another? If they are not independent, decreases in decision time or reductions in awareness might be expected to increase threat. Similarly, high threat or almost complete surprise may reduce decision time. Some international situations undoubtedly involve dependence between these dimensions. To discover the degree of relationship between the dimensions in the simulation, Pearson product moment correlations[29] were computed for the simulation data. The results indicate no significant relationship between either the time and awareness dimensions ($r =$ .02) or the threat and awareness dimensions ($r = .07$); however, a significant correlation did occur between decision time and threat ($r =$ .55; $p = .001$). Despite this one correlation in the simulation data, we contend that it is theoretically possible for situations to involve one of these dimensions without engaging the other two in any substantial manner.

Several examples may help to illustrate this point. In the latter part of the 1960s, Communist China continues to develop a nuclear capability and intercontinental missile system which are a considerable threat to the United States, but the decision time for meeting this threat is relatively extended. The conditions are reversed when a nonpermanent member of the United Nations Security Council is required to vote in a matter of hours (short decision time) on a resolution toward which his government is indifferent (low threat). Independence between the awareness and threat dimensions is demonstrated by the sudden death of Dag Hammarskjold in 1961. Like other governments, American policy makers were completely surprised by the airplane crash that took the life of the Secretary-General of the United Nations. His death, however, created little immediate threat for the United States.

A new problem arises if we contend, as we do, that crisis involves the interaction of three separate traits. The predictive and explanatory value of the concept is weakened if a hypothesis associating crisis with

---

[29] The Pearson product moment correlation *(r)* is a measure of the degree of relationship between two variables. It can vary from 1.00 (a perfect positive correlation) through .00 (no correlation) to − 1.00 (a perfect negative correlation). In a positive correlation one variable, Y, increases as the other variable, X, increases; in a negative correlation Y decreases as X increases. This measure of association is described in any standard text on statistics. See, for example, H. M. Blalock, *Social Statistics* (New York: McGraw-Hill, 1960), pp. 285–311.

some decision-making process produces a relationship no different in degree or direction from that resulting when only one or two of the crisis traits are present. In other words, the question is: Do the results that occur in crisis differ from those produced by its traits acting separately (e.g., high threat) or in combinations of two (e.g., high threat and short time)? To check on the effects of each separate characteristic and each combination of two traits, six more pairs of samples were drawn in which the presence of either one or two of the three dimensions was controlled.

By paired sample is meant two samples (each involving 24 of the 462 experimental situations) between which we will look for differences. In addition to the crisis-noncrisis paired samples, the others are:

> high vs. low threat *(time and awareness controlled)*
> short vs. extended time *(threat and awareness controlled)*
> surprise vs. anticipation *(threat and time controlled)*
> high threat-short time vs. low threat-extended time *(awareness controlled)*
> high threat-surprise vs. low threat-anticipation *(time controlled)*
> short time-surprise vs. extended time-anticipation *(threat controlled)*

The procedure for choosing the additional paired samples is illustrated by the selection of the high threat-low threat samples in which the other two dimensions are controlled. All the situations selected for the threat samples were either in the top or bottom third of the threat distribution, but on the other two dimensions the samples included an approximately equal number of situations from the top, middle, and bottom thirds of the time and awareness distributions. More specifically, in the low threat sample all of the 24 situations were in the bottom third of the threat distribution—that is, they were perceived to be among the least threatening situations experienced. Thus, they all are located in section A of Figure 3. Eight of these 24 situations also were located in the lowest third of the time and awareness distributions (sections D and G respectively), eight more from the middle third of these distributions (sections E and H), and the final eight from the highest third of each of the two distributions (sections F and I). For the contrasting high threat sample, all 24 situations were from the highest third on threat, but were evenly divided between each third of the other two dimensions. The other paired samples were established by a similar procedure. The size of the samples was largely determined by the limited number of situations with threat in one extreme third and time in the other, given their positive correlation. Moreover, uniform samples of 24 lent themselves to equal three-way divisions among the dimensions to be controlled.

Sections B through G of Table 3 display the results of Mann-Whitney U tests performed on the three dimensions in each set of paired samples. In section B, the sample of high threat situations is compared to the sample of low threat situations. These paired samples were selected to differ from each other on threat, but not on decision time or awareness. Table 3 confirms a statistically significant difference on threat, but not on the other two dimensions. As intended, the other five paired samples also show a significant difference between uncontrolled dimensions but not between controlled dimensions. In brief, Table 3 reveals seven pairs of samples. The crisis-noncrisis pair differs on all three dimensions; the pairs in sections B-D each differ on one dimension, whereas the pairs in sections E-G differ on two dimensions. When hypotheses are tested in Chapters 4–7 they will be investigated not only with the crisis-noncrisis samples but also with the other six paired samples. If the proposed definition of crisis has a distinctive influence on the decision-making process, the results using the crisis-noncrisis samples should be different from the others.

Summary. In the last part of this chapter, the research design was described for a study of crisis through simulation. Eleven replications of the ten-hour simulation were conducted with Navy petty officers as decision makers. In each run, the six nations manned by Navy personnel experienced seven experimental situations. Although the situations were designed to represent three levels of threat, and two levels of both decision time and awareness, the current analysis is based on the participants' perceptions of the three crisis dimensions. The decision makers' perceptions were measured through a questionnaire administered after every induced situation. For each dimension, the individual scores were aggregated to form a composite score for every nation. Based on these national scores, a sample of 24 crisis and 24 noncrisis situations were assembled. Six additional pairs of samples of equal size were drawn. These (1) represented opposite extremes on one or two dimensions, and (2) did not differ significantly on the remaining dimension(s). Now, we can begin to explore the results obtained through the research design.

Chapter 4

CRISIS AND ACTION

A Basic Hypothesis

Action-Inaction as Policy Alternatives

Introduction. During the critical days in 1965 when the India-Pakistan struggle over Kashmir broke into war, President Lyndon Johnson sought the counsel of Dean Acheson. The President asked the former Secretary of State what action he thought the United States should take. Acheson replied, "Mr. President, have you ever thought of doing nothing?"[1] This comment illustrates an important issue concerning crises. Do crises increase the pressure on the political leadership of a nation to take some kind of action—a pressure for action which, in the India-Pakistan war, Acheson was urging President Johnson to recognize and resist?

This question can be recast in broader terms. Do policies, developed during crises, tend to differ in a consistent manner from those formed under more normal conditions? If differences do exist, ultimately we will want to know what specific kinds of actions are more often found in crisis periods. Is Quincy Wright correct, for example, in suggesting that the probability of war increases with each crisis?[2] Or, are com-

---

[1] Quoted in E. Weintal and C. Bartlett, *Facing the Brink: An Intimate Study of Crisis Diplomacy* (New York: Scribner's, 1967), p. 16.

[2] According to Wright, the probability of war between two nations over a period of time is a function of the number of crises and the probability of

promises and bargaining more likely to result under such conditions? The first question to be asked is: Are the decision makers more prone to action in crisis—regardless of its specific content? Thus, for the most part, Chapters 4–6 will investigate the impact of crisis on the probability and frequency of action.

Action-Inaction. Several scholars propose that action involves deliberate behavior directed toward the achievement of some objective. For example, Parsons and Shils define action as behavior "oriented to the attainment of ends in situations, by means of the normatively regulated expenditure of energy."[3] Sprout and Sprout observe that action is "behavior that is consciously purposeful: that is, pointed or directed toward some state of affairs, consciously envisaged by the person whose activities are under observation."[4] The latter part of the Sprouts' statement incorporates into the action concept the perspective of the person performing the action. That feature is essential in the decision-making formulation of action:

Basically, action exists (analytically) when the following components can be ascertained: actor (or actors), goals, means, and situation. The sit-

---

avoiding war in each crisis. He formalizes this hypothesis in the expression:

$$P = 1 - (1-p_1)(1-p_2)(1-p_3) \ldots (1-p_n)$$

Even when the probability of war in any given crisis $(p_1, p_2, p_3 \ldots p_n)$ is quite small, the accumulative probability of war (P) approaches certainty as the number of crises becomes quite large. See Q. Wright, *A Study of War*, 2nd ed. (Chicago: University of Chicago Press, 1965), p. 1272. Alternatively, Charles McClelland states in "The Acute International Crisis," *World Politics*, 14 (October 1961), 188, that the experience with previous encounters will improve the likelihood of successful management in each successive crisis. He reverses Wright's equation to indicate that the probability of war decreases as the number of crises increase, in the expression:

$$P_i = \frac{P_1}{i},$$

where P_i is the probability of war after a given number of crises (i), and P_1 is the likelihood of war during the first crisis.

[3] T. Parsons and E. Shils, eds., *Toward a General Theory of Action* (New York: Harper and Row, 1962), p. 53.

[4] H. Sprout and M. Sprout, *The Ecological Perspective on Human Affairs with Special Reference to International Politics* (Princeton: Princeton University Press, 1965), p. 23.

uation is defined by the actor (or actors) in terms of the way the actor (or actors) relates himself to other actors, to possible goals, and to possible means, and in terms of the way means and ends are formed into strategies of action subject to relevant factors in the situation.[5]

Action is a product of decision. Action becomes an integral part of the decision process because it is conscious, purposive, choice behavior with at least one alternative available, i.e., inaction. In the present simulation, action is a response to a situation, by one or more decision makers, intended to affect some goal through either (1) the allocation of national resources, or (2) a statement indicating an intention to commit national resources under certain conditions. Inaction in a situation occurs either as (1) a conscious deferral by decision makers from taking a position or allocating resources, or (2) indecision or failure to reach a decision regarding a position or resource allocation.

Situations and Action. The decision to act can be explained in terms of stimulus and response; that is, action is the response to a situation which serves as a stimulus. A strong argument can be made that in complex organizations, such as those involving a nation's foreign policy, action-inaction decisions are not made until authoritative policy makers recognize some change in the current state of affairs. Cyert and March have conjectured that "organizations make decisions by solving a series of problems; each problem is solved as it arises; the organization then waits for another problem to appear."[6] A fire department pays little attention to a particular piece of property until it is endangered by fire. Similarly, a foreign policy organization, charged with managing a complex set of national goals or interests, takes new action on a specific goal only when it realizes that a situation can create major threats or opportunities for that interest.

In the decision-making approach, an occasion for decision (that is, a choice between action and inaction) develops when a new event is recognized in the decision makers' definition of the situation. Stated another way, for the connection between stimulus (situation) and response (action) to be complete in conscious decision making, the stimu-

―――――――
[5] R. C. Snyder, H. W. Bruck, and B. Sapin, eds., *Foreign Policy Decision Making* (New York: Free Press, 1962), p. 64.
[6] R. M. Cyert and J. G. March, *A Behavioral Theory of the Firm* (Englewood Cliffs: Prentice-Hall, 1963), p. 119.

lus must enter the decision makers' view of the external environment (their definition of the situation). Exploring this relationship further, we propose that new action may result if the definition of the situation establishes a disparity between the decision makers' expectations for their national goals and the existing level of national performance. The imbalance may result from a change in the level of expectations. For instance, as Indonesia became less closely affiliated with Communist China, American policy makers increased their expectations as to what kinds of relations would be possible between Indonesia and the West. Alternatively, an imbalance may result from a change in the existing level of a nation's performance toward some goal. If, for example, the Soviet Union developed a successful antiballistic missile defense, United States officials could be expected to downgrade the performance of their existing strategic deterence system. In either instance, action results when the definition of the situation held by the leadership is modified in such a way that some behavior is thought possible which will increase their satisfaction. According to the "satisficing" concept,[7] the action need not maximize the nation's position on the affected goal, that is, it need not be the best possible action; it must only be looked upon by the decision makers as an improvement. As soon as a solution is found that appears satisfactory to the policy makers, search for a further, perhaps even better, solution will be discontinued.

So far, the relationship between situations and action could be interpreted as indicating that every new definition of the situation would produce new action. If this condition existed, the distinction between crisis and noncrisis would not be relevant. Noncrises, as well as crises, could be expected to bring about action responses. However, even when a situation arises that creates a recognized imbalance between expectations and performance, the result may be inaction. Inaction may result when the foreign policy organization cannot reach a decision before the situation is transformed.[8] Inaction also results when the imbalance between expectations and performance is accepted.

---

[7] H. A. Simon, *Models of Man* (New York: Wiley, 1957), pp. 204–205.

[8] A high-level official in the Eisenhower administration, who was interviewed for illustrative material on actual crises, offered an example of inaction which resulted because the situation was transformed before a decision could be reached. At the time of the Hungarian uprising in 1956, a controversial proposal for United States action was developed within the

When policy makers accept imbalance—which may eventually reduce expectations—no action is identifiable at tolerable costs. Costs, as used here, are those recognized by the decision makers. The costs associated with action may be more visible and immediate than the cost of lost opportunity that is associated with inaction. A variety of factors may be perceived by the decision makers as costs, such as the displacement of other national objectives by any action, as when action to defend an ally against aggression runs counter to reducing military expenditures or avoiding foreign military engagements. When the decision makers' dissatisfaction does not exceed their judgment of the costs, then no action will be taken.

March and Simon note that "the distinction between action and inaction . . . is more important in some situations than in others."[9] In crisis the distinction is vital because crisis contains traits which, if examined separately, could have radically different effects on the likelihood of action. High threats to major goals can produce extreme dissatisfaction and, therefore, an incentive for action. "When a power is threatened it will respond to that threat by an effort to create offsetting strength."[10] On the other hand, short decision time can increase the probability that foreign policy agencies will be unable to act quickly enough. Furthermore, a situation characterized by surprise disrupts established programs and prepared agendas; therefore, it is less likely to receive the attention from policy makers necessary for action than is an anticipated situation. It is plausible that if each dimension of crisis were considered separately, two crisis characteristics would reduce the likelihood of action, whereas the third would increase it. This explanation may or may not be sufficient to account for the competing reports on the relationship between crisis and action.

---

government. While various agencies attempted to build a consensus for the proposal, word came of the British-French-Israeli action in the Middle East. Critical parties, whose support was required for the proposal, became absorbed in the Suez crisis. Many hours later when attention was again directed to Hungary, the Soviet Union had moved to reestablish its control over the breakaway nation. The proposal was no longer applicable.

[9] J. G. March and H. A. Simon, with H. Guetzkow, *Organizations* (New York: Wiley, 1958), p. 175.

[10] A. M. Scott, "Challenge and Response: A Tool for the Analysis of International Affairs," in J. N. Rosenau, ed., *International Politics and Foreign Policy* (New York: Free Press, 1961), p. 377.

Conflicting Accounts. In Chapter 2, some definitions of crisis were reviewed that made the increased propensity for action one of the defining characteristics. Others have suggested that action is a consequence of crisis and not a property of the definition. In describing the impact of administrative structure on decision making, Kissinger contends, "Decisions can be avoided until a crisis brooks no further delay, until the events themselves have removed the element of ambiguity."[11] Of course, even if crises force decisions, the choice could be for inaction. More directly applicable is the hypothesis by North and his associates that the tension of a crisis makes action appear desirable to policy makers:

> The higher the tension, the stronger the tendency to assess the probable rewards of early action high and the danger of punishment low; concomitantly, the tendency will be to estimate the probable rewards of delay as low and the dangers of punishment as high.[12]

The language of this hypothesis is consistent with the satisfaction-cost interpretation of action. Punishment is a cost, whereas rewards are a source of increased satisfaction. In their study of the crisis preceding World War I, from which their hypothesis is derived, Zinnes, North, and Koch[13] found that Germany and Austria-Hungary ignored their earlier estimates concerning the questionable ability of the Central Powers to defeat the Triple Entente in 1914. Unfavorable consequences (costs) were disregarded when action was taken against Serbia. In addition to the pre-World War I crisis, the two case studies presented in Chapter 1 support the proposition that crises lead to action. Both the Korean and Cuban decisions represent strong actions taken by the United States.

---

[11] H. A. Kissinger, "Domestic Structure and Foreign Policy," *Daedalus*, 95 (Spring 1966), 507–508. Here as elsewhere when the relevant literature is searched for evidence to support a hypothesis, it should be recognized that the material cited does not define crisis in the manner used in this book. These citations should be treated as illustrations which are used to demonstrate that a certain proposition has received some consideration and is plausible at the general, nonoperational level of discourse.

[12] R. C. North, O. R. Holsti, M. G. Zaninovich, and D. A. Zinnes, *Content Analysis* (Evanston: Northwestern University Press, 1963), p. 173.

[13] D. A. Zinnes, R. C. North, and H. E. Koch, Jr., "Capability, Threat, and the Outbreak of War," in J. N. Rosenau, ed., *International Politics and Foreign Policy* (New York: Free Press, 1961), pp. 469–482.

It can be argued, however, that a crisis reduces the probability of action:

Change may look more attractive as the situation becomes more threatening and exigent. This may dispose decision-makers to action in crises. However, many factors press for conservatism, or for relative inaction. These factors are in addition to the psychological consequences of the decision-maker's possibly increased anxiety or emotional involvement; they are intrinsic to the structure of choices in "crisis" as distinguished from "non-crisis" situations.[14]

Among the crisis situations examined by Charles McClelland is the 1958 shelling of Quemoy, in which he identifies four "decisional opportunities" for the United States. In two of these periods for decision no action was taken; in the other two, the American response is described as one of "restraint." From this analysis, McClelland concludes that the United States attempted "to fend off the challenge there with the lowest workable level of countering responses."[15] That decision makers occasionally withdraw during organizational crises also might lead to deferment of action.[16]

Testing the Hypothesis

The material just reviewed contains observations that appear to conflict as to the effect of crisis on the probability of national action. Nevertheless, we should recognize that these studies contain variables that are not quite identical; therefore, they may not exhibit contradictory hypotheses. Policy makers' perceptions of action constituted the

[14] A. J. Wiener and H. Kahn, *Crisis and Arms Control* (Hudson Institute, 1962), p. 176.

[15] C. A. McClelland, "Decisional Opportunity and Political Controversy: The Quemoy Case," *Journal of Conflict Resolution*, 6 (September 1962), 211; also see C. A. McClelland, "Action Structures and Communication in Two International Crises: Quemoy and Berlin," *Background*, 7 (February 1964), 201–215.

[16] C. F. Hermann, "Some Consequences of Crisis Which Limit the Viability of Organizations," *Administrative Science Quarterly*, 8 (June 1963), 73.

variable used in the hypothesis by North and his colleagues, whereas McClelland reconstructed crises from the observer's perspective by drawing upon public documents of foreign policy actions. Moreover, in terms of the proposed definition of crisis, the Quemoy situation may be quite different from the invasion of Korea or the placement of missiles in Cuba. Finally, if conservatism involves protecting the status quo, then crises threatening radical changes may require active rather than passive behavior. Despite these possible explanations, the relationship between crisis and action remains highly ambiguous. The Korean and Cuban decisions, however, were situations that conformed to our proposed definition of crisis and they both resulted in action. For that reason, the following hypothesis was investigated in the Inter-Nation Simulation.

Hypothesis 1: In crisis as compared to noncrisis, a nation's decision makers are more likely to take action.

Measurement. The conceptual and operational definitions of crisis and noncrisis, as used in the simulation, were presented in Chapters 2 and 3. The action variable has been defined conceptually in this chapter, but we must establish how it was measured in the simulation. All the participants' forms, messages, and conference transcripts[17] were examined to determine whether a simulated nation took action in response to either a crisis or a noncrisis. In this analysis, as in others based on communication in the simulation, it first was necessary to establish which forms, messages, and conferences pertained to a particular experimentally-induced situation. Relevance was separately judged by two staff members who had assisted in the operation of the simulation. When disagreements occurred, a third coder (the author) judged the disputed communication. If several topics were treated in a message or conference, material unrelated to the experimental situation was excluded. Communication concerning situations used in the paired samples constituted the data from which judgments were made as to whether action had been taken.

Action in the simulation was defined as any allocation of the

---

[17] The only conference transcripts not available for this analysis were those of the International Organization meetings and sessions of the World Bank.

nation's resources or any external communication indicating what the nation had done (or would do) about the situation. By external communication was meant any statement addressed to someone outside the nation of the communicating decision maker. In other words, action responses were (1) resource-allocating forms (e.g., trades, blockades, military attacks, budget allocations, etc.) or (2) external communications indicating the nation's position on the situation.

Three separate measures of action were used to test Hypothesis 1. Two of the three techniques drew upon the appearance of action in the relevant communications (forms, messages, and conferences). In one measure the experimental situations were divided between those which involved action and those which did not. The second technique went beyond the dichotomy between action and inaction, and recorded the number of actions, if any, taken in each experimental situation. Both of these measures were used to check for differences in action between the crisis and noncrisis samples and also between each of the six other paired samples in which one or two of the crisis dimensions were controlled. It will be recalled that analysis with these additional paired samples permits estimates of the contribution made by each separate dimension of crisis.

The third technique for measuring action as opposed to inaction was a questionnaire administered after the simulation (Post-Simulation Questionnaire, see Appendix I-C). Participants were asked to select from their simulation experience two situations—one characterized by the three dimensions used to define crisis and the other by the opposite extremes of these dimensions (noncrisis). Each respondent completed a set of multiple-choice items that was identical for both situations. One item (Appendix I, item C5 for both situations) asked whether, in response to the situation, definite action had been taken or deferred. Responses indicating action in crisis but inaction in noncrisis were compared to those reporting inaction in crisis but action in noncrisis. The third measure of action, therefore, was not confined to the experimental situations or sampling procedures described at the end of Chapter 3. Action or inaction was judged by the participants themselves.

Results. In brief, the three tests of Hypothesis 1 produced some inconsistencies. Both measures of action based on messages, conferences, and forms indicated that more action occurred in times of crisis than in

TABLE 4 **Chi Square Differences in the Action-Inaction Dichotomy Between Crisis-Noncrisis and Other Paired Samples (Hypothesis 1)**

	Paired Samples	Action	Inaction	Total	Chi Square	p if ≤.10	Reject Null Hypothesis
A.	Crisis	18	6	24	1.46		no
	Noncrisis	13	11	24			
	Total	31	17	48			
B.	High Threat	16	8	24	0.00		no
	Low Threat	15	9	24			
	Total	31	17	48			
C.	Short Time	19	5	24	1.55		no
	Extended Time	14	10	24			
	Total	33	15	48			
D.	Surprise	12	12	24	2.22		no
	Anticipation	18	6	24			
	Total	30	18	48			
E.	High Threat-Short Time	19	5	24			
	Low Threat-Extended Time	10	14	24	4.43	.04	yes
	Total	29	19	48			
F.	High Threat-Surprise	12	12	24			
	Low Threat-Anticipation	17	7	24	1.39		no
	Total	29	19	48			
G.	Short Time-Surprise	15	9	24			
	Extended Time-Anticipation	10	14	24	1.34		no
	Total	25	23	48			

NOTE: Except for the crisis-noncrisis samples (for which a directional hypothesis was formed), the reported p values are 2-tailed; therefore, the null hypothesis can be rejected even when the results are the reverse of those predicted for the crisis-noncrisis situations.

noncrisis. However, only the measure which recorded the number of actions taken in each situation was statistically significant. Furthermore, the questionnaire results were the reverse of those predicted by the hypothesis. The participants reported significantly more action in noncrisis.

Table 4, section A, shows that 18 of the 24 crisis situations and 13 of the 24 noncrisis situations involved action. With this dichotomized measure of action, a chi-square statistic was used to determine if the difference between the number of action situations in the two samples was sufficiently great to reject the null hypothesis (i.e., no difference other than sampling error) and accept Hypothesis 1. The obtained value of the chi square was not large enough to reject the null hypothesis at the designated significance level.[18] Although the results were in the predicted direction, Hypothesis 1 was not confirmed by the dichotomized action-inaction measure. Section E of Table 4 reveals an action-inaction difference in one set of paired samples. Situations characterized by high threat-short time resulted in action a significantly greater number of times than did the situations in the low threat-extended time sample.

The second measure, in which the number of actions taken in each situation are counted, indicates that the frequency of action was significantly greater in crisis than in noncrisis. Table 5, section A, displays the findings of a Mann-Whitney U test that supports Hypothesis 1. The table also reveals that there were either significant or nearly significant

---

[18] A research hypothesis will be reported as statistically confirmed if the probability (p) value obtained from the statistical test is equal to or less than .05. In other words, the null hypothesis will be rejected if its likelihood of occurrence is five times or less out of 100. Phrases employing the word "significant" will be used only when these conditions are met. Values of p between .10 and .05 will be reported as *approaching* the significance level. One-tailed tests are reported for the crisis-noncrisis samples (for which the direction of the difference has been hypothesized) and 2-tailed tests are given for all other paired samples. This procedure has several implications for the data as reported in the Tables. A statistic of a given value may produce a significant result for the crisis-noncrisis samples, but not be sufficient for the others. Furthermore, only in those paired samples using 2-tailed tests are results significant regardless of the direction of the difference found between samples. Appendix III contains an introduction to the three primary statistics used in this analysis. Tables 4, 5, and 6 are referred to in that Appendix as illustrations of the manner in which the results are displayed.

TABLE 5   **Mann-Whitney *U* Differences in the Frequency of Action Between Crisis-Noncrisis and Other Paired Samples (Hypothesis 1)**

	Paired Samples	N	Data Range	Normalized U	p if ⪅.10	Reject Null Hypothesis?
A.	Crisis*	24	0–7	1.80	.04	yes
	Noncrisis	24	0–5			
B.	High Threat	24	0–4	0.35		no
	Low Threat*	24	0–4			
C.	Short Time*	24	0–4	1.67	.10	no
	Extended Time	24	0–4			
D.	Surprise	24	0–3	1.93	.06	no
	Anticipation*	24	0–4			
E.	High Threat-Short Time*	24	0–4	2.71	.006	yes
	Low Threat-Extended Time	24	0–2			
F.	High Threat-Surprise	24	0–7	1.33		no
	Low Threat-Anticipation*	24	0–4			
G.	Short Time-Surprise*	24	0–4	1.72	.08	no
	Extended Time-Anticipation	24	0–2			

NOTE: Except for the crisis-noncrisis samples (for which a directional hypothesis was formed), the reported *p* values are 2-tailed; therefore, the null hypothesis can be rejected even when the results are the reverse of those predicted for the crisis-noncrisis situations.

* Indicates which type of situation in each set of paired samples had greater frequency of action.

differences in the frequency of action between four of the other paired samples. With the exception of the awareness dimension (section D), the situations in these paired samples involving one or two of the crisis traits led to more action than the situations possessing the noncrisis traits.

TABLE 6 **Participant Replies to Action vs. Inaction Question when Describing a Crisis and a Noncrisis (Hypothesis 1)**

		Crisis		
		Inaction	Action	Total
Noncrisis	Inaction	15	18	33
	Action	32	57	89
	Total	47	75	122

McNemar $X^2 = 3.38$; $p = .04$; (more action in noncrisis)

NOTE: In this table, as in all others involving the McNemar test, the values in each cell represent individuals who completed the questionnaire. Appendix III explains how the McNemar test is used here and why the total respondents for any question are less than 325. See p. 223.

The third test of the relationship between crisis and action results in the reverse of the predicted hypothesis. The results achieved by comparing action and inaction as reported by the simulation participants on the Post-Simulation Questionnaire are found in Table 6. Here the critical entries appear in the diagonal formed by the lower-left and upper-right cells. These two entries or cells indicate people who shifted from action to inaction depending on whether the situation was a crisis or noncrisis. Thirty-two simulation decision makers said that they acted in noncrisis, but not in crisis. Only slightly more than half as many (18) indicated the opposite; that is, they acted in crisis and remained inactive in noncrisis. The questionnaire made no provision for exploring behavior in situations involving only one or two of the crisis dimensions.

In the questionnaire the participants indicated they had taken *less* action in crisis, whereas in the actual verbal statements and physical allocations the frequency of action was *greater* in crisis. These first simulation results, like the findings of the crisis literature, offer conflicting evidence on the relationship between crisis and action.

Hostile, Exploratory, and Cooperative Actions

Let us consider the findings reported in Tables 4–6. Other than the possibility of some experimental error, several explanations can be offered for the general pattern of divergent relationships discovered between crisis and action. One interpretation is that no difference actually exists in the likelihood of taking action in crisis as compared to noncrisis. In deciding whether they should act, policy makers are unaffected by the crisis nature of the situation they face. An alternative explanation suggests that what people actually do in crisis deviates sharply from their subsequent perceptions of this behavior. Hence, the questionnaire results were different from the other measures. Policy makers may believe that they were more cautious and inactive in times of crisis than they actually were because they do not wish to recall the danger involved in their actions, or because they lacked a referent with which to compare their activity in unusual and extreme situations. Still another interpretation is that the probability of action in crisis depends upon the conditions under which a nation experiences the crisis. When these circumstances, or intervening variables, are ignored in a simple, unmediated relationship between crisis and action, the unrecognized factors account for the inconsistent results. Actually, the third alternative is a more general explanation which could include the objective-perceptual difference as one kind of intervening variable.

One extension of the first explanation—that crises and noncrises do not differ in the probability of action—explores the content of policy. This interpretation suggests that what is distinctive about crises is not the *quantity* of action, but rather the *kind* of action. Although decision makers may take as many actions in noncrisis as crisis, the substantive character of actions in the two situations may be quite different. As an initial exploration of this argument in the simulation, three hypotheses that classified actions as hostile, exploratory, or cooperative were investigated.

Hypothesis 2: In crisis as compared to noncrisis, a nation's decision makers are more likely to take hostile actions toward the agent initiating the situation.

Hypothesis 3: In crisis as compared to noncrisis, a nation's decision makers are more likely to take exploratory actions toward the agent initiating the situation.

Hypothesis 4: In crisis as compared to noncrisis, a nation's decision makers are less likely to take cooperative actions toward the agent initiating the situation.

Neither the missile crisis nor the Korean invasion appears to have been a situation of pure conflict for the United States; that is, in the terminology of game theory they were "variable-sum" and not "constant-sum" situations. In both cases the conflicting parties cooperated at least tacitly to avoid World War III. The actions of the United States, however, cannot be considered as cooperative except in this limited sense. Within the boundaries imposed by the desire to avoid general war, the actions of American policy makers were hostile to the objectives of the Soviet Union and to the satellite states involved. Despite the hostility, some American actions in each situation were exploratory. In the first days of the Korean invasion, special care was taken not to charge the Soviet Union with responsibility for the aggression—even though the leadership of the United States was convinced that the invasion had been instigated by the U.S.S.R.[19] The first American communication to the Soviet government sought to probe the Russian position by urging them to influence the North Koreans to stop the aggression. After the blockade was established by the United States during the missile crisis, a number of communications that sought a solution to the confrontation were exploratory. One clear example was Kennedy's letter to Khrushchev the day before an agreement was reached. In the letter American policy makers proposed a settlement that ignored the most recent communication received from Moscow. Thus, when we examine the two crises, evidence can be found for both hostile and exploratory acts, but American behavior can be characterized as cooperative only in the sense that it sought to avoid mutually undesirable outcomes.

To classify simulation actions into these three categories, each action taken in response to one of the experimental situations was recorded on a separate index card. A mutually exclusive system of

---

[19] Assistant Secretary of State for Public Affairs Edward W. Barret was away from Washington when South Korea was invaded, and therefore, when contacted by the press, was unaware of the policy not to blame the Soviet Union. "Secretary Barret told reporters that the North Korean invasion demonstrated the 'rank hypocrisy of the Kremlin's so-called peace offensive.' He further explained that the relationship between the Soviet Union and the North Koreans was the same as that between 'Walt Disney and Donald Duck.' He soon received an urgent telegram from the State Department telling him to 'pipe down.' " G. D. Paige, *The Korean Decision* (New York: Free Press, 1968), pp. 117–118.

classificati n required coders to sort the action cards as hostile, exploratory, cooperative, or "none of these." To guide their coding of the actions, judges r ceived a detailed definition of each kind of action. Briefly, hostility was defined as a statement or another type of behavior which had the expressed intent of injuring or obstructing the nation or actor who initiated the situation. Cooperation was any statement or another type of behavior that expressed either open agreement or acceptance without protest of the requests or proposals made by the originator of the situation. Exploratory actions were those that did not commit the nation to any position regarding the program of the agent responsible for the situation, but rather took the form of an inquiry (for example, requests for assistance, more time, further information, or the statement of counterproposals). To estimate intercoder reliability, the two judges classified a common set of 116 actions. With a phi coefficient[20] the correlation representing the degree of agreement between the coders on hostility was .81, on exploration was .94, and on cooperation was .82.

All three hypotheses are confirmed with the simulation data. Actions taken in crisis are more likely to be hostile or exploratory and less likely to be cooperative than actions taken in noncrisis. As shown in Table 7, section A, all but two of the 15 hostile actions were taken in crisis. Eighteen of the 22 exploratory actions presented in Table 8, section A, occurred in crisis. Less than a third (4 out of 15) of the cooperative actions reported in Table 9, section A, were responses to crisis. The chi-square values computed for these differences were sufficiently large in each case to reject the null hypothesis in favor of the appropriate research hypothesis. The results for the situations characterized by one or two of the crisis traits also are reported in Tables 7–9 (sections B-G). When actions are classified as either hostile or nonhostile, there are no significant differences except for the crisis-noncrisis samples. With the exploratory and cooperative categories, several other paired samples produce substantial differences. Actions in surprise situations are more likely to be exploratory and less likely to be cooperative than actions in anticipated situations (Tables 8–9, section D). High

---

[20] The phi coefficient, like the Pearson product moment correlation, is a measure of the degree of association between two variables. It is used when the variables are measured on a nominal or ordinal scale, and when each variable is a dichotomy. See Q. McNemar, *Psychological Statistics*, 3rd ed. (New York: Wiley, 1962), pp. 197–198.

TABLE 7 **Chi Square Differences in the Number of Hostile and Non-Hostile Actions Between Crisis-Noncrisis and Other Paired Samples (Hypothesis 2)**

Paired Samples	Hostile Action	Non-Hostile Action	Total	Chi Square	p if ⩽.10	Reject Null Hypothesis?
A. Crisis	13	27	40	3.63	.03	yes
Noncrisis	2	22	24			
Total	15	49	64			
B. High Threat	2	20	22	0.16		no
Low Threat	3	28	31			
Total	5	48	53			
C. Short Time	3	32	35	0.65		no
Extended Time	2	17	19			
Total	5	49	54			
D. Surprise	1	20	21	0.20		no
Anticipation	1	30	31			
Total	2	50	52			
E. High Threat-Short Time	7	26	33	0.00		no
Low Threat-Extended Time	4	12	16			
Total	11	38	49			
F. High Threat-Surprise	4	22	26	0.44		no
Low Threat-Anticipation	2	29	31			
Total	6	51	57			
G. Short Time-Surprise	2	25	27	0.36		no
Extended Time-Anticipation	1	13	14			
Total	3	38	41			

NOTE: Except for the crisis-noncrisis samples (for which a directional hypothesis was formed), the reported p values are 2-tailed; therefore, the null hypothesis can be rejected even when the results are the reverse of those predicted for the crisis-noncrisis situations.

TABLE 8 **Chi Square Differences in the Number of Exploratory and Non-Exploratory Actions Between Crisis-Noncrisis and Other Paired Samples (Hypothesis 3)**

Paired Samples	Exploratory Action	Non-Exploratory Action	Total	Chi Square	p if ⪕.10	Reject Null Hypothesis?
A. Crisis	18	22	40	4.16	.02	yes
Noncrisis	4	20	24			
Total	22	42	64			
B. High Threat	5	17	22	0.32		no
Low Threat	4	27	31			
Total	9	44	53			
C. Short Time	5	30	35	1.53		no
Extended Time	0	19	19			
Total	5	49	54			
D. Surprise	9	12	21	3.29	.08	no
Anticipation	5	26	31			
Total	14	38	52			
E. High Threat-Short Time	15	18	33	2.12		no
Low Threat-Extended Time	3	13	16			
Total	18	31	49			
F. High Threat-Surprise	12	14	26	9.98	.002	yes
Low Threat-Anticipation	2	29	31			
Total	14	43	57			
G. Short Time-Surprise	5	22	27	0.01		no
Extended Time-Anticipation	2	12	14			
Total	7	34	41			

NOTE: Except for the crisis-noncrisis samples (for which a directional hypothesis was formed), the reported p values are 2-tailed; therefore, the null hypothesis can be rejected even when the results are the reverse of those predicted for the crisis-noncrisis situations.

TABLE 9 **Chi Square Differences in the Number of Cooperative and Non-Cooperative Actions Between Crisis-Noncrisis and Other Paired Samples (Hypothesis 4)**

Paired Samples	Cooperative Action	Non-Cooperative Action	Total	Chi Square	p if ≤.10	Reject Null Hypothesis?
A. Crisis	4	36	40			
Noncrisis	11	13	24	8.83	.002	yes
Total	15	49	64			
B. High Threat	11	11	22			
Low Threat	18	13	31	0.91		no
Total	29	24	53			
C. Short Time	21	14	35			
Extended Time	10	9	19	0.55		no
Total	31	23	54			
D. Surprise	6	15	21			
Anticipation	21	10	31	6.21	.003	yes
Total	27	25	52			
E. High Threat-Short Time	5	28	33			
Low Threat-Extended Time	7	9	16	3.34	.08	no
Total	12	37	49			
F. High Threat-Surprise	2	24	26			
Low Threat-Anticipation	22	9	31	20.70	.001	yes
Total	24	33	57			
G. Short Time-Surprise	9	18	27			
Extended Time-Anticipation	5	9	14	0.04		no
Total	14	27	41			

NOTE: Except for the crisis-noncrisis samples (for which a directional hypothesis was formed), the reported p values are 2-tailed; therefore, the null hypothesis can be rejected even when the results are the reverse of those predicted for the crisis-noncrisis situations.

threat-short time situations also lead to actions which are less cooperative than actions in low threat-extended time situations (Table 9, section E). Finally, high threat-surprise situations lead to actions that are more likely to be exploratory and less likely to be cooperative than are actions in low threat-anticipated situations (Tables 8–9, section F). In each set of paired samples where a significant or nearly significant difference was found in one of the categories of action, it was in the same direction as the crisis-noncrisis difference.

These findings lend considerable support to the argument that the content of actions taken in crisis differs from the content of noncrisis actions. They suggest that our initial hypothesis would be confirmed if we considered either hostile or exploratory actions. Hypothesis 1 would be reversed, however, if the sample were confined to cooperative responses, for under those circumstances action would be more probable in noncrisis than in crisis. The results do not eliminate the possibility that intervening variables play an important role. Under certain specified conditions both the frequency and content of action in crisis as compared to noncrisis might be dramatically altered. With the present simulation data we cannot examine the impact of intervening variables on the three substantive categories of policy because of the small number of cases that would result from such a division of our samples. For example, if the analysis were limited to hostile actions, we would have only two cases in our noncrisis sample. With two cases it would be exceedingly difficult to establish whether any intervening variable produced a significant pattern. But if we do not differentiate between different kinds of actions, the samples remain reasonably large. In this way we can investigate what effects selected intervening variables have on the probability of any action in crisis.

Intervening Variables: An Overview

Ten intervening variables were introduced in the simulation to determine whether these variables differentiated the occasions for action in crisis from actions in noncrisis. The crisis-noncrisis samples and the other paired samples were reformed to include only those experimental situations in which action was taken. Hypotheses, each introducing an additional variable, were tested with these data. The conditions, or intervening variables, were separated into two classes—definition of the situation and properties of the decision unit. These two analytical categories represent different types of influences on the decision and different means of measurement in the simulation.

Definition of the Situation. We already have mentioned that before a change in an external situation can lead to a decision to act, the stimulus must be recognized and interpreted by the policy makers— it must enter their definition of the situation. "The key to political action lies in the way decision-makers as actors define their situation"; that is, their "selection and evaluation of objects, events, symbols, conditions, and other actors."[21] Given the intermediary role of definition of the situation between the external situation and action, it is not surprising that one group of intervening variables would concern the decision makers' perceptions. "It is particularly important for the investigator who seeks to analyze short term changes in the international system— such as the crisis situation—to incorporate subjective data into his model."[22] Harold and Margaret Sprout introduce a concept quite similar to definition of the situation called the "psycho-milieu." This concept consists of the individual decision maker's "images or ideas, derived from some sort of interaction between what he selectively receives from his milieu (via his sensory apparatus) and his scheme of values, conscious memories, and subconsciously stored experience."[23] The Sprouts distinguish the psycho-milieu from the "operational milieu" by noting that the latter is the environment relevant to the decision outcome as it is defined by observers rather than by decision makers.

The importance of the definition of the situation, or psychological milieu, is illustrated by the discussions to decide whether the weapons in Cuba were offensive or defensive. Analysts have disagreed as to whether the military manpower build-up—the MIG-15 fighter aircraft, and the surface-to-air missiles known to exist in Cuba early in 1962—

---

[21] R. C. Snyder, "A Decision-Making Approach to the Study of Political Phenomena," in R. Young, ed., *Approaches to the Study of Politics* (Evanston: Northwestern University Press, 1958), p. 17.

[22] O. R. Holsti, R. A. Brody, and R. C. North, "Measuring Affect and Action in International Reaction Models," *Journal of Peace Research*, 3–4 (July 1964), 176.

[23] Sprout and Sprout, *Ecological Perspective on Human Affairs*, p. 28.

constituted an offensive capability that threatened the United States. In explaining the American response, however, the important factor is that the governmental decision makers interpreted (defined) such capability as defensive, whereas they interpreted (defined) the IL-28 bombers, the medium and intermediate range ballistic missiles they discovered in Cuba as offensive capability. In brief, the differentiation of defensive and offensive capability was not important because it represented an "objective" characteristic of the environment, but because it represented a critical distinction in the American policy makers' definition of the Cuban situation.

Similarly, analysts have discussed whether the defense of Korea was vital to the security of the United States. Some writers have noted statements in the early months of 1950 by Secretary of State Acheson and other officials that document their position that Korea was not of major importance to America. To account for the United States' decision to intervene in Korea, however, we must concede that, in late June, the American decision makers thought it vital to the interests of the United States to protect Korea.

Five of the intervening variables used in the research are included in the definition of the situation category. They are the following: (1) the past friendliness or hostility of the nation precipitating the crisis; (2) the characterization of the events as deliberately planned or accidental; (3) the degree of ambiguity in the situation; (4) the involvement of national survival; and (5) the previous importance of any threatened goal.[24]

These five variables were not selected because they were judged to reflect an adequate sample of the various aspects of a decision maker's definition of the situation. Each variable was included because some of the material—to be introduced with each hypothesis—suggests its relevance to action in crisis. The simulation measure for each definition of the situation variable was drawn from reports made by the participants. The simulation decision makers gave their assessment of the five

---

[24] We have measured the three properties in the crisis concept from the viewpoint of the decision makers; therefore, crisis properties also are definition of the situation variables. In contrast to most of the intervening variables just described, however, the crisis traits refer to the decision maker's interpretation of a specific, external event. Four of the five selected intervening variables involve perceptions of actors and goals, not situational attributes.

variables by means of questionnaires completed at various points during the exercise. The variables classified as properties of the decision unit were measured in a different way.

Properties of the Decision Unit. This class of variables includes structural qualities of the decision unit and the processes it employs in reaching decisions. A decision unit can be either a large organization or a single individual. Even when a foreign policy decision involves only a small set of individuals, they almost always are members of the complex bureaucracies which conduct foreign affairs in contemporary states. Snyder and his associates have emphasized the importance of this organizational setting:

Therefore, the definitions of the situation which we consider to be central to the explanation of state behavior result from decision-making processes in an organizational context. . . . To ignore this context omits a range of factors which significantly influence the behavior of decision-makers (and therefore state behavior), including not only the critical problem of how choices are made but also the conditions under which choices are made.[25]

That crises affect the organizational context, and, more specifically, the decision unit, can be illustrated by the composition of the decision-making groups in the Korean as well as the Cuban decisions. In both cases the Presidents relied upon a small, ad hoc group of trusted advisors. Truman, it will be recalled, instructed Acheson to assemble key officials to join him for dinner at Blair House as soon as he returned to Washington. With few exceptions this same group met with Truman in the series of meetings held in the following days. Similarly, when informed of the missiles in Cuba, President Kennedy immediately named those whose counsel he thought would be most valuable. Not until the National Security Council met after the blockade decision had been made, did this group acquire formal status as the Executive Committee of the Council. Most foreign policy personnel had no knowledge of the crisis decision until the President spoke to the nation.

It is not difficult to speculate how the size and structure of the unit involved in a foreign policy decision influences the substance of

---

[25] Snyder *et al.*, eds., *Foreign Policy Decision Making*, p. 87.

policy. For instance, a decision made in a small group rather than through inter-agency negotiation might reflect more clearly the values of those individuals involved; extensive bargaining might be less necessary to reach agreements; decisions might be made more quickly; previous policies might more readily be reversed.[26] These and other consequences of the composition of the decision unit would occur whether the policy makers were aware of their presence and implications or not.

Whereas the definition of the situation variables were estimated by the participants, the variables characterizing the decision unit were assessed by outside observers. Content analysis, observer rating forms, and output from the simulation calculators were the measuring techniques used to operationalize the variables independently of the simulation decision makers. The five variables measured in this manner and classified as properties of the decision unit were: (1) the quantity of national capabilities available to the decision unit; (2) the amount of search for alternative solutions; (3) the number of alternative solutions considered; (4) the extent of affective conflict among members of the decision unit; and (5) the size of the decision unit.

---

[26] Small decision groups can have negative effects on the decision process as well as positive ones. It has been suggested that the weaknesses in the plan to invade the Bay of Pigs would likely have been caught if the proposal had been reviewed more broadly. "There was so deep a commitment, indeed, that there was an *unconscious* effort to confine consideration of the proposed operation to as small a number of people as possible, so as to avoid too harsh or thorough a scrutiny of the plans." [Italics mine.] R. Hilsman, *To Move a Nation* (Garden City: Doubleday, 1967), p. 31.

Chapter 5

CRISIS AND ACTION

Definition of the Situation

The hypotheses involving intervening variables in this chapter and the next follow the same format. Each hypothesis will be considered in sections on illustrations, measurement, and results. After the hypothesis is formally stated, the plausibility of the proposed relationship is suggested by illustrations from international politics. For several reasons, the reader must not construe this material as rigorous evidence. First, these illustrations constitute only a few of the many examples that are found in world politics, and they may represent cases that are atypical of the class of situations relevant to the hypothesis. Second, although the hypotheses compare crisis with noncrisis situations, most of the material exemplifies the operation of the intervening variables only in international crises without demonstrating that the process differs in noncrises. Third, the definition of crisis stipulated in this research differs from the formulation of the concept found in some of the previous studies from which examples are drawn. Nevertheless, the illustrations section connects the proposed hypothesis with broadly related materials taken from sources outside the simulation. The second section for each hypothesis—measurement—deals with the means of measuring the intervening variable in the simulation. Finally, a statistical analysis summarizes the results of the hypothesis as contained in the simulation.

For all hypotheses, results will be reported not only for the crisis-noncrisis samples, but also for the six other paired samples (as was done in Tables 4 and 5). For the analysis of these additional samples, no predictions will be made as to the manner in which they are related to the dependent variable. A final evaluation to determine if the proposed definition of crisis explains more than can be done with one or two of its traits will be deferred until the findings from all the hypotheses have been presented.

A Friendly or Hostile Agent of Crisis

Hypothesis 5: In crisis as compared to noncrisis, if the decision makers perceive the situation as originating from a friendly agent, then action is less likely to occur.

Hypothesis 6: In crisis as compared to noncrisis, if the decision makers perceive the situation as originating from a hostile agent, then action is more likely to occur.

Illustrations. The closely related variables, "friendly" and "hostile," are the decision makers' perceptions of the agent or actor assumed to be responsible for creating the situation. In Hypothesis 5, friendliness is intended to convey much the same meaning as that associated with the term responsiveness as it has been used in several recent studies of international politics.[1] Responsiveness is the attentiveness and assistance offered by one nation to meet the needs of another. Dean Pruitt proposes that when two nations obtain some stability in their mutual responsiveness, a momentary disturbance will not alter the established pattern.[2] If crisis is equated with a short-term disturbance, and if actions taken in crisis tend to be hostile (Hypothesis 2), then a possible means by which the decision makers in one nation could demonstrate their responsiveness to a friendly, second nation is by taking no action in reply to a crisis triggered by that second country. In noncrisis, during

---

[1] K. W. Deutsch, S. A. Burrell, R. A. Kann, M. Lee, Jr., M. Lichterman, R. E. Lindgren, F. L. Loewenheim, and R. W. VanWagenen, *Political Community and the North Atlantic Area* (Princeton: Princeton University Press, 1957); D. G. Pruitt, "National Power and International Responsiveness," *Background,* 7 (February 1964), 165–178; and B. M. Russett, *Community and Contention: Britain and America in the Twentieth Century* (Cambridge: MIT Press, 1963).

[2] Pruitt, *ibid.*

which any action is more likely to be cooperative according to Hypothesis 4, the probability of action in reply to the overtures of a friendly nation increases.

With respect to the relative probability of action in crisis and noncrisis, Hypothesis 6 proposes the reverse of the previous proposition. The cooperative action, which we found to increase in noncrisis, is less likely to be directed toward a hostile agent. In crisis, however, "delayed response will be less likely if . . . the categorization of the core-event [i.e., the event triggering the crisis] in terms of negatively valued previous experience precedes the full revelation of the objective situation."[3] Research by both Zinnes and Zaninovich substantiates the hypothesis that a nation's decision makers express hostility when they perceive their nation as the target of another state's hostility.[4] Hostile actions might reasonably be expected to be associated with the expressions of hostility reported in these studies.

A comparison of the United States' response to the Suez Canal crisis in 1956, and its response to the Korean and Cuban crises is helpful for understanding Hypotheses 5 and 6. Before 1956 the United States' leadership felt Britain, France, and Israel to be relatively friendly to American objectives. Therefore, although the United States acted against these countries in the United Nations by calling for the withdrawal of their forces, the U.S. resisted stronger action such as the use of force proposed by the Soviet Union. In Korea, on the other hand, American policy makers perceived the North Korean invasion as directed by the Soviet Union—their Cold War opponent and a nation recognized as hostile to the United States. Similarly, in the missile crisis, the decision makers in the United States did not hesitate to identify the principal antagonist as the U.S.S.R. In both instances, the American policy makers believed that the crisis originated from a hostile source, and they responded with immediate action.

---

[3] R. C. Snyder, "The Korean Decision (1950) and the Analysis of Crisis Decision-Making," *Working Group Reports, Military Operations Research Society*, 1963, p. 245.

[4] D. A. Zinnes, "The Expression and Perception of Hostility in Prewar Crisis: 1914," in J. D. Singer, ed., *Quantitative International Politics* (New York: Free Press, 1968), pp. 85–158; and M. G. Zaninovich, "An Empirical Theory of State Response: The Sino-Soviet Case." Unpublished doctoral dissertation, Stanford University, Stanford, California, 1964.

Measurement. In the simulation, the questionnaire used to estimate friendliness and hostility was the same as that used to measure
threat and time (Chapter 3). Immediately after the deadline for responding to an experimental situation, the decision makers characterized that
event by rating the relevance of a series of descriptive phrases (Appendix
I, item B6). Each phrase was rated on a four-point scale ranging from
"not applicable" (scale score of 0) to "considerably applicable" (scale
score of 3). With the exception of the ADMs, the responses of a nation's
decision makers were averaged to obtain a national estimate of the
saliency of each phrase. The ADM was excluded because his opposition
to governmental policies frequently resulted in different evaluations
of events. The friendliness of the agent who initiated the situation was
measured by the phrase "from a friendly source." The more applicable
that phrase was rated, the more friendliness the decision makers were
assumed to perceive. The phrase "from a hostile source" measured the
perception of hostility.

Originally, the experimenters thought that hostility and friendliness
were antonyms describing opposite extremes of the same type of human
emotion. We anticipated a high negative correlation between the two
ratings in the simulation, which would allow us to combine them into
a single measure. Although a negative correlation was found, it was not
sufficiently large to warrant aggregating the measures.[5] Because participants found a number of nations that showed a mixture of friendship
and hostility toward them, a combination of the separate scales would
have introduced these ambiguous judgments.

A second problem in the measurement of these two variables concerns a discrepancy between the conceptual definition and the operational measure. These variables are intended to represent a government's
perception of the friendliness or hostility of other simulation actors
before the latter initiated the experimental situation. The variables,
however, were measured *after* the induced situation had occurred. Confronting the situation might influence the decision makers' recollections
of previous interactions with the source of the experience. Given the
threat characteristic of crisis, for example, the tendency for policy

---

[5] A rank-order correlation was computed between hostility and friendliness in each of the fourteen samples (two samples in each of seven paired
samples). The average correlation was −.50 ($p < .01$).

makers to increase the estimate of their prior hostility could be particularly acute.

To ask participants to complete friendliness-hostility ratings of all agents initiating experimental situations before each event developed would raise suspicions about the confederates. (Recall that in addition to the confederate nations, such positions as the newspaper and the International Organization chairman were used as agents.) During each period, however, the participants indicated on a single, ten-point scale the friendliness-hostility of all nations including the two confederate nations (Appendix I, item A2). High ratings indicated friendship, low ratings reflected hostility. For those experimental situations introduced by confederate nations, a rank-order correlation was computed between the recipient nation's estimates of the friendliness or hostility of the confederate source before and immediately after the experimental situation. The higher the positive correlation between the "before" and "after" ratings of friendliness, the more acceptable the assumption that the data for Hypothesis 5 reflected previous responsiveness; the higher the negative correlation between the before and after ratings of hostility, the more acceptable the assumption in Hypothesis 6. With the post-situation measure of friendliness, the earlier rating correlated .67; with the post-situation estimate of hostility, the earlier rating correlated −.63. Both correlations are significant at beyond the .001 level.

Results. Hypothesis 5 was confirmed. Significantly fewer decision makers who take action in crisis, as compared to those who take action in noncrisis, perceive the initiator of the situation as friendly to their nation. In none of the paired samples, which controlled for one or two of the crisis dimensions, did the friendliness variable make any significant, or nearly significant, difference in the number of actions. These findings are summarized in Table 10. The absence of any significant results for the other paired samples suggests that all three crisis traits must be present for the intervening variable to make any difference.

The companion proposition, Hypothesis 6, also was supported by the simulation data. The agent that triggered the situation was more likely to be considered as hostile in crisis situations that led to action than in comparable noncrises. Unlike Hypothesis 5, however, the hostility variable made a significant difference in two other sets of paired action samples. Strong perceptions of hostility occurred more often in situations

TABLE 10   **Mann-Whitney *U* Differences in Agent's Friendliness Between Paired Samples Involving Action (Hypothesis 5)**

Paired Action Samples	N	Data Range	U	p if ≥.10	Reject Null Hypothesis?
A. Crisis	18	0.0–1.0	49.0	.004	yes
Noncrisis*	13	0.0–1.8			
B. High Threat	16	0.0–2.0	81.0		no
Low Threat*	15	0.2–2.2			
C. Short Time*	19	0.0–2.8	123.0		no
Extended Time	14	0.0–2.2			
D. Surprise	12	0.0–1.5	92.0		no
Anticipation*	18	0.0–2.2			
E. High Threat-Short Time	19	0.0–2.2	81.0		no
Low Threat-Extended Time*	10	0.0–2.5			
F. High Threat-Surprise	12	0.0–3.0	65.0		no
Low Threat-Anticipation*	17	0.0–2.2			
G. Short Time-Surprise*	15	0.0–2.8	45.0		no
Extended Time-Anticipation	10	0.0–1.0			

NOTE: Except for the crisis-noncrisis samples (for which a directional hypothesis was formed), the reported *p* values are 2-tailed; therefore, the null hypothesis can be rejected even when the results are the reverse of those predicted for the crisis-noncrisis situations.

* Indicates which type of situation in each set of paired samples contains the higher friendliness scores.

characterized by high threat-short time or by high threat-surprise than in the situations with which they were paired (low threat-extended time and low threat-anticipation, respectively). Table 11 shows that every type of situation involving the interaction of threat with one or both

TABLE 11 **Mann-Whitney *U* Differences in Agent's Hostility Between Paired Samples Involving Action (Hypothesis 6)**

	Paired Action Samples	N	*Data Range*	U	p *if* $\leq$*.10*	*Reject Null Hypothesis?*
A.	Crisis*	18	1.2–3.0	4.0	<.001	yes
	Noncrisis	13	0.0–2.0			
B.	High Threat*	16	0.2–3.0	79.0		no
	Low Threat	15	0.0–2.0			
C.	Short Time*	19	0.0–3.0	132.5		no
	Extended Time	14	0.0–3.0			
D.	Surprise*	12	0.0–2.8	92.5		no
	Anticipation	18	0.0–3.0			
E.	High Threat-Short Time*	19	0.8–3.0	13.5	.002	yes
	Low Threat-Extended Time	10	0.0–1.5			
F.	High Threat-Surprise*	12	1.0–3.0	23.5	.002	yes
	Low Threat-Anticipation	17	0.0–1.5			
G.	Short Time-Surprise	15	0.0–3.0	60.0		no
	Extended Time-Anticipation*	10	0.2–3.0			

NOTE: Except for the crisis-noncrisis samples (for which a directional hypothesis was formed), the reported *p* values are 2-tailed; therefore, the null hypothesis can be rejected even when the results are the reverse of those predicted for the crisis-noncrisis situations.

* Indicates which type of situation in each set of paired samples had greater amount of perceived hostility from agent.

of the other crisis traits produced a significant result. By itself, however, the threat dimension was not significant. Taken together, Hypotheses 5 and 6 suggest that the prior disposition of the policy makers toward the source of the crisis makes a difference in how they respond. The next two hypotheses also concern perceptions of the agent responsible for the situation, and therefore, they allow a further opportunity to examine the importance of the source of the crisis in explaining action.

Accidental or Deliberate Behavior of the Agent

Hypothesis 7: In crisis as compared to noncrisis, if the decision makers perceive that the agent originated the situation accidentally, then action is less likely to occur.

Hypothesis 8: In crisis as compared to noncrisis, if the decision makers perceive that the agent originated the situation deliberately, then action is more likely to occur.

Illustrations. At the height of the Cuban missile crisis, the pilot of an American U-2 aircraft, who was on a routine air-sampling mission near the North Pole, picked the wrong star for his navigation. Soon he was over the Soviet Union. Later, in agreeing to withdraw the missiles, Khrushchev recalled the incident. "The question is, Mr. President, how should we regard this? . . . Is it not a fact that an intruding American plane could be easily taken for a nuclear bomber, which might push us to a fateful step?"[6] Although Russian interceptors undoubtedly established that no bomber was involved, the Soviets still faced the question of whether this was an accident or a deliberately planned reconnaissance mission to gather last-minute intelligence before a nuclear strike. It can only be inferred from Khrushchev's decision not to take a "fateful step" that the Soviet government concluded that the trespassing was accidental.

Some scholars have contended that crises are, by definition, deliberate. "A crisis is not some accidental or brief flare-up in the relationship of two hostile systems [such as] a row at Checkpoint Charlie. . . . A crisis normally implies a deliberate challenge and a deliberate response, of the kind which both sides hope will change the course of history in their favour."[7] Triska takes a different position and suggests that a crisis may be deliberately initiated "or the action may be accidental, or

---

[6] Quoted in H. M. Pachter, *Collision Course: The Cuban Missile Crisis and Coexistence* (New York: Praeger, 1963), p. 225.

[7] A. Buchan, *Crisis Management* (Boulogne-sur-Seine, France: The Atlantic Institute, 1966), p. 21.

erroneous; or it may be of a habitual or semiautonomous sort, as when a man, in sheer anger, takes a swing at a member of an occupying army."[8] Though the agent's intent is not part of our proposed crisis definition, Hypotheses 7 and 8 indicate that perception of intent influences likelihood of action. Again we turn to our earlier finding that actions made in response to crises are frequently hostile. Hostile action is unlikely to be the response to accidental behavior, but it might well be the reply to a deliberate move. Thomas Schelling makes a similar observation:

> The distinction is between a game of chicken to which one has been deliberately challenged by an adversary, with a view to proving his superior nerve, and a game of chicken that events, or the activities of bystanders, have compelled one into along with one's adversary. If one is repeatedly challenged, or expected to be, by an *opponent* who wishes to impose dominance or to cause one's allies to abandon him in disgust, the choice is between an appreciable loss and a fairly aggressive response. If one is repeatedly forced by *events* into a test of nerve along with an opponent, there is a strong case for developing techniques and understandings for minimizing the mutual risk.[9] [*Italics his.*]

Although he does not suggest the complete absence of response, Snyder hypothesizes that "tolerance of ambiguity and uncertainty on the part of decision makers, and exploratory rather than reactive responses, will be more likely if . . . the crisis is perceived as induced by chance or accident."[10] The Korean decision in 1950 and the Cuban crisis in 1962 were recognized by American policy makers as deliberate moves, and, as we have noted, these crises were met with vigorous action by the United States. "The Budapest uprising of 1956 was as near to the opposite pole as one could expect, neither East nor West having deliberately created the situation as a test of nerve, and the Soviet response not appearing as a direct test of Western resolve to intervene."[11] As

---

[8] J. F. Triska, *Studies in Deterrence XIII: Pattern and Level of Risk in Soviet Foreign Policy-Making, 1945–1963*, NOTS TP 3880, U.S. Naval Ordnance Test Station, China Lake, California (October 1966), p. 8.

[9] T. C. Schelling, *Arms and Influence* (New Haven: Yale University Press, 1966), p. 121. Reprinted with permission of the publisher.

[10] Snyder, "The Korean Decision (1950)," p. 245.

[11] Schelling, *Arms and Influence*, p. 121.

could be expected, the Hungarian uprising, in contrast to the Korean and Cuban situations, led to minimal action on America's part.

Measurement. The participants' definition of the situation as accidental or deliberate was measured in the same way that friendliness and hostility were. The relevant phrases on the questionnaire were "deliberate or planned" and "accidental" (Appendix I, item B6). As before, the ratings by the four government decision makers on each phrase were totaled and a mean was used to represent the national estimate. (The ADM's rating was excluded.) A rank-order correlation did not produce a statistically significant relationship between the two variables; therefore, no attempt was made to form a single scale from the two measures.[12] For Hypothesis 7, crisis actions were compared with noncrisis actions to determine if the situations differed in the degree to which they were judged as initiated by accident. Similar comparisons were made on deliberateness ratings for Hypothesis 8.

Results. Crisis situations that involved action did not differ significantly from comparable noncrisis situations in the degree to which the decision makers thought the events were accidentally initiated by another international actor. Thus, Hypothesis 7 was not confirmed. The variable, "accidentally initiated situation," made neither a significant nor a nearly significant difference between situations represented in the other paired samples.[13] At least as it was measured in the simulation, an agent, who was perceived as initiating a situation more or less by accident, had no effect on action in crisis. However, the findings presented in Table 12 confirm Hypothesis 8. These positive results found with the "deliberate" variable stand in striking contrast to the negative results found with the "accidental" variable. The crises resulting in action are more frequently seen as deliberately initiated situations than the occasions for action in noncrisis. Other situations, in which the threat dimension is combined with one other crisis dimension, differ in perceived deliberate-

---

[12] The average rank-order correlation was —.32 between accidental and deliberate ratings in the 14 samples. This correlation is not significant at the .05 level.

[13] When none of the seven paired samples results in a difference that at least approaches the significance level (that is, when no $p \lessgtr .10$), then no table is presented in reporting the findings on that hypothesis.

TABLE 12 **Mann-Whitney *U* Differences in Deliberateness Between Paired Samples Involving Action (Hypothesis 8)**

Paired Action Samples	N	Data Range	U	p if ≲.10	Reject Null Hypothesis?
A. Crisis*	18	2.0–3.0	15.5	.001	yes
Noncrisis	13	0.0–3.0			
B. High Threat*	16	0.5–3.0	85.0		no
Low Threat	15	0.5–3.0			
C. Short Time	19	0.2–3.0	115.0		no
Extended Time*	14	0.5–3.0			
D. Surprise*	12	1.5–3.0	86.0		no
Anticipation	18	0.8–3.0			
E. High Threat-Short Time*	19	1.8–3.0	12.0	.002	yes
Low Threat-Extended Time	10	0.0–2.5			
F. High Threat-Surprise*	12	0.8–3.0	43.5	.01	yes
Low Threat-Anticipation	17	0.0–2.8			
G. Short Time-Surprise	15	0.1–3.0	65.0		no
Extended Time-Anticipation*	10	1.2–3.0			

NOTE: Except for the crisis-noncrisis samples (for which a directional hypothesis was formed), the reported *p* values are 2-tailed; therefore, the null hypothesis can be rejected even when the results are the reverse of those predicted for the crisis-noncrisis situations.

* Indicates which type of situation in each set of paired samples had the greater amount of deliberateness.

ness (Table 12, sections E and F). When the decision makers take action, they are more likely to consider a situation to be deliberately initiated if it is high threat-short time or high threat-surprise than if it contains the opposite traits.

The results from these two hypotheses may indicate that the participants found it easier to characterize situations as more or less deliberately started by someone else than they did to describe them as the result of accidental moves. Whatever the reason, deliberateness was the more important variable in differentiating the conditions under which simulation participants took action. Hypotheses 5–8 suggest that the manner in which one group of decision makers interprets the intentions of another actor is important in distinguishing reactions to crises from reactions to noncrises. It is also evident that the threat dimension has a prominent part in differentiating situations.

Ambiguity in the Situation

Hypothesis 9: In crisis as compared to noncrisis, the more the decision makers perceive a situation to be ambiguous, the less likely is action to occur.

Illustrations. In late summer of 1963, United States policy makers were deeply troubled by events in Vietnam. The Buddhist protest had resulted in extreme measures from the Diem government. Several Vietnamese Army generals had asked the American mission what the United States' position would be in the event of a *coup d'etat.* In Washington, the government was sharply divided on what the future course of American policy toward Vietnam should be. Early in September, President Kennedy sent Marine General Victor H. Krulak of the counterinsurgency task force, and Joseph A. Mendenhall of the State Department's Far Eastern Bureau on a fact-finding mission to Vietnam. When the two men reported to the National Security Council on September 10, their assessments of the situation sharply differed. Krulak reported that antiwar demonstrations had little effect on the successful prosecution of the war. Mendenhall insisted that the political dissent threatened to unravel the entire war effort. After listening to the reports the President inquired, "Were you two gentlemen in the same country?"[14] The background of the two officials may have influenced their conflicting interpretations, but the essential ambiguity of the Vietnamese situation

---

[14] A. M. Schlesinger, Jr., *A Thousand Days* (Boston: Houghton Mifflin, 1965), p. 993.

was reflected in the continuous stream of conflicting reports from other observers. When Kennedy was killed in November, the United States was still struggling to reach a consensus on a new course of action.

Of course, as a situation becomes more ambiguous, the policy makers become more uncertain about its meaning. This uncertainty can result from various information problems such as too much information (an overload of physical or human facilities), too little information, or conflicting information. During the Cuban missile crisis, once the photographic evidence was available, the American decision makers thought that the situation was relatively unambiguous. The initial invasion of the South by the North Koreans, on the other hand, illustrated an ambiguous situation created by limited information. In the first days of the Korean war, the information that reached Washington was extremely limited. Was it an invasion or a border skirmish? Were the South Korean forces sufficient or not? Under these circumstances, the initial responses of the United States were modest. Later, with the advantage of additional information—particularly MacArthur's inspection report—strong actions were taken. The decisions on what course to take in Korea are consistent with the hypothesis that the "probability that the response of a given group of decision-makers to a crisis situation will be inaction varies inversely with the amount of intelligence available with which the situation can be defined."[15]

However, not all ambiguous situations result from the absence of information. For this reason Hypothesis 9 differs from the proposition advanced by Welsh. The information available before the attack on Pearl Harbor is an example of too much information and conflicting accounts. In her analysis of these circumstances, Roberta Wohlstetter identifies information that could have alerted American intelligence officials to the impending air strike. These clues, as we know, went unnoticed:

The mass of signals grows increasingly dense and freighted with ambiguities as we move to the larger assemblage of agencies in Washington. In both places [Honolulu and Washington] signals announcing the Pearl

---

[15] W. Welsh, "The Analysis of Crisis: A Comparison of Five Cases." Unpublished manuscript, Northwestern University, Evanston, Illinois, 1961, p. 21.

Harbor attack were always accompanied by competing or contradictory signals, by all sorts of information useless for anticipating this particular disaster.[16]

Whether or not the ambiguity results from inadequate information (as in the first days of the Korean conflict) or from contradictory information and information overload (as in the days before Pearl Harbor), the lack of clarity reduces action in times of crisis. Because the responses to crises generally result in hostile actions, the decision makers are momentarily blocked by the ambiguity. In noncrisis, the consequences of error resulting from action taken in a situation that looks ambiguous may not be so severe.

Measurement. On the questionnaire completed by the participants immediately after each experimental situation, a single descriptive phrase was designed to record how they saw situational ambiguity. A national estimate was made by averaging the extent to which the four governmental decision makers saw the situation as "ambiguous and unclear" (Appendix I, item B6). To test Hypothesis 9, the ambiguity ratings of nations that acted in times of crises were compared with those of nations that acted in times of noncrises.

Results. The data, as summarized in Table 13, do not support Hypothesis 9. In the simulation, the crisis actions were substantially more ambiguous than the noncrisis actions—which is the reverse of our prediction. Three other paired samples do yield significant differences (sections C, F, and G) and another approaches the significance level (section B). These additional findings indicate that when the crisis trait of high threat is involved, a high degree of ambiguity in a situation is associated with action; whereas if the situation involves short time— another crisis trait—actions occur when the ambiguity is low.

One explanation for why Hypothesis 9 came out the opposite to what was predicted is that ambiguous situations do increase the probability of a certain kind of action—exploratory acts designed to clarify the circumstances. The fact-finding mission to Vietnam as well as Mac-

---

[16] R. Wohlstetter, *Pearl Harbor: Warning and Decision* (Stanford: Stanford University Press, 1962), p. 3.

TABLE 13 **Mann-Whitney** U **Differences in Ambiguity Between Paired Samples Involving Action (Hypothesis 9)**

Paired Action Samples	N	Data Range	U	p if ≲.10	Reject Null Hypothesis?
A. Crisis*	18	0.0–3.0	74.0		no
Noncrisis	13	0.0–1.5			
B. High Threat*	16	0.0–2.5	75.5	.08	no
Low Threat	15	0.0–1.2			
C. Short Time	19	0.0–1.5	67.0	.02	yes
Extended Time*	14	0.0–2.5			
D. Surprise*	12	0.0–1.5	87.0		no
Anticipation	18	0.0–2.0			
E. High Threat-Short Time*	19	0.0–3.0	71.5		no
Low Threat-Extended Time	10	0.0–2.5			
F. High Threat-Surprise*	12	0.5–2.5	34.0	.002	yes
Low Threat-Anticipation	17	0.0–1.5			
G. Short Time-Surprise	15	0.0–2.2	34.5	.02	yes
Extended Time-Anticipation*	10	0.2–1.5			

NOTE: Except for the crisis-noncrisis samples (for which a directional hypothesis was formed), the reported p values are 2-tailed; therefore, the null hypothesis can be rejected even when the results are the reverse of those predicted for the crisis-noncrisis situations.

* Indicates which type of situation in each set of paired samples had the greater amount of ambiguity.

Arthur's inspection of Korea could be described as actions of this kind. As previously noted, we cannot make a full investigation of this explanation given the sample sizes that occur when the situations are divided into kinds of actions. In this particular case, however, we can offer evidence sufficient to question the proposed interpretation. The crisis actions were classified as either high or low in ambiguity depending on each government's rating of the ambiguity scale. The median of the ambiguity ratings was used as the dividing point. We then determined what proportion of the actions in each group was exploratory. If the explanation were correct, we would expect most of the actions taken in highly ambiguous situations to be exploratory. In the highly ambiguous situations 43 per cent of the actions were exploratory (10 out of 23), but 47 per cent of the actions in the low ambiguity situations were exploratory also (8 out of 17). Although the absolute number of exploratory actions did increase slightly as the situations became more ambiguous, other types of actions increased even more rapidly. For example, only one of the 17 actions (7 per cent) taken in the situations which registered low ambiguity was hostile, whereas over half of the actions (52 per cent) taken in highly ambiguous situations were hostile.

An inability to tolerate ambiguity in crisis as compared to noncrisis is an alternative explanation. This interpretation parallels certain findings on individual behavior that indicate as stress increases, tolerance of ambiguity decreases.[17] If crises do make an ambiguous situation harder to withstand, then taking a definite position, through an action response, may provide a method of reducing the ambiguity. Whatever the explanation, actions in crises were not reduced in the simulation because there was situational ambiguity.

Danger to National Survival Goal

Hypothesis 10: In crisis as compared to noncrisis, the more the decision makers perceive their national survival to be endangered, the more likely is action to occur.

Illustrations. The physical and political security of a nation is represented in the variable called "national survival." It is one of two intervening variables, in this study, which is concerned with goals as

---

[17] Two experimental studies which report this finding are J. W. Moffitt and R. Stagner, "Perceptual Rigidity and Closure as Functions of Anxiety," *Journal of Abnormal and Social Psychology,* 52 (May 1956), 354–357; and C. D. Smock, "The Influence of Psychological Stress on the 'Intolerance of Ambiguity,'" *Journal of Abnormal and Social Psychology,* 50 (March 1955), 177–182.

they are incorporated in the decision makers' definition of the situation. Specifically, Hypothesis 10 applies to crisis the widely accepted notion that policy makers will initiate whatever action they believe necessary when they perceive their nation in jeopardy. Some students of politics have described the particular relationship between crisis, national survival, and action: "Delayed response will be less likely if the event-core of a rapidly unfolding crisis is perceived to be an aggressive action which threatens safety."[18] A similar hypothesis states, "The degree of probability that the response of a given group of decision-makers to a crisis situation will be inaction varies inversely with the degree to which the decision-makers envision their national entity to be threatened by the crisis."[19]

In a recent book, two journalists observe that "only a few of the crises involving the United States in the last three administrations faced the country with a sudden and direct threat to its security."[20] Even if the proposed definition requires that every crisis involve a severe threat to a national goal, the comment of the journalists is valid because the goal threatened need not be national survival. For example, when the Chinese Communists began to shell Quemoy in September 1954, United State officials saw this action as a challenge to their objective of protecting Nationalist China, but they concluded that no direct threat to the security of the United States was involved. Proposals for military action against the Chinese artillery were rejected by President Eisenhower and Secretary of State Dulles. With respect to national goals, the situation was similar in the 1958 Quemoy-Matsu crisis. Again American action was restrained.[21]

As they apply to Hypothesis 10, the decisions that led the United States to intervene in Korea are less clear. President Truman and his advisors considered the possibility that the invasion of Korea might be designed by the Soviet Union as a prelude to general war. This, of

---

[18] Snyder, "The Korean Decision (1950)," p. 245.

[19] Welsh, "Analysis of Crisis," p. 21.

[20] E. Weintal and C. Bartlett, *Facing the Brink: An Intimate Study of Crisis Diplomacy* (New York: Scribner's, 1967), p. 16.

[21] See C. A. McClelland, "Decisional Opportunity and Political Controversy: The Quemoy Case," *Journal of Conflict Resolution,* 6 (September 1962), 201–213; and S. Alsop, "The Story Behind Quemoy: How We Drifted Close to War," *Saturday Evening Post,* 231, 24 (December 13, 1958), 26 ff.

course, would be a direct threat to the security of the United States. By the second meeting at Blair House on Monday, June 26, this interpretation had been rejected. Thus, the commitment of American military force to the South Koreans can only be viewed as a response to an indirect threat to America's survival as a nation. Truman's later remarks confirm that he viewed such an indirect danger to be acute:

> I remembered how each time that the democracies failed to act it had encouraged the aggressors to keep going ahead. Communism was acting in Korea just as Hitler, Mussolini, and the Japanese had acted ten, fifteen, and twenty years earlier. . . . If this was allowed to go unchallenged it would mean a third world war, just as similar incidents had brought on the second world war.[22]

The Cuban missile confrontation is an even clearer illustration of a crisis which resulted in action when the nation's safety was perceived to be in immediate danger. Questions such as whether the crisis actually threatened to alter the balance of strategic power, and whether a nuclear exchange was actually imminent are not relevant. Evidence from a number of sources suggests that during the crisis the American decision makers perceived that the danger to the physical security of the United States was quite real.[23]

---

[22] Harry S. Truman, *Years of Trial and Hope: 1946–1952* (Garden City: Doubleday, 1956), p. 333.

[23] During the crisis, Dean Rusk reportedly said that a misstep might mean, "the 'incineration' of the entire Northern Hemisphere." (R. Hilsman, *To Move a Nation* [Garden City: Doubleday, 1967], p. 226.) The morning after the blockade was announced, the Secretary of State commented to George Ball, "We have won a considerable victory. You and I are still alive." (E. Abel, *The Missile Crisis* [Philadelphia: Lippincott, 1966], p. 127.) Douglas Dillon, commenting on the atmosphere at the first ExCom meeting, recalled, "We didn't know, that day, if the country would come through it with Washington intact." (*Ibid.*, p. 48.) Paul Nitze commented at an ExCom meeting the morning the blockade was established, "The greatest danger of war as we saw it then was that we would sink a Russian ship trying to run the blockade." (*Ibid.*, p. 153.) During the crisis the President told his aide, David Powers, "If it weren't for these people that haven't lived yet, it would be easy to make decisions of this sort." (Schlesinger, *Thousand Days*, p. 819.) Speaking of the mood on the last night of the crisis, Robert Kennedy said, "If the Russians were ready to go to nuclear war over Cuba, they were

The reader may conclude that, generally, national survival is free from danger in a noncrisis situation. Admittedly, a contradiction exists when the same noncrisis situation is described as menacing to national survival as well as involving no threat. If we relax our requirements, however, it is possible to conceive of a situation which involves little immediate threat, but which could lead to national disaster if the proper decision is not reached. Some governments face this type of situation on the issues of population growth and birth control. The debate in 1950 on the issues presented in a National Security Council paper, NSC 68, is another example. A quotation describing this situation in some detail is relevant:

The document submitted to the President included a brief analysis of the purposes of the United States and the Soviet Union in world politics, the nature of the conflict between them, and an evaluation of their respective capabilities. The West, it argued, lacked conventional forces and was critically weak in Europe. The Soviet Union, on the other hand, possessed overwhelming superiority in ground troops and an expanding economy. By 1954, it was estimated, the Soviet Union would have the nuclear capability to launch a devastating attack upon the United States. The potential dangers confronting the United States and its allies were manifold: general war, piecemeal aggression, subversion, disunity in the western alliance, and loss of American will. . . . The report urged the expansion of American capabilities for both limited war and all-out war and the strengthening of the allies of the United States. All this would require a vast expansion of the security effort. . . . NSC 68 was rational in terms of international goals, but was it feasible in terms of domestic politics? This issue confronted the Administration in the spring of 1950. . . . The Administration was identified with austerity in the defense program. It was an election year. Presumably Congress was in no mood to approve larger defense expenditures or higher taxes. The Ways and Means Committee was changing an Administration tax revi-

---

ready to go to nuclear war, and that was that." (*Ibid.*, p. 829.) Even the Wohlstetters, who argue that both sides maintained control over a number of choice points before they had to resort to nuclear weapons or general war, state, "Nor was Cuba a case in which there was no danger of military action. There were possibilities of escalation, of the spread and intensification of violence. The risks of nuclear war are never zero. But the President was aware also of the risks of escalation in inaction." See A. Wohlstetter and R. Wohlstetter, *Controlling the Risks in Cuba.* Adelphia Papers No. 17, Institute for Strategic Studies, London, England (April 1965), p. 14.

sion bill into a tax reduction bill. In addition, the danger toward which NSC 68 was directed was still four years in the future: the drafters of the report did not expect major or minor Soviet aggressions until the Soviets obtained operational nuclear capabilities. Here was the crux of the issue: Without an immediate challenge or threat was it possible for a democracy to embark on a large and long-term program of rearmament designed primarily to meet a danger which would not become real for several years?[24]

No action was taken on NSC 68 at that time, however. The problem was resolved by the outbreak of the Korean War—an external event which made the threat which was detailed in that document visible to most Americans.

Measurement. One goal that was given to all the governments in the simulation was to maintain their nation as an entity independent from the other nations in their world. On the questionnaire, distributed shortly after each experimental situation, participants were given a list of their assigned national goals, including one presented as "preserve nation as separate unit" (Appendix I, item B2). The decision makers indicated which of the goals listed, if any, were more difficult to achieve during the experimental situation. National survival was said to be endangered when at least three of the four decision makers in the government (the ADM was excluded) reported that the goal appeared obstructed. In this manner, all action situations in the crisis and non-crisis samples were divided into those that endangered national survival, and those that did not endanger it.

Results. Chi square tests were performed on the dichotomous data created by the separation of the situations according to their effect on the goal of national survival. Table 14 gives the statistical results. Significantly more crises that involved action were perceived to menace national survival than were noncrises that involved action. Even though Hypothesis 10 was confirmed, situations differing only in degree of threat did not produce significant results. Intuitively we might have assumed that when national survival was involved, high threat alone would be sufficient

---

[24] S. P. Huntington, *The Common Defense* (New York: Columbia University Press, 1961), pp. 50–52. Reprinted with permission of the publisher.

Paired Action Samples	Survival Involved	Survival not Involved	Total	Chi Square	p if ≤.10	Reject Null Hypothesis?
A. Crisis	15	3	18			
Noncrisis	1	12	13	14.40	<.001	yes
Total	16	15	31			
B. High Threat	4	12	16			
Low Threat	2	12	14	0.08		no
Total	6	24	30			
C. Short Time	3	15	18			
Extended Time	1	13	14	0.73		no
Total	4	28	32			
D. Surprise	4	8	12			
Anticipation	2	16	18	1.05		no
Total	6	24	30			
E. High Threat-Short Time	12	7	19			
Low Threat-Extended Time	1	7	8	3.94	.04	yes
Total	13	14	27			
F. High Threat-Surprise	7	5	12			
Low Threat-Anticipation	1	16	17	7.25	.008	yes
Total	8	21	29			
G. Short Time-Surprise	2	12	14			
Extended Time-Anticipation	1	9	10	0.10		no
Total	3	21	24			

NOTE: Some samples in this table contain smaller N's than in other tables because situations were deleted when three of the four governmental decision makers did not agree that the goal was endangered. Except for the crisis-noncrisis samples (for which a directional hypothesis was formed), the reported p values are 2-tailed; therefore, the null hypothesis can be rejected even when the results are the reverse of those predicted for the crisis-noncrisis situations.

to trigger action. In the simulation, however, threat had to interact with at least one of the other dimensions of crisis. High threat-short time and high threat-surprise situations resulted in significantly more action when national survival was endangered than did the situations with which they were paired (low threat-extended time and low threat-anticipation, respectively).

The Previous Priority of a Goal

Hypothesis 11: In crisis as compared to noncrisis, the greater the priority attached by the decision makers to a goal before it is endangered, the more probable is the occurrence of action.

Illustrations. This hypothesis attempts to generalize to other goals the effect associated with the intervening variable, national survival. This variable is widely proclaimed as the objective of maximum importance to policy makers in most states. "National security, then, is the irreducible minimum that diplomacy must defend with adequate power without compromise."[25] But, obviously, governments have other goals toward which they devote extensive efforts from time to time. The present variable considers any national goal that, for at least a short time, is assigned extremely high priority by the government. What happens when such a goal is entangled in a crisis? Although, in our definition, all crises contain threat to valued national goals, the present hypothesis proposes that the higher the priority that decision makers assign to a goal, the greater the probability of action in a crisis in which the goal is involved.

Both the Korean and the Cuban situations jeopardized goals which were of extreme importance to American foreign policy leaders in the months immediately preceding these crises. However, it may not be immediately evident that in Korea some American objectives which were threatened by the North Korean invasion were of prime importance *before* the attack. In a major policy address on January 15, 1950, Secretary of State Acheson had indicated that the defense of South Korea was the responsibility of the United Nations. In this way, he

---

[25] H. Morgenthau, *Politics Among Nations*, 3rd ed. (New York: Knopf, 1962), pp. 562–563.

invited the conclusion that the protection of that nation was not suffi-ciently vital to the goals of the United States as to warrant a direct American commitment. At approximately the same time, the Joint Chiefs of Staff reached "decisions as to the use or non-use of U. S. military forces to ensure the defense of these areas [the Far East] . . . in terms of their strategic importance to the security of the United States. From such a standpoint, Korea was clearly not of strategic importance."[26]

As we have already indicated, however, the protection of South Korea was not the only American objective jeopardized by the attack. The invasion threatened the principle of collective security and the peace-keeping role of the United Nations, both of which the United States had been working to establish. Of even greater importance, the aggres-sion confirmed for American policy makers the character of Soviet foreign behavior which was described in NSC 68. Just at the time when President Truman and his foreign policy advisors were debating what might be done about the possible future inadequacy of American military preparedness that the document warned about, the military capability of the nation was challenged in Korea.

In Korea the affected goals that had been most vital to American policy makers before the crisis did not concern the Republic of Korea. This, as we know, was not the case in the 1962 Cuban missile crisis. Of course national security—a goal that always receives high priority—was imperiled by the ballistic missile bases that were so near the United States. In addition to that objective, the specific position of the United States toward Cuba had become a political issue of increasing impor-tance in the months and weeks before October 16, 1962:

The fact of the matter was that President Kennedy and his adminis-tration were peculiarly vulnerable on Cuba. He had used it in his own campaign against Nixon to great effect, asking over and over why a Commu-nist regime had been permitted to come to power just ninety miles off our coast. Then came the Bay of Pigs, and now the Soviets were turning Cuba into an offensive military base. Senator Keating, Senator Goldwater, and others had attacked the administration's posture toward Cuba and the Soviet program of arms aid as a 'do-nothing' policy. . . . Keating, Goldwater, and the others had beaten the drums so loudly that Kennedy had been forced not

---

[26] A. L. George, "American Policy Making and the North Korean Aggression," *World Politics*, 7 (January 1955), 218.

only to deny that 'offensive' weapons were in Cuba but to put himself on the public record that his administration would not tolerate their being put there.[27]

It is plausible that any situation—noncrisis as well as crisis—increases the probability of action when it focuses attention on a goal already of vital concern to policy makers. The reasoning on which Hypothesis 11 is based, however, contends that action is most likely to occur if the situation involves a high threat to a high priority goal.

Measurement. To measure goal priority, two steps were necessary. First, we had to determine the relative importance of each goal, and second, we had to decide which goals, if any, the participants judged to have been affected by the situation after it occurred. It will be recalled that goals were assigned to nations at the outset of the simulation. Although validators might protest if goals were neglected, the participants were free to give as much or as little attention to each national objective as they saw fit. Once during each sixty-minute period, the participants rated their five national goals on a ten-point scale indicating the importance they currently attached to each (Appendix I, item A1). A mean of the ratings, made by the governmental decision makers just before the experimental situation, was used to indicate the importance they assigned to each objective.

The procedure that established when a national goal was endangered by a situation was the same as that used for the variable, national survival, in Hypothesis 10. After the experimental situation, participants indicated whether they thought any of the goals had been made more difficult to achieve, that is, whether any goals were endangered (Appendix I, item B2). If at least three out of the four governmental decision makers judged a goal to be endangered, the most recent priority score assigned that goal was used in the analysis. When a majority of the decision makers marked several goals as obstructed, the goal with the highest priority score was selected.

Results. A Mann-Whitney U test was used to determine if significant differences existed in the goal priority scores between each set of

---

[27] Roger Hilsman, *To Move a Nation* (New York: Doubleday & Company, Inc., 1964, 1967), pp. 196–197. Reprinted with permission of the publisher.

TABLE 15 **Mann-Whitney** U **Differences in Goal Priority Between Paired Samples Involving Action (Hypothesis 11)**

Paired Action Samples	N	Data Range	U	p if $\leqq.10$	Reject Null Hypothesis?
A. Crisis*	18	1.0–3.7	36.5	.01	yes
Noncrisis	9	1.2–4.5			
B. High Threat*	16	1.2–3.2	64.5		no
Low Threat	9	1.2–5.3			
C. Short Time*	15	1.0–4.0	48.5		no
Extended Time	10	1.2–3.8			
D. Surprise	11	1.5–4.5	69.0		no
Anticipation*	15	1.2–3.0			
E. High Threat-Short Time	18	1.0–5.2	18.0	.02	yes
Low Threat-Extended Time*	6	2.3–4.0			
F. High Threat-Surprise	12	1.2–3.2	55.5		no
Low Threat-Anticipation*	10	1.2–5.0			
G. Short Time-Surprise*	12	1.2–5.0	53.5		no
Extended Time-Anticipation	9	1.5–3.0			

NOTE: Some samples in this table contain smaller N's than in other tables because situations were deleted when three of the four governmental decision makers did not agree on which goal was endangered. Except for the crisis-noncrisis samples (for which a directional hypothesis was formed), the reported p values are 2-tailed; therefore, the null hypothesis can be rejected even when the results are the reverse of those predicted for the crisis-noncrisis situations.

* Indicates which type of situation in each set of paired samples had the greater amount of goal priority.

paired action samples. Table 15 shows that Hypothesis 11 is confirmed. Crises which resulted in action were more likely to involve goals that had been previously rated as extremely important than were noncrisis situations which resulted in action. We had expected that threat would be a critical dimension in distinguishing crisis from noncrisis according to the policy makers' prior sensitivity to the affected goal. It was reasoned that if an extremely important goal was subjected to high rather than low threat the incentive for action would be greater. In the simulation, however, the difference between high and low threat situations was not significant; in situations that resulted in action, the priority of goals was no different in high threat than in low threat. Furthermore, the interaction of threat and time is significant in the reverse direction from the crisis hypothesis (Table 15, section E). The importance of goals is significantly greater in low threat-extended time situations that lead to action than in comparable high threat-short time situations. Thus, by knowing all three crisis traits, the result is the opposite of that obtained with only two of the traits. No other differences between paired samples were significant.

Summary

In this chapter we have interposed seven definitions of the situation variables between crisis-noncrisis and action. Four of these intervening variables (friendliness, hostility, accidental action, deliberate action) concerned the agent whom the decision makers believed to have precipitated the event. One variable (ambiguity) characterized the situation itself. The last two variables (national survival, goal priority) dealt with the way the decision makers saw their own goals. Five of the seven hypotheses involving these variables were statistically significant. These findings suggest that a crisis is more likely to result in action than a noncrisis if the decision makers perceive that (1) the agent was not friendly, (2) the agent was hostile, (3) the agent acted deliberately, (4) the goal of national survival was endangered, or (5) the goal imperiled was of high priority before the incident. Contrary to our hypothesis, ambiguity in the situation may increase the likelihood of action in crisis. The participants' ratings of situations as more or less accidentally initiated by the agent did not distinguish between action in crisis and action in noncrisis.

Two of the other paired samples produced four significant results in relationships involving the same seven intervening variables. By itself, the threat dimension accounted for only one difference between situations, and that finding only approached the significance level. But when high threat interacted with *either* short time *or* surprise the results were comparable to those predicted with crisis when the definition of the situation included hostility, deliberate action, or national survival. High threat-short time produced a result which was the reverse of that predicted for crisis with goal priority, whereas high threat-surprise led to a finding similar to crisis for ambiguity. With the definition of the situation variables, if crisis had been replaced by any *one* of its traits or by the combination of short time and surprise, no more than one significant result would have been obtained. We will consider the possible meaning of all these findings more thoroughly after examining the impact of five operational environment variables classified as properties of the decision unit.

Chapter 6

CRISIS AND ACTION

Properties of the Decision Unit

Quantity of National Capabilities

Hypothesis 12: In crisis as compared to noncrisis, the more capabilities a nation has in relation to other nations, the more likely is action to occur.

Illustrations. National capabilities are the quantifiable human and nonhuman resources which are available to the policy makers of a nation for use in the pursuit of foreign policy objectives. To make authoritative foreign policy decisions, a decision unit must have control over some of the nation's resources. Thus, we can consider the quantity of capabilities which are available to the policy makers as a property of their decision unit. We wish to determine whether the amount of usable resources has a different influence on the decision to act in crisis as compared to noncrisis. Before reviewing studies that examine capabilities, we should repeat that this intervening variable, like the others that will be considered in this chapter, was measured in the simulation without asking the participants for their estimation of its influence.

Conclusions of studies that deal with the *perceptions* of this variable differ. In their examination of the 1914 crisis, Zinnes, North, and Koch found that policy makers in the major European states communicated more frequently about the danger they felt their nation to be in than about the relative capability of their countries to cope with the problem. On the basis of their research, the authors contend that in crisis the perceptions of injury to one's country are much more important than perceptions of that country's relative capabilities when it is deciding whether or not to go to war.[1] On the other hand, after studying 25 major wars, Abel concludes that policy makers seldom make a commitment to enter a war without "a careful weighting of chances and of anticipated consequences . . . such as relative military strength, available resources, ability to stir up community sentiment, reliability and extent of outside support, and so forth."[2] A similar position is assumed by Bernard who observes, "A modern war is not, then, a blind, emotional outburst, the result of subjective hatreds or hostilities; it is, rather, a matter of strategy which may even be provoked, timed."[3] Moreover, other research conducted with the Inter-Nation Simulation found that participants perceived their national strength to increase when they had the capacity to delay response—that is, when their retaliatory forces were invulnerable to a first strike. This addition to national capability also increased the frequency and magnitude of wars occurring in the simulation.[4]

Hypothesis 12 examines the issues in a different way from these studies that deal with the decision makers' perception of national capabilities. It proposes that even if the policy makers do not discuss capabilities, differences in the quantity of resources influence their decision to act or not. One possible explanation as to the way capabilities are important is that they expand the range of possible actions. "Small powers have a narrower range of interests, and fewer alternative means of resolving conflicts short of violence, than the great powers."[5] Although the capabilities themselves may not be recognized, they make more options visible; nations with more capabilities provide their decision makers with more possible alternatives for action. Findings from a

---

[1] D. A. Zinnes, R. C. North, and H. E. Koch, Jr., "Capability, Threat, and the Outbreak of War," in J. N. Rosenau, ed., *International Politics and Foreign Policy* (New York: Free Press, 1961), p. 470.

[2] T. Abel, "The Element of Decision in the Pattern of War," *American Sociological Review*, 6 (December 1941), 855.

[3] J. Bernard, "Parties and Issues in Conflict," *Journal of Conflict Resolution*, 1 (June 1957), 111n.

[4] J. R. Raser and W. J. Crow, "Winsafe II: An Inter-Nation Simulation Study of Deterrence Postures Embodying Capacity to Delay Response" (mimeo, Western Behavioral Sciences Institute, La Jolla, California, 1964).

[5] J. L. Richardson, "International Crises: A Research Project" (mimeo, University of Sydney, Sydney, Australia, n.d.), p. 20.

psychological study of individuals who were involved in taking risks provide another possible explanation for the proposition that the greater one's capabilities are, the greater is the probability that action will occur. The more resources people had, the more they were willing to commit their resources on a "risky" bet—presumably because the risk of action represented a smaller proportion of their total wealth.[6] An analogy can be drawn between individual bet making and foreign policy making with respect to their common requirement for commitment under considerable uncertainty. National decision makers, like individual gamblers, are more willing to take definite action if the resources available to their nation are proportionately greater.

So far, we have considered the effect of capabilities on action without paying much attention to crisis. McClelland, commenting on crises between nations, suggests that "advanced modernizing societies" are more likely to engage in "stalemates, standoffs, postponements, and no-win, no-solution outcomes."[7] On this point, however, we are inclined to draw the opposite conclusion. It is precisely in times of crisis that industrial societies, whose foreign policy is directed by complex bureaucracies, are more likely to act. "In general, the inertia that is characteristic of such large organizations as governments is greatly diminished during a crisis. . . ."[8] Kissinger concludes that "bureaucratic-pragmatic" type leaders are much more likely to act on a problem in times of crisis.[9] The converse of this proposition is that in noncrisis situations, industrial nations with complex organizations for the operation of foreign policy are less likely to take action.

The strong actions taken by the United States as a result of the Korean and Cuban decisions support Hypothesis 12. There can be little doubt about the high level of national capabilities available to America during those crises in comparison to the capabilities of the vast majority

---

[6] D. G. Pruitt, "Three Experiments on Decision Making Under Risk," Program of Graduate Training and Research in International Relations, (mimeo, Department of Political Science, Northwestern University, August 1961). Of course, under some circumstances, the failure to act would also be quite risky.

[7] C. A. McClelland, "The Acute International Crisis," *World Politics*, 14 (October 1961), 199–200.

[8] H. Kahn, *On Escalation* (New York: Praeger, 1965), p. 241.

[9] H. A. Kissinger, "Domestic Structure and Foreign Policy," *Daedalus*, 95 (Spring 1966), 515.

of the nations in the world. By contrast, we might consider the Chinese People's Republic whose national capabilities are modest in comparison to those of the superpowers. Despite extremely belligerent statements, many observers conclude that in their foreign policy the Communist Chinese have been cautious and circumspect. "Even in the two major crises in the Straits, their action has been limited to artillery fire and some light use of PT boats. They have refrained from bombing the islands or any ships heading for them."[10] Because some action was taken, the Chinese behavior in these crises is not strictly in keeping with the hypothesis, but the evident constraint and hesitation are consistent with the spirit of the proposition.

Measurement. Capabilities were operationally defined as the total amount of Basic and Force Capabilities (conventional and nuclear) available to a nation's decision makers at the time they experienced the experimental situation. Nuclear Force Capability units were multiplied by a constant before they were combined with Conventional Force Capability units to adjust for their greater destructive potential. Because we were interested in relative rather than absolute national strength, the target nation's capabilities were represented in the calculations as a proportion of the capabilities of the largest nation in the simulation at the time of the experimental situation. To investigate Hypothesis 12, the relative strength quota of nations that took action in crisis was contrasted with the quota of nations that took action in noncrisis.

Results. No comparison of national capabilities between crisis and noncrisis or between any of the other paired samples produced a difference that approached the significance level. The Mann-Whitney U's were recalculated with the relative strength of the nation replaced by the relative strength of any alliance to which the nation belonged. Still no statistically significant results were found. Several other explanations, left unexplored because of the current simulation data, may account for the absence of differences. For example, the important

---

[10] M. H. Halperin, *China and the Bomb* (New York: Praeger, 1965), p. 15. For other examples of the limited action the Chinese have taken in foreign policy, see A. L. Hsieh, *Communist China's Strategy in the Nuclear Era* (Englewood Cliffs: Prentice-Hall, 1962), and H. C. Hinton, *Communist China in World Politics* (New York: Houghton Mifflin, 1966).

environmental factor may not be the quantity of national capabilities relative to those of the largest nation in the simulation, but rather a comparison of a nation's capabilities with those of the agent precipitating the situation. Alternatively, in the simulation an increase in capabilities may not expand the range of options in a manner comparable to international politics. Barring some such explanation, the simulation results suggest that the relative quantity of national capabilities does not distinguish crisis action from noncrisis action.

Restricted Search for Alternative Proposals

Hypothesis 13: In crisis as compared to noncrisis, a restricted search for alternative proposals is less likely to prevent action from occurring.

Illustrations. Beginning with this hypothesis, we consider four intervening variables whose presence under normal conditions of decision making could be expected to obstruct a decision to act. Although they may impede action in times of crisis, we contend that these variables are less likely to do so than in noncrisis. Search for alternative proposals also is the first of two variables concerned with the alternatives or choices involved in any decision. Despite the fundamental importance of alternatives in the formation of policy, little research has been conducted on the role of alternatives in determining actions (or inactions) in foreign affairs. The immediate hypothesis concerns the decision makers' attempts to seek out methods of coping with the problem created by the experimental situation.

The decisions involving Korea taken in late June 1950 illustrate the hypothesis. At the Blair House meetings, the Secretary of State recommended a series of steps. The merits of these actions were evaluated by those present, but no efforts were made to seek alternatives to Acheson's recommendations. The policy makers accepted the proposals of the Secretary of State. From their study of that decision, Snyder and Paige conclude that "the shorter the decision period, the less thorough is a search for information within the communication system likely to be."[11] That no search for alternatives took place in the Korean decision

---

[11] R. C. Snyder and G. D. Paige, "The United States Decision to Resist Aggression in Korea: The Application of an Analytical Scheme," *Administrative Science Quarterly*, 3 (December 1958), 362.

is consistent with the theory of organizational search described by James March, "In simplest terms, the theories specify that an organization will search for new alternatives when its current goals exceed its current achievement; that it will examine alternatives sequentially and in a more or less predictable order until a satisfactory one is obtained; and that it will then stop searching."[12] The course of action proposed by Acheson at the outset was acceptable to Truman and his advisors; therefore, the search to find alternatives was never begun.

A crisis situation may increase the tendency of decision makers to accept the first or second option they consider; we will explore this possibility later. When making decisions in times of noncrisis, however, the absence of search for alternatives may indicate a lack of interest in resolving the problem rather than satisfaction with the first alternative examined. Cyert and March, who studied the decision-making process of business firms, conclude that under normal circumstances search becomes quite intensive after a tentative decision to act is made. "If a problem area is recognized, there is ordinarily a search for possible alternatives. . . . In most cases a rather firm commitment to an action was taken before the search for information proceeded very far, but the search became more and more intensive as the decision approached implementation."[13]

The absence of such vigorous search in noncrisis might reasonably be attributed to a lack of interest on the part of the decision makers in resolving the problem. Therefore, a limited amount of alternative search in noncrisis can be associated with inaction. In times of crisis, however, the explanation for a limited search for alternatives is likely to be different. If examined separately, each of the crisis traits appears to inhibit the search for alternative proposals. *Short decision time* imposes a physical restriction on the amount of search that can be undertaken. Research on individual behavior indicates that under *threat* people find it more difficult to recognize alternative solutions. "The evidence suggests that (at least for some individuals) search becomes less fruitful as stress

---

[12] J. G. March, "Some Recent Substantive and Methodological Developments in the Theory of Organizational Decision-Making," in A. Ranney, ed., *Essays on the Behavioral Study of Politics* (Urbana: University of Illinois Press, 1962), p. 197.

[13] R. M. Cyert and J. G. March, *A Behavioral Theory of the Firm* (Englewood Cliffs: Prentice-Hall, 1963), p. 79.

and time pressure are pushed to the limit."[14] Since a *surprise* situation is one that is considered improbable, contingency plans are less likely to be available—thus, a search of the organization's files would probably not turn up possible programs of action.

However, these restrictions on search were, apparently, overcome in the Cuban missile crisis. At the outset, several policy makers made deliberate attempts to discover new solutions:

> On the first Tuesday morning the choice for a moment seemed to lie between an air strike or acquiescence—and the President had made clear that acquiescence was impossible. Listening to the discussion the Attorney General . . . said aloud that the group needed more alternatives: surely there was some course in between bombing and doing nothing; suppose, for example, we were to bring countervailing pressure by placing nuclear missiles in Berlin? . . . All these considerations encouraged the search for alternatives. When the Executive Committee met on Wednesday, Secretary McNamara advanced an idea which had been briefly mentioned the day before and from which he did not thereafter deviate—the conception of a naval blockade designed to stop the further entry of offensive weapons into Cuba and hopefully to force the removal of the missiles already there. Here was a middle course between inaction and battle. . . .[15]

Despite the search for alternatives in this crisis, the incident does not conflict with Hypothesis 13. The relationship proposed in this hypothesis indicates that *if* a search for alternatives is limited—and in some cases, it may not be—then action is more likely to result in crisis than in noncrisis.

Measurement. The "memories" of complex organizations take such forms as filing systems, reference staffs, and computer retrieval systems. In conducting a search, alternative proposals may be sought from persons who augment their personal memories with access to such organizational facilities for the storage and recall of information. In the simulation the primary, detectable materials used in searching for alternatives were the records of the decision makers in the form of mes-

---

[14] J. G. March and H. A. Simon with H. Guetzkow, *Organizations* (New York: Wiley, 1958), p. 116.

[15] A. M. Schlesinger, Jr., *A Thousand Days* (Boston: Houghton Mifflin, 1965), pp. 803–805. Reprinted by permission of the publisher.

sages and conferences. Therefore, to measure search, a content analysis was performed on conference transcripts and messages pertaining to the experimental situations. The unit of analysis was the simple sentence; compound sentences were divided into separate, simple statements. A sentence was coded as containing search for alternatives if it involved an inquiry that asked another person or group for a means of coping with a problem created by the experimental situation.[16]

The number of alternative search statements, made by all the decision makers in a nation during a given experimental situation, was divided by their total number of statements (simple sentences) during that time. This conversion to proportions was undertaken to control for the differences in actual decision time between various induced situations. Many of the situations perceived as short time by the decision makers were 15 minutes in duration, whereas many of the extended time situations allowed 50 minutes for response. Without the proportions the difference in time alone may have resulted in sharp contrasts in the number of search statements. Furthermore, the use of proportions controls for the differences in fluency between nations. For example, it differentiates between a government that made only three statements in a crisis, all of which were search for alternatives, and another government that issued 12 statements in a crisis, only three of which were search for alternatives. To test Hypothesis 13, the proportion of alternative search statements made in crisis situations that resulted in action was compared to the proportion of search statements in noncrisis situations that resulted in action.

Results. The hypothesis that action would be more likely to occur in crises involving a restricted search for alternatives than in comparable noncrisis situations was not supported. No significant differences were found in the frequency of alternative search between the crisis and noncrisis action samples. Moreover, none of the paired samples in which

---

[16] The inter-coder reliability for alternative search was determined by a Pearson product moment correlation and resulted in an average reliability of .81. To establish the reliability, the two coders selected a sample of fifty decision makers from the total of 325 that participated in the eleven runs. Both coders checked all the communications of these fifty decision makers in each of the seven experimental situations given a nation. Thus, the reliability sample is based on messages and conferences dealing with 350 situations.

one or two of the crisis dimensions were controlled produced a result that even approached the significance level. In general, the participants' records revealed very little search for alternatives in any type of situation. The simulation decision makers apparently either thought out their own alternatives, waited for others to volunteer solutions, or recognized no choice but inaction to the policy they pursued.

Limited Alternative Proposals

Hypothesis 14: In crisis as compared to noncrisis, the consideration of only a few alternative proposals by the decision makers is less likely to prevent action from occurring.

Illustrations. In discussing Hypothesis 13, we concluded that simulation participants could enumerate alternative proposals without conducting organized search. When the decision makers themselves identify various options or when other individuals or groups volunteer alternatives, then the necessity for search is reduced. These circumstances can arise in actual foreign-policy organizations as well as in the simulation. To investigate these sources of alternatives, we extend the argument made in support of Hypothesis 13; namely, that the conditions under which decision makers are likely to discuss only a few alternatives are different in crisis than in noncrisis situations, and that this distinction influences the probability of action.

When only one or two means of coping with a problem are enumerated in noncrisis situations, it can indicate that the policy makers fortuitously arrived at an acceptable solution when they had reached the first or second alternative. On the other hand, the development of only a few alternatives in noncrisis may reveal that the decision makers are, for one reason or another, not fully attentive to the problem. Given the continuous and varied demands on a foreign-policy organization and the complexity of that bureaucracy, it is quite plausible that many decisions necessary for action are neglected or postponed. On this subject, the previously cited observation of Kissinger bears restating in fuller detail. "Success consists in moving the administrative machine to the point of decision, leaving relatively little energy for analyzing the merit of this decision. . . . Attention tends to be diverted from the act of choice.

. . . Decisions can be avoided until a crisis brooks no further delay, until the events themselves have removed the element of ambiguity."[17]

If only a few alternatives are considered in a crisis situation, it is less likely a result of organizational sources which impede action, than what psychological research has found is a tendency for individuals to experience "cognitive rigidity" when exposed to severe stress. One consequence of this mental closure is an increased inability to recognize alternative means of coping with a problem.[18] Some scholars contend that this individual behavior can also afflict groups and organizations:

> What holds true of people considered in isolation should also apply to people who hold beliefs in common and form groups, movements, or institutions. Here we would expect that if a threat to the collective belief system occurs, the people who hold it should develop a closed system. And we might predict that the degree to which this occurs should also vary with the extent of the threat.[19]

Rokeach and his associates found systematic evidence of institutional closure in religious organizations that were confronted with a threat to their beliefs.

Aside from cognitive rigidity, the number of alternatives considered in crisis situations may be limited by the decision makers' willingness to accept the first alternative examined. As we will indicate in the next

---

[17] Kissinger, "Domestic Structure and Foreign Policy," pp. 507–508.

[18] Examples of the psychological literature on this topic are: E. L. Cowen, "The Influence of Varying Degrees of Psychological Stress on Problem-Solving Rigidity," *Journal of Abnormal and Social Psychology*, 47 (April 1952), 512–519; C. W. Eriksen and H. Wechsler, "Some Effects of Experimentally Induced Anxiety upon Discrimination Behavior," *Journal of Abnormal and Social Psychology*, 51 (November 1955), 458–463; S. Pally, "Cognitive Rigidity as a Function of Threat," *Journal of Personality*, 23 (March 1955), 346–355; I. G. Sarason, "The Effects of Anxiety and Threat on the Solution of a Difficult Task," *Journal of Abnormal and Social Psychology*, 62 (January 1961), 165–168. For a study of this behavior in simulation, see M. J. Driver, "Conceptual Structure and Group Processes in an Inter-Nation Simulation," Research Bulletin RB–62–15, Educational Testing Service and Princeton University, Princeton, New Jersey, 1962.

[19] M. Rokeach, H. H. Toch, and T. Rottman, "The Effect of Threat on the Dogmatization of Catholicism," in M. Rokeach, *The Open and Closed Mind* (New York: Basic Books, 1960), p. 377.

chapter, crises increase the pressure on policy makers to come to a consensus; therefore, participants may be less willing in a crisis decision than in other situations to argue against a suggested course of action. If a proposal is accepted, the need to consider other alternatives is eliminated.

We have already shown that at each of the decision points in the Korean crisis the recommended course of action was debated and accepted without any serious examination of possible alternatives. In the Cuban decision, in which we found evidence of search, estimates of the number of alternatives considered by the ExCom run as high as six.[20] Although the number of options was soon narrowed to either a blockade or an air strike, the missile crisis does not seem relevant to the present hypothesis.

Measurement. The number of alternative proposals considered by a decision group was determined by a content analysis of the relevant messages and conference transcripts. Only communications that originated in the nation experiencing the induced situation were examined. A sentence was coded as an alternative proposal if it contained a procedure for treating the situation that confronted the nation. The difference between this variable and the search for alternative proposals depended upon whether the speaker offered a solution (alternative proposal) or looked for one (alternative search). Two or more statements were coded as separate alternatives if they differed on any of the following features: (1) the types of action proposed; (2) the actors involved in the proposal; (3) the time specified for action; or (4) the situations of concern in the proposal.[21] For each experimental situation the number of alternatives identified by the members of a nation were represented as a proportion of their total number of statements—the same procedure used in alternative search. The proportion of alternative statements expressed in crisis situations that led to action was compared with the proportion of alternatives in noncrisis situations that led to action.

---

[20] T. C. Sorensen, *Kennedy* (New York: Harper and Row, 1965), p. 682; E. Abel, *The Missile Crisis* (Philadelphia: Lippincott, 1966), pp. 60–63.

[21] The average inter-coder reliability as determined by a Pearson product moment correlation was .93. The reliability for number of alternatives was computed from a sample of 126 experimental situations examined by two coders.

TABLE 16 **Mann-Whitney U Differences in Number of Alternatives Between Paired Samples Involving Action (Hypothesis 14)**

Paired Action Samples	N	Data Range	U	p if ≶.10	Reject Null Hypothesis?
A. Crisis*	18	.08–.40	107.5		no
Noncrisis	13	.00–.50			
B. High Threat*	16	.00–.44	118.5		no
Low Threat	15	.00–.47			
C. Short Time*	19	.06–.40	97.0		no
Extended Time	14	.00–.40			
D. Surprise	12	.00–.39	96.5		no
Anticipation*	18	.05–.44			
E. High Threat-Short Time*	19	.10–.50	83.0		no
Low Threat-Extended Time	10	.00–.50			
F. High Threat-Surprise*	12	.08–.31	56.5	.04	yes
Low Threat-Anticipation	17	.00–.47			
G. Short Time-Surprise	15	.00–1.0	64.5		no
Extended Time-Anticipation*	10	.07–.40			

NOTE: Except for the crisis-noncrisis samples (for which a directional hypothesis was formed), the reported p values are 2-tailed; therefore, the null hypothesis can be rejected even when the results are the reverse of those predicted for the crisis-noncrisis situations.

* Indicates which type of situation in each set of paired samples had the greater proportion of alternatives.

Results. As shown in Table 16, in only one set of the seven paired samples is the difference in the number of alternatives statistically significant. More alternatives were discussed by the participants in high threat-surprise situations that led to action than in comparable low threat-extended time situations. Although these two crisis traits did result in a significant relationship, when the third characteristic was added to form crisis, the difference did not occur. Thus, Hypothesis 14 is not confirmed. In this simulation neither the search for alternatives nor the number actually considered by the decision makers proved to be useful variables for distinguishing crisis and noncrisis actions.

Affective Conflict

Hypothesis 15: In crisis as compared to noncrisis, the occurrence of affective conflict among the decision makers is less likely to prevent action from occurring.

Illustrations. Affective conflict refers to the differences that arise among those participating in policy decisions. It does not include substantive disagreement over issues, but only emotional or affective conflict involving interpersonal antagonisms. Affective conflict is frequently associated with the loss of temper, name-calling, and abuse of other individuals also engaged in making the decision. We exclude disagreement over the content of issues because of the substantial overlap it would have with the preceding variable—the number of alternatives considered by a group. When two or more alternative proposals are actively evaluated by decision makers, disagreements occur among the participants over the merits of each option. Were it otherwise, all but one option would be quickly dropped. However, disagreements over the consequences of one course of action as compared to another can be done dispassionately; if not, then personal antagonisms develop and affective conflict is present.

One study of a large number of business and governmental conferences provides us with some insight into the consequences of affective conflict in noncrisis situations. Trained observers recorded instances of personal antagonism in these decision-making bodies as well as how the conferences disposed of agenda items. It was discovered that inaction frequently occurred in groups with affective conflict. "There was a striking proclivity of the groups to withdraw from the problem itself— either by becoming less interested in it or by postponing its consideration."[22] Another research project surveyed American foreign service

22 H. Guetzkow and J. Gyr, "An Analysis of Conflict in Decision-Making Groups," *Human Relations*, 7 (1954), 379.

officers. These men were asked, "When disagreement erupts into personal antagonisms, what is the best thing for a leader to do?" Among the most common replies were, "Get them back to the facts." "Keep personalities out of the discussion." *"Call off the meeting."* [Italics mine.][23] Other studies of the political process have commented on the postponement technique as a means of avoiding or reducing conflict—though not necessarily affective conflict. In his characterization of the National Security Council and the Joint Chiefs of Staff as "strategic legislatures," whose processes are not unlike those of Congress, Huntington comments, "If an issue appears highly controversial, members of the strategic committees, like members of Congress, attempt to avoid considering it."[24] The policies formed under such conditions led another author to remark, "Their conflict can result in pure stalemate. Equally obvious are the possibilities for 'compromised policy,' where alternatives may be so watered by accommodation that the direction of choice is hardly evident. . . ."[25]

We have already mentioned the divided councils that existed in the United States government over Vietnam policy in the summer and fall of 1963. Various sources suggest that the endless meetings on that issue were emotionally charged. "These differences became personal and rather mean as time went on. At one briefing in the Cabinet room, Hilsman needled General Lemnitzer so hard that McNamara told him brusquely to give the chairman of the Joint Chiefs a chance to finish."[26] In late August, one cluster of officials responded favorably to an inquiry from Vietnamese generals who were contemplating a coup against the Diem regime. This supportive action was possible because opponents

---

[23] C. Argyris, *Some Causes of Organizational Ineffectiveness in the Department of State*, Center for International Systems Research, Department of State Publication 8180 (January 1967), p. 11.

[24] S. P. Huntington, *The Common Defense* (New York: Columbia University Press, 1961), p. 162.

[25] W. R. Schilling, "The Politics of National Defense: Fiscal 1950," in W. R. Schilling, P. Y. Hammond, and G. H. Snyder, *Strategy, Politics, and Defense Budgets* (New York: Columbia University Press, 1962), p. 25.

[26] E. Weintal and C. Bartlett, *Facing the Brink: An Intimate Study of Crisis Diplomacy* (New York: Scribner's, 1967), p. 81. Referring to this problem, Sorensen has commented that "Kennedy's advisers were more deeply divided on the internal situation in Saigon than on any previous issue. . . . There were bitter disputes, with each side often trying to commit the President in the other's absence." *Kennedy*, pp. 659–660.

of the action in Washington were not fully aware of the implications that were contained in a critical cable sent to Saigon on a Saturday:

> By Monday, John Kennedy's administration had, as he phrased it, "fallen apart" over the cable. It had ignited the simmering split in the government—McNamara, McCone, and Taylor were furious. Kennedy quickly summoned a meeting of his key advisers. Nolting, who had weekended in Virginia after his return from Honolulu, was on hand and he bluntly denounced the Harriman-Hilsman-Forrestal cable as an improvident act. Harriman yelled at him to shut up.[27]

When the coup did not occur, officials in Washington debated whether or not to countermand the cable, to reinterpret it, or to take some entirely different action. No decision was reached.

In crisis situations efforts are made to minimize affective conflict. When such divisions cannot be avoided, participants in the decision tend to emphasize the need to put the national interest ahead of their personal feelings. One method of avoiding emotional conflict is to exclude from the decision process those individuals between whom animosity exists. An interview study in the Department of State found that in situations characterized by the crisis trait of short decision time, fewer people were consulted. In part, the reason for this pattern was "to save the time that would otherwise be lost in trying to resolve the controversies that are bound to arise when people are consulted."[28] Just before the outbreak of the Korean War, some animosity is reported to have existed between Secretary of Defense Johnson and Secretary of State Acheson. At the first Blair House meeting a brief conflict may have flared between the secretaries:

---

[27] Weintal and Bartlett, *Facing the Brink*, p. 87. One of the persons deeply involved in this conflict has described how individuals tended to identify opposition with personal criticism. "But it was the question of how the war was going that stirred up the most emotion. McNamara and Taylor, especially, had made so many public statements that we were winning that they interpreted any suggestion that we were not as a criticism of their judgment and of the whole Pentagon effort." R. Hilsman, *To Move a Nation* (Garden City: Doubleday, 1967), p. 496.

[28] D. G. Pruitt, *Problem Solving in the Department of State*, No. 2, 1964–1965, Monograph Series in World Affairs, The Social Science Foundation and the Department of International Relations, University of Denver, Denver, Colorado, p. 25.

Some participants insist they have no recollection of the incident, and some deny emphatically that it occurred. Others say Johnson pressed the issue of Formosa and stressed the necessity of a new relationship with Generalissimo Chiang and his anti-Communist forces. Acheson flared up and repeated his well-known assessment of the Generalissimo as one who had lost the confidence of the Chinese people and had been surrounded by incompetency. Johnson is said to have retorted: "I can say more bitter things about robber barons than you. But all I'm concerned about is the security of the United States."[29]

The veracity of the specific incident may be uncertain, but what is not in doubt is that personal differences failed to prevent action in that crisis. As we have seen, both men agreed in recommending intervention in Korea.

Equally difficult is the task of ascertaining the degree of affective conflict that may have been present in the discussions of the Executive Committee during the Cuban missile crisis. A member of that group, Theodore Sorensen, wrote, "Despite the fatiguing hours and initially sharp divisions, our meetings avoided any loss of temper and frequently were lightened by a grim humor."[30] By the last full day of the crisis, the same author commented:

We stayed in session all day Saturday, and finally, shortly after 8 P.M., noting rising tempers and irritability, the President recessed the meeting for a one-hour dinner break. Pressure and fatigue, he later noted privately, might have broken the group's steady demeanor in another twenty-four or forty-eight hours.[31]

Whatever affective conflict did occur did not obstruct the decision to establish the blockade.

Measurement. In the simulation, affective conflict was estimated by the staff observers who tape-recorded the conferences. After each

---

[29] A. L. Warner, "How the Korea Decision was Made," *Harpers*, 202 (June 1951), 102.

[30] Sorensen, *Kennedy*, p. 680.

[31] *Ibid.*, p. 716. Sorensen also describes the disagreement over the diplomatic moves to accompany the blockade as "bitter," see p. 695. Also see the description of a conflict between Robert Kennedy and Dean Acheson and between Robert McNamara and Admiral Anderson in Abel, *Missile Crisis*, pp. 64–65, 154–156.

conference held between two or more participants in the same nation, observers rated the degree of emotional conflict.[32] For each nation an average affective conflict score was derived from all the internal conferences. Upon examination, scores were found to be concentrated near that end of the scale that indicated minimal conflict. Rather than discard the variable, the data were dichotomized into those nations with the lowest possible affective conflict scores (average rating of 10) and those in which some affective conflict was registered (average rating less than 10). To test Hypothesis 15, the crisis and noncrisis situations that resulted in action were each divided into "affective conflict" and "no affective conflict" samples.

Results. Once again the hypothesis was not confirmed. The difference between crisis and noncrisis was statistically nonsignificant; further, the trend was the opposite of that predicted. Action in noncrisis rather than crisis occurred somewhat more often when affective conflict existed among the decision makers. As shown in Table 17, the chi square values for all seven paired samples were insufficient to reject the null hypothesis at the accepted significance level. One set of samples, however (Table 17, section E), neared the significance level. Affective conflict was less often present in the action situations characterized by high threat and short time than in action situations characterized by low threat and extended time. The situations with any crisis traits produced action in the absence of affective conflict more often than noncrises. All crisis situations, regardless of the decision to act, may less often involve affective conflict than noncrises, thus making it an unsatisfactory variable for distinguishing action from inaction.

---

[32] Observers were given forms for each conference with the following instructions:

> Rate the conference on its affective conflict (the amount of personal or emotional disputing which went on—name-calling, flares of temper, shouting, etc.).

:	:	:	:	:	:	:	:	:	:	:
1	2	3	4	5	6	7	8	9	10	
Quite a Bit									Very Little	

The inter-coder reliability as determined by a phi coefficient was .51, the lowest reliability in the present research. The reliability estimate was based on 44 conferences rated by two observers.

TABLE 17 **Chi Square Differences in Affective Conflict Between Paired Samples Involving Action (Hypothesis 15)**

	Paired Action Samples	Affective Conflict	No Affective Conflict	Total	Chi Square	p if ≲.10	Reject Null Hypothesis?
A.	Crisis	7	11	18			
	Noncrisis	8	4	12[a]	1.25		no
	Total	15	15	30			
B.	High Threat	9	7	16			
	Low Threat	8	7	15	0.04		no
	Total	17	14	31			
C.	Short Time	9	10	19			
	Extended Time	7	7	14	0.04		no
	Total	16	17	33			
D.	Surprise	6	6	12			
	Anticipation	9	8	17[a]	0.05		no
	Total	15	14	29			
E.	High Threat-Short Time	5	14	19			
	Low Threat-Extended Time	7	3	10	3.52	.06	no
	Total	12	17	29			
F.	High Threat-Surprise	5	7	12			
	Low Threat-Anticipation	10	7	17	0.28		no
	Total	15	14	29			
G.	Short Time-Surprise	5	10	15			
	Extended Time-Anticipation	7	3	10	1.93		no
	Total	12	13	25			

NOTE: Except for the crisis-noncrisis samples (for which a directional hypothesis was formed), the reported *p* values are 2-tailed; therefore, the null hypothesis can be rejected even when the results are the reverse of those predicted for the crisis-noncrisis situations.

[a] Data for one situation not available in this sample.

Contraction of Authority

Hypothesis 16: In crisis as compared to noncrisis, the contraction of authority in making a decision is less likely to prevent action from occurring.

Illustrations. Contraction of authority is a reduction in the number of individuals who share responsibility for making the decision. When the active participants in a decision are fewer than in most other situations, then contraction of authority has occurred. The standard procedure in devising foreign policy—usually adhered to in noncrises—involves extensive coordination within the agency with primary responsibility for formulating the policy as well as between the various agencies that have an interest in the issue. "The basic principle underlying programmed lateral consultation is that every branch of the government whose area of specialty is directly involved in a problem must be consulted during the development of policy recommendations."[33] In noncrisis situations a contraction of authority frequently leads to inaction. For example, in the Department of State "failure by a desk officer to obtain clearance from other bureaus in the Department or from other governmental agencies with direct interest in a note, telegram, or policy paper means that agreement must be sought at a higher level or the matter dropped."[34] Often the net effect of referring an issue to a higher level for coordination is identical to the termination of the proposal, because the higher the official in the organizational hierarchy, the more problems there are which compete for his attention, and, of course, only the most urgent can be acted upon.

The contraction of authority in noncrisis leads to inaction for various other reasons. A recent study of the United States Foreign Service found a tendency for "participants to minimize interpersonal threat by minimizing risk-taking, being open and being forthright, as well as minimizing their feelings of responsibility. . . . Under these conditions people soon learn the survival quotient of 'checking with everyone.' "[35] When the opportunity for wide consultation is closed, risk and

---

[33] Pruitt, *Problem Solving*, p. 23.

[34] R. E. Elder, *The Policy Machine* (Syracuse: Syracuse University Press, 1960), p. 35.

[35] Argyris, *Ineffectiveness in the Department of State*, p. 33.

responsibility can frequently be avoided by inaction. Moreover, other officials often desire to be consulted on problems which relate to their field, hence they may use various means to punish an officer who fails to discuss recommendations with them. One method is to obstruct future policies that the officer advocates.

In crisis, the pressures for inaction that are normally associated with a contraction of authority are substantially less. "Evidence suggests that in times of emergency an officer is less likely to be punished for failing to consult branches of the government that are marginally involved."[36] Furthermore, those individuals who do exercise authority in crisis situations tend to be at the highest levels of government; therefore, they are able to commit agencies without seeking the approval of others. We have emphasized the small size of the decision-making groups in both the Korean and Cuban decisions. Late Thursday evening, in the first week of the missile crisis, most members of the ExCom left the State Department to rejoin the President at the White House. Only one individual elected to walk, while nine others climbed into a single limousine to avoid attracting attention which would result if a caravan of cars arrived at the White House at that hour. "In the crush of bodies, someone remarked: 'What if we get into a collision?' "[37] From the standpoint of Hypothesis 16, this humorous quip is revealing. The decisional unit was so small that an automobile accident at that moment would have involved almost the entire group responsible for recommending action against the missile threat.

Measurement. The number of decision makers who were actively involved in resolving an experimental situation was measured by using a variation of the content analysis category devised for alternative proposals (see the measurement discussion for Hypothesis 14). A participant was defined as active if he recommended one or more alternatives for resolving the problem. He need not have been the first to advocate a specific proposal, but he was required to speak for it if he was to be counted. Unlike the measure of alternative proposals, the number of persons suggesting solutions—not the number of different proposals—determined the value of the variable. With the ADM excluded because he was not a member of the government, total participation occurred

---

[36] Pruitt, *Problem Solving*, p. 26.
[37] Abel, *Missile Crisis*, p. 81.

when each of the remaining four decision makers in the nation made at least one recommendation. When the number of participants who suggested proposals was less than four, then contraction of authority was said to exist. For Hypothesis 16, the crisis and noncrisis samples involving action were compared for the frequency of contracted decisional units as opposed to noncontracted units.

Results. Although contractions of authority outnumbered noncontractions in crises that led to action, the tendency was more pronounced in noncrisis-action situations. Therefore, Hypothesis 16 was not confirmed. No significant differences in contraction of authority were found between the situations in any other paired samples. Several other methods of measuring the variable were tried including an estimate based on the number of participants necessary to account for 75 per cent of the alternative proposals and a count of the number of decision makers who individually took action in the situation. With both these measures, contraction was defined as any number of participants less than four. As with the original operational definition, contraction was somewhat more frequent in noncrisis situations that led to action than in comparable crises, whereas none of the other paired samples resulted in any significant differences.[38]

Summary

Each of the five hypotheses examined in this chapter have introduced a property of the decision unit as an intervening variable between crisis and action. When these hypotheses were examined using the simulation data, none was statistically significant. In addition to those performed on the hypothesized relationships, 30 other statistical tests were conducted between simulated situations that differed on only one or two of the traits that comprise the definition of crisis. Only one result was significant; a second was nearly so. It would be inappropriate

---

[38] Another operational definition of contraction, inappropriate for a chapter using measures that are independent of the participants, was based on the questionnaire administered after each experimental situation. Every participant was asked whether he participated in the situation (Appendix I, item B5). No significant differences were found.

to conclude from these nonsignificant findings that all properties of the decision unit are unimportant in distinguishing action in crisis from action in noncrisis. Although the new variables in this chapter were classified as decision unit properties, they are not representative of all the attributes of an individual, group, or organization that might influence its decisions. What we can say is that in this simulation these specific intervening variables were ineffective.

One possible explanation for why these variables proved ineffective is the method by which they were measured. As we have noted, all these variables were measured indirectly, that is, independently of the participants. The specific techniques for estimating each variable, however, were not the same. National capabilities were data that already existed in quantitative form. Contraction of authority and the two variables concerned with alternatives were measured through a content analysis of the participant messages and conference transcripts. The degree of affective conflict was judged by observers of the participant conferences. Furthermore, with several of these variables (capabilities, contraction, and number of alternatives) different operational definitions were explored when the original procedure failed to produce significant results. In each case the substitute measures also yielded findings that were not significant. Unless we are prepared to reject the appropriateness of indirect methods of measuring decision unit properties regardless of the specific technique, the plausibility of attributing the results to the measuring procedure is reduced.

Another explanation is introduced if the means of measuring the intervening variables in this chapter can be associated exclusively with the perspective of the *observers* and not the *actors*. The Sprouts have contended that the environment in which policy makers operate—including properties of the decision unit—will affect their decision only as it is perceived by the decision makers:

Environmental factors become related to the attitudes and decisions which comprise a state's foreign policy only by being perceived and taken into account in the policy-forming process. . . . What matters is how the policy maker imagines the milieu to be, not how it actually is.[39]

---

[39] H. Sprout and M. Sprout, "Environmental Factors in the Study of International Politics," in J. N. Rosenau, ed., *International Politics and Foreign Policy* (New York: Free Press, 1961), p. 112.

If we assume that these decision unit properties were not perceived by the participants in the simulation, then the finding that these environmental variables had no effect on the decision to act is consistent with the position stated by the Sprouts. Differences in a nation's capabilities, for example, may well influence the *consequences* of a decision to take action, but if the property is not perceived by the policy makers it will have no effect whatsoever on the decision itself. Unfortunately, no data were collected on the hypotheses enumerated in this chapter which would reveal whether the participants perceived the five variables in the same manner as the observers who content analyzed messages or judged conferences. As we will see in Chapter 7, however, the observers and participants did not agree on their estimates of other variables.

Some implications of Chapter 6 can best be understood when the findings are compared with those for the previous chapters. Figure 4 presents in schematic form the conditions discussed in Chapters 4–6 as possible influences on the probability of action. The proposed definition of crisis is shown to have been a part of six statistically significant relationships. (This does not include the finding from the Post-Simulation Questionnaire which was significant in the opposite direction from that predicted in Hypothesis 1.) In the number of significant relationships, the crisis-noncrisis distinction does better than any of the other paired samples except the combination of threat and time. Situations involving the dimensions of threat and time—but with the awareness dimension controlled—also produce six significant results. A seventh relationship with these two traits approaches the significance level.

In four relationships the results obtained with crisis (all three traits) parallel those found with threat and time; that is, the results would have been similar regardless of whether the situation was defined by the proposed crisis concept or by only threat and time. In four other relationships, however, the two formulations of the situation led to different results. In those four tests the addition of surprise to high threat and short time cancelled a previously significant relationship, reversed the direction of the relationship, or produced a significant relationship where none had previously existed.

Together with the crisis-noncrisis and the threat-time findings, Figure 4 summarizes the four significant relationships obtained by the combination of threat and awareness. Three of the relationships are similar to those found with crisis-noncrisis. No other situational trait

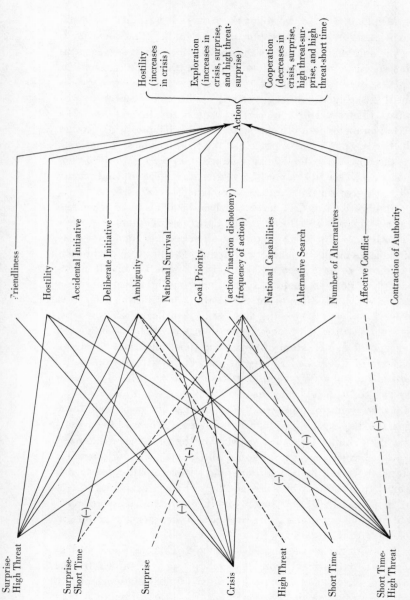

FIGURE 4 **Summary of Relationships Between Crisis (or Its Components) and Action When Intervening Variables Are Introduced**

NOTE: Solid lines between variables indicate a statistically significant relationship ($p \leq .05$). Broken lines represent rela-

or combination of traits is involved in more than two significant results. In summary, Chapters 4–6 provide some data on the proposed definition of crisis. A more complete evaluation will be possible after examining the results of the next chapter.

In addition to their implications for a definition of crisis, the data we have considered provide some information about crisis decisions. When faced with a crisis, the simulation participants placed considerable emphasis on past experience in deciding whether or not to take action. For example, in a crisis the prior attitude of hostility or friendliness of the agent precipitating the situation played a larger part in deciding whether or not to act than it did in noncrisis. Furthermore, the past priority of a national objective was more relevant in crisis than in noncrisis. The interpretation of the crisis findings as emphasizing past experience is consistent with observations made by Pool on communications in crisis:

> Crisis communications will not change existing attitudes or identifications much, but they can provide a context that will lead people who have given attitudes and identifications to act in desired ways. These propositions have been documented by research on election campaigns. It has been shown that campaigns persuade very few individuals. What they do is to increase interest in and attention to certain topics, triggering off latent responses that people already have to those topics.[40]

The findings from Chapters 4–6 also indicate that in response to a crisis, friendly action is less likely to occur, whereas exploratory or hostile action is more likely. Although it could not be established with the available simulation data, we suspect that hostile rather than exploratory action is more probable (1) when the agent is perceived to have deliberately triggered the crisis, or (2) when national survival is endangered. The data did confirm that these two variables distinguished crisis from noncrisis actions.

---

[40] I. S. Pool, *Studies in Deterrence VI: Human Communication and Deterrence*, NOTS TP 2841, U. S. Naval Ordnance Test Station, China Lake, California (September 1963), p. 45.

Chapter 7

A MODEL OF CRISIS
DECISION MAKING

The initial data from this study dealt with the direct impact of crisis as a situational variable on the decision to act. The hypotheses in Chapters 5–6 extended this relationship by introducing mediating variables, one at a time. Even in Chapters 5 and 6, the assumed connection between crisis and action has been relatively uncomplicated. Some important consequences of a crisis, however, may be more complex. For example, a crisis could alter procedures and structures normally involved in the decision process, and these modified variables, in turn, could combine in a way that would change the decision. With evidence drawn from the simulation data, this chapter explores a more complex model of interrelated hypotheses.

The Model

In brief, the model proposes that a crisis creates among the decision makers substantial incongruity or dissonance between their accelerated commitment to take effective action toward a specific goal and their decreased expectation that a policy which advances a specific goal can be formed. In other words, at the same time that a crisis increases the policy makers' desire to do something it increases their conviction that the situation severely restricts the opportunity for positive action. Many occasions for decision confront the decision makers with a conflict between the commitment to act and the belief that action will be ineffective. A crisis makes this incongruity severe. Regardless of the decision taken in a crisis, the dissonance reduces the confidence of the policy makers that their response will protect the threatened goals. To reduce that dissonance, the decision makers begin an extensive search for support; that is, they initiate efforts to gain assurances of support for the decision from others. When combined with the flow of instructions for executing the decision, the search for support increases the volume of communication that occurs in a crisis after a decision has been made.

Figure 5 is a diagram of the basic relationships contained in the model. At the top of the diagram, the two variables linked to crisis are postulated to increase the decision unit's commitment to act toward a specific goal. As a result of the crisis, a consensus emerges among the decision makers as to the nature of the objective that is jeopardized (Hypothesis 17). A crisis also increases the priority assigned by policy makers to the goal or goals that are threatened by the situation (Hypothesis 18). Together the increase in these two variables overcomes some of the aspects of bureaucracy that normally obstruct goal-oriented actions. In contrast to many noncrisis situations, the members of the organization are agreed as to what issues demand their immediate attention. Internal divisions and differences in priorities are temporarily set aside. This increases the commitment of the decision makers to take effective action. (See the dotted line at the top of Figure 5.)

Crisis reduces two kinds of search processes that foreign policy organizations go through as part of the policy-making procedure. First, decision makers gather less information necessary to establish the nature of the occasion for decision; that is, crisis causes the search for the definition of the situation to decrease (Hypothesis 19). Second, in times of crisis decision makers conduct less search for alternative solutions, or different responses, to the situation (Hypothesis 20). Closely related to the reduction in search for alternatives is the tendency of the decision-making unit to consider fewer alternative responses in a crisis (Hypothesis 21). Hypotheses 20 and 21 are different since imaginative policy makers may be able to conceive of a number of possible responses to a situation without engaging in an extensive search of the organizational memory. Hypothesis 21 suggests that this enumeration of options without organizational search is less likely in crisis. The fourth hypothesis in this section of the model contends that crisis leads to a contraction

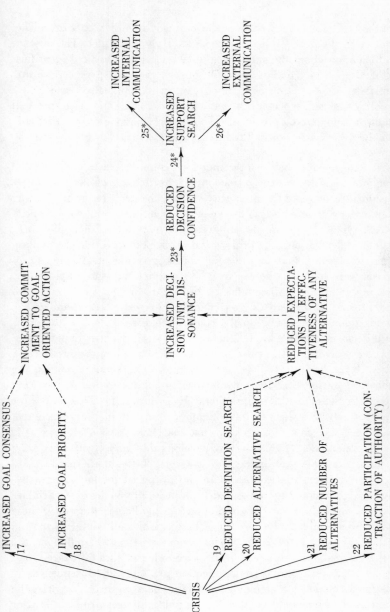

FIGURE 5 A Diagram of a Model Indicating the Impact of Crisis on Foreign Policy Decision Making

NOTE: The broken lines represent relationships not investigated with the simulation data. Those hypotheses whose numbers are followed by an asterisk (*) involve dependent variables that were explored only in a direct relationship with crisis.

of authority, or, a crisis reduces the number of individuals exercising authority in the decision-making process (Hypothesis 22). The absence of information about the situation, the lack of search for and identification of alternative solutions, and the limited range of perspectives that result from a contraction of authority, all are hypothesized to decrease the policy makers' expectations that a response can be devised that will sustain the endangered objective. (The dotted line in Figure 5 that connects the four variables to "reduced expectations" represents this relationship.)

The incongruity between the increased commitment to goal-oriented action and the reduced expectations in the effectiveness of any alternative is assumed to increase the dissonance within the decision unit. The way policy makers cope with this dissonance can influence their decision. If different types of individuals employ different means of handling these conflicting dispositions, then this variation in personality might explain the earlier finding that in some simulated governments the responses to crisis were hostile, whereas in others the actions were exploratory. The possible effects of dissonance on the nature of decisions are investigated further at the end of this chapter. For the moment, the model depends upon the assumption that policy makers respond to the crisis with a decision of some kind. Whatever that decision, it is hypothesized that the dissonance reduces the confidence of the policy makers in their choice (Hypothesis 23). The decision makers attempt to reduce the dissonance, or increase their confidence in their decision, by seeking support for their position from others (Hypothesis 24). This search for support accelerates the rate of communication within the government (Hypothesis 25) as well as to other nations (Hypothesis 26).

The remainder of this chapter develops this model with data from the simulation. Several limitations, however, prevent an inquiry into all of the relationships contained in the proposed model. Certain hypotheses (represented by the dotted lines in Figure 5) involve variables for which no data from the simulation are available; therefore, these relationships cannot be included. Furthermore, those hypotheses that do not directly involve the crisis variable pose another restriction on the simulation analysis. Although decision confidence, support search, and both internal and external communication are indirect consequences of crisis in the model, the amount of available data requires that crisis be treated as the immediate independent variable in each proposition. For example, in the model Hypothesis 24 proposes that an increase in search for support is the direct result of a reduction in decision confidence, but the simulation data establish only whether an increase in search for support occurs in a crisis. If we are able to confirm that the dependent variables do change in the predicted manner in crisis situations, we will not have confirmed the role of such intervening variables as decision confidence, but we will have established a first approximation that is consistent with the model.

Commitment to Goal-Oriented Action

Hypothesis 17: In crisis as compared to noncrisis, the frequency of consensus among decision makers as to the national goals affected by the situation is increased.

Hypothesis 18: In crisis as compared to noncrisis, the priority assigned by decision makers to the most affected national goal(s) is increased.

Illustrations. These two hypotheses provide the basis for assuming that crises increase the commitment of decision makers to take action toward a specific goal. Both the emplacement of the missile bases in Cuba and the invasion of South Korea offer examples of consensus on the nature of the nation's goals that can develop among policy makers during a crisis. Among the ExCom participants in the Cuban missile crisis consensus on goals was reflected by their agreement as to what the American response should be. It was decided that the missiles must be removed and that the Soviets were responsible for putting them there. The objective was not to remove Castro, nor to hold the Cubans responsible. The ExCom members disagreed not on the goals, but on the feasible means of achieving them. Similarly, when the United States decision makers confronted the crisis in South Korea, they thought that the threat was directed at the American investment in the principle of collective security and at the United Nations which was established to maintain security. In Korea, the policy makers' "definition of the situation included agreement on the basic general values involved."[1] These

---

[1] R. C. Snyder and G. D. Paige, "The United States Decision to Resist Aggression in Korea: The Application of an Analytical Scheme," *Administrative Science Quarterly*, 3 (December 1958), 375.

two crises illustrate the generalization posed by Kissinger, "Agreement on what constitutes a problem generally depends on an emerging crisis. . . ."[2] Cuba and Korea also confirm the broader observation that "in general crisis concentrates, noncrisis disperses attention."[3] Others have contended that a crisis will "clarify relevant values."[4] The tendency of a crisis to narrow or focus attention as well as to clarify values probably increases the consensus as to which goals are involved in the situation.

Hypothesis 18 concerns changes in the priority of goals that result from a crisis. Although Cuba undoubtedly was a sensitive problem in the wake of the attempted invasion at the Bay of Pigs, the leadership of John F. Kennedy's administration seemed preoccupied in the fall of 1962 with the forthcoming elections as well as with the future of Berlin —this latter problem had been recently aggravated by Soviet threats. The discovery of the missiles changed the immediate priorities assigned to these issues. In the months before the invasion of South Korea, American policy makers had indicated that the Republic of Korea was peripheral to the strategic interests of the United States. However, when the North Koreans attacked, the relative importance of Korea to our overall strategic goals increased. Dramatic changes in the priorities of several European states during the summer of 1914, led North to conclude:

At a certain threshold of high tension the value hierarchy of the state is likely to "flip," that is, preferences that were low on the hierarchy move to the top and replace preferences that formerly were considered primary.[5]

---

[2] H. A. Kissinger, "Domestic Structure and Foreign Policy," *Daedalus*, 95 (Spring 1966), 517.

[3] H. D. Lasswell, D. Lerner, and I. S. Pool, *The Comparative Study of Symbols* (Stanford: Stanford University Press, 1952), p. 21.

[4] R. C. Snyder and J. A. Robinson, *National and International Decision-Making* (New York: Institute for International Order, 1961), p. 31. Also see R. W. Mack and R. C. Snyder, "The Analysis of Social Conflict—Toward an Overview and Synthesis," *Journal of Conflict Resolution*, 1 (June 1957), 234, and J. D. Thompson and R. W. Hawkes, "Disaster, Community Organization, and Administrative Process," in G. W. Baker and D. W. Chapman, eds., *Man and Society in Disaster* (New York: Basic Books, 1962), p. 278.

[5] R. C. North, O. R. Holsti, M. G. Zaninovich, and D. A. Zinnes, *Content Analysis* (Evanston: Northwestern University Press, 1963), p. 174.

Another scholar calls attention to the emergence, during a crisis, of previously dormant attitudes. Pool suggests that it is not that totally new attitudes appear during a crisis but that "what does happen, which sometimes gives the impression of total change, is a drastic change in priorities and in the conclusions drawn from latent attitudes long present. . . ."[6] Whereas students of international politics occasionally propose that crises create shifts in the priority of goals, to some policy makers this is completely obvious.[7]

Measurement. The previously undefined variables in Hypotheses 17 and 18 are (1) the consensus among the decision makers as to which goal is threatened and (2) the change in priority of the threatened goal. Questionnaires issued to the participants provided the means for determining whether the simulation decision makers agreed on which goals were endangered by the situation. Consensus existed if at least three of the four national decision makers—excluding the ADM—agreed that one or more goals had become more difficult to attain during the experimental situation (Appendix I, item B2). If less than three participants agreed on what goals were endangered by the situation, then that situation involved no consensus.

Those national goals threatened by an experimental situation—as perceived by three of the four governmental decision makers—were analyzed further to ascertain if the priority assigned to the goals by the participants had shifted. Periodically the participants ordered their nation's goals according to importance (Appendix I, item A1); they also made similar ratings of their goals after each experimental situation (Appendix I, item B3). The differences in the ratings made shortly before and immediately after the situation indicated whether a particular goal had become more important and, if so, by how much. To obtain a goal priority score for the government as a unit, the differences in rat-

---

[6] I. S. Pool, *Studies in Deterrence VI: Human Communication and Deterrence*, NOTS TP 2841, U. S. Naval Ordnance Test Station, China Lake, California (September 1963), p. 42.

[7] In interviews with high-level policy makers concerning their crisis decisions, the author asked whether crisis tended to elevate the priority of objectives jeopardized by the situation. In affirming this effect of crisis, a number of respondents suggested that such a consequence was so evident that systematic inquiry was unnecessary.

ings acquired from each governmental decision maker were averaged. If the decision makers agreed that the situation affected more than one goal, then the mean change in all threatened goals constituted the measure of the goal priority variable.

Results. The simulation data support Hypothesis 17. Decision makers concur more frequently in times of crisis about which are the endangered goals than they do in noncrisis. The participants reached a consensus in all the crises, but in only half the noncrises. The results of the chi square tests displayed in Table 18 also indicate that consensus occurred with significantly greater frequency in high threat than in low threat situations. Similarly high threat-short time situations produced significantly more consensus on the goals than did low threat-extended time situations.

The effect of crisis on goal priority remains less certain. The importance of goals increased more in crisis than in noncrisis, but this difference only approached the established significance level with a Mann-Whitney U test. Situations having two of the crisis characteristics (high threat and surprise) resulted in significantly higher goal priorities than those found in situations with the two comparable noncrisis characteristics. Table 19 shows these findings. Although the change in goal priority that resulted from crisis remained small in the samples, this change represented the predicted shift in the importance of goals. Thus, the crises in the simulation produced the changes proposed in the model for both variables associated with increased commitment to goal-oriented action. Now let us consider the other hypotheses that, when combined with those already discussed, create dissonance for the decision makers.

Reduced Expectations in the Effectiveness of Alternatives

Hypothesis 19: In crisis as compared to noncrisis, the amount of search conducted by the decision makers for information with which to define the situation is decreased.

Hypothesis 20: In crisis as compared to noncrisis, the amount of search conducted by the decision makers for differentiated alternative solutions to the situation is decreased.

TABLE 18 **Chi Square Differences Between Goal Consensus and No Goal Consensus in Crisis-Noncrisis and Other Paired Samples (Hypothesis 17)**

Paired Samples	Consensus	Non-Consensus	Total	Chi Square	p if ≶ .10	Reject Null Hypothesis?
A. Crisis	24	0	24			
Noncrisis	16	8	24	7.17	.004	yes
Total	40	8	48			
B. High Threat	23	1	24			
Low Threat	14	10	24	7.58	.008	yes
Total	37	11	48			
C. Short Time	19	5	24			
Extended Time	18	6	24	0.00		no
Total	37	11	48			
D. Surprise	20	4	24			
Anticipation	22	2	24	0.19		no
Total	42	6	48			
E. High Threat-Short Time	23	1	24			
Low Threat-Extended Time	11	13	24	12.20	< .001	yes
Total	34	14	48			
F. High Threat-Surprise	20	4	24			
Low Threat-Anticipation	14	10	24	2.52		no
Total	34	14	48			
G. Short Time-Surprise	18	6	24			
Extended Time-Anticipation	19	5	24	0.00		no
Total	37	11	48			

NOTE: Except for the crisis-noncrisis samples (for which a directional hypothesis was formed), the reported p values are 2-tailed; therefore, the null hypothesis can be rejected even when the results are the reverse of those predicted for the crisis-noncrisis situations.

TABLE 19 **Mann-Whitney U Differences in Priority of National Goals Between Crisis-Noncrisis and Other Paired Samples (Hypothesis 18)**

Paired Samples	N	Data Range[a]	Normalized U	p if $\leqslant .10$	Reject Null Hypothesis?
A. Crisis*	24	− 0.4 to + 2.7	1.31	.10	no
Noncrisis	16	− 2.5 to + 4.5			
B. High Threat*	23	− 1.2 to + 2.5	1.44		no
Low Threat	14	− 1.3 to + 3.5			
C. Short Time	19	− 1.3 to + 2.5	156.5[b]		no
Extended Time*	18	− 0.3 to + 2.0			
D. Surprise*	20	− 1.5 to + 2.1	0.05		no
Anticipation	22	− 1.3 to + 2.2			
E. High Threat-Short Time*	23	− 1.0 to + 4.0	0.61		no
Low Threat-Extended Time	11	− 2.5 to + 3.3			
F. High Threat-Surprise*	20	− 1.1 to + 2.1	74.5[b]	.02	yes
Low Threat-Anticipation	14	− 2.0 to + 2.0			
G. Short Time-Surprise*	18	− 2.7 to + 3.0	162.0[b]		no
Extended Time-Anticipation	19	− 1.0 to + 2.6			

NOTE: N's are less than 24 in some samples because of lack of agreement among the decision makers as to which goals were involved. These situations were deleted. Except for the crisis-noncrisis samples (for which a directional hypothesis was formed), the reported p values are 2-tailed; therefore, the null hypothesis can be rejected even when the results are the reverse of those predicted for the crisis-noncrisis situations.

* Indicates which type of situation in each set of paired samples had the higher goal priority.

[a] Minus values in the range of data scores result from nations which reduced goal priority after the experimental situation was introduced. In no sample did this occur in more than one-fourth of the situations.

[b] Sample size was not sufficient to calculate a normalized U; therefore, U is uncorrected for ties.

Hypothesis 21: In crisis as compared to noncrisis, the number of alternative solutions to the situation identified by the decision makers is decreased.

Hypothesis 22: In crisis as compared to noncrisis, the number of decision makers exercising authority in the decision process is decreased; that is, a contraction of authority occurs.

Illustrations. In apparent contradiction to Hypothesis 19, both the Korean and the Cuban crises involved increased search for definitional information. President Truman requested General MacArthur to make an immediate inspection of the Korean conflict. President Kennedy ordered an acceleration in the number of photographic reconnaissance flights over Cuba. The public record, however, suggests that in both incidents a search for information that would help define the situation was limited to these channels alone. Furthermore, the policy makers did not await further evidence that would assist in interpreting the situations. As Snyder and Paige observed in the Korean decision, "Limited information did not prevent an initial definition of the situation which included elements beyond the objective situation per se."[8]

The dependent variables in Hypotheses 20 and 21—the search for alternatives and number of alternatives—originally appeared in Chapter 6 as intervening variables between crisis actions and noncrisis actions. At that time, relevant illustrations drawn from the Korean and Cuban crises conflicted with one another. In June 1950, the American policy makers made few inquiries as to the possible alternative responses to the invasion of South Korea. Nor did they differentiate multiple courses of action in their deliberations. By contrast, the decision makers in the Cuban crisis not only sought options, they actively discussed various courses of action. Several explanations might account for the discrepancy between these two historical cases. The somewhat longer time available for decision in the Cuban situation provided an increased opportunity for the search and the enumeration of alternatives. That each side possessed deliverable nuclear weapons may have increased the policy makers' incentive to develop alternatives in 1962 as compared to 1950.[9] For these or other reasons, the Cuban situation may not have been a typical crisis with respect to alternatives.

---

[8] Snyder and Paige, "Decision to Resist Aggression," p. 349.

[9] Thomas Schelling has mentioned the importance of nuclear capability on the generation of policy alternatives in crisis situations. See his *Arms and Influence* (New Haven: Yale University Press, 1966), p. 96.

Other crises, such as the political events that led up to the outbreak of World War I, lend support to Hypotheses 20 and 21. Drawing his conclusion from the 1914 crisis, one scholar proposes that "the higher the tension, the less the ability to seek new solutions for a conflict and the stronger the tendency to choose an alternative habitually associated with the kind of crisis that is perceived."[10] In another study of the same crisis, the investigator content analyzed diplomatic communiqués for statements by the policy makers which described a particular action as necessary and as one that offered no choice. The frequency of such statements was significantly greater for both the Dual Alliance and the Triple Entente in the period immediately preceding the outbreak of war than it was earlier in the summer.[11]

The 1965 crisis in the Dominican Republic offers a recent American decision that was characterized by restricted search for definitions and alternatives as well as a limited examination of alternative solutions. Late in the afternoon of April 28, 1965, the United States Ambassador to the Dominican Republic, W. Tapley Bennett, sent a critical message to the State Department:

> When Bennett's "critic" cable was brought into the President's office, a call had been made to Tom Mann [Thomas C. Mann, Under Secretary of State for Economic Affairs], who was meeting with his staff at State. Meanwhile at the White House, there was a brisk, brief discussion. One man who was there reported later that nobody felt much need to say anything. "One or two spoke up, and the general conclusion was that there was no real choice. The President asked if there was any other view. By the time Mann called back with his recommendation, the decision had really been made to send in the Marines."[12]

This description of the American decision process during the Dominican Republic crisis also supports the proposition that a crisis creates a contraction of authority (Hypothesis 22). Earlier chapters have emphasized this behavior in the Korean and Cuban decisions. What has not been previously reported is the evidence of contraction of

---

[10] North *et al.*, *Content Analysis*, p. 173.

[11] O. R. Holsti, "The 1914 Case," *American Political Science Review*, 59 (June 1965), 365–378.

[12] P. Geyelin, *Lyndon B. Johnson and the World* (New York: Praeger, 1966), pp. 251–252.

authority among the Soviet leaders during the Cuban missile crisis. Khrushchev, reportedly, consulted mainly with an inner group of five or six members of the Party Presidium (now the Politburo).[13] The contraction hypothesis is probably the most widely reported proposition about the effects of crisis. An inventory of social science research includes this relationship as an established finding.[14] Two men who have occupied positions as Assistant Secretaries in the Department of State have independently substantiated this phenomenon in foreign policy crises.[15] Although the present hypothesis does not stipulate that the exercise of authority must necessarily shift to higher levels of an organization, contraction of this kind is frequently mentioned as the following statement by Buchan illustrates, "As a period of tension grows towards its crisis point, the handling of decisions becomes more centralized and elevated within national governments."[16] Of course, in most studies the exact nature of a crisis remains undefined; therefore, the specific circumstances leading to a contraction of authority remain vague.

Measurement. The two variables that dealt with search measured the efforts of the simulation participants to gather certain kinds of information. Search for definition consisted of the policy makers' requests for information about the present nature of a situation they confronted. Search for alternatives comprised those inquiries by policy makers for information about the possible means for coping with the situation. The measurement procedure for alternative search appeared in Chapter 6. The same method established the amount of search for definition; that is, the experimenters content analyzed each participant's messages and conference statements pertaining to an experimental situation. If a simple sentence—the basic unit of analysis—contained a request for

---

[13] *Staffing Procedures and Problems in the Soviet Union,* Committee on Government Operations, U. S. Senate (88 Cong., 1 Sess., 1963), p. 25.

[14] B. Berelson and G. A. Steiner, *Human Behavior* (New York: Harcourt, Brace and World, 1964), p. 370.

[15] See R. Hilsman, "The Foreign Policy Consensus: An Interim Research Report," *Journal of Conflict Resolution,* 3 (December 1959), 372; and H. Cleveland, "Crisis Diplomacy," *Foreign Affairs,* 41 (July 1963), 638.

[16] A. Buchan, *Crisis Management* (Boulogne-Sur-Seine, France: The Atlantic Institute, 1966), pp. 40–41.

information about the nature of the situation, then it was coded as a definition search statement.[17]

Chapter 6 also included the procedures used to measure the number of alternatives as well as the amount of contraction of authority. These two variables constituted part of Hypothesis 14 and 16 respectively. In summary, the experimenters identified an alternative proposal as a statement by a participant that advanced some means of handling or disposing of an experimental situation. In this content analysis, two proposals were classified as separate alternatives if they involved different actions, actors, times, or situations. To establish a proportion, the number of sentences containing different alternatives offered by all members of a nation were divided by the total number of sentences they made in the situation.

To determine if a contraction of authority occurred, the experimenters counted the number of individuals in a simulated nation who actively participated in deciding how the government should respond to a situation. If a participant wrote or spoke at least once for a specific means of dealing with the problem, he was considered active. Excluding the opposition leader (the ADM), each simulated government consisted of four individuals; thus, contraction took place when the number of active participants was three or less.

The simulation data provided another means of exploring each hypothesis in this section of the model. After the simulation, every individual selected one crisis and one noncrisis in which he had participated. He chose both situations according to the definitions of crisis and noncrisis used in this study. Then the participant responded to a questionnaire that contained an identical set of questions about the decision-making process in the crisis and the noncrisis situations. The question

---

[17] The reliability between coders for definition search statements was .88 (Pearson product moment correlation). The sampling procedure for checking the reliability of the coding is described in Chapter 6, footnote 16. As indicated in that footnote, the correlation between coders of alternative search inquiries was .81. Initially both definition and alternative search sentences were measured as a proportion of the total number of sentences made by participants during a given experimental situation. Because of the large number of situations in which neither type of search occurred, the measures were reconstructed as dichotomies (i.e. some search, no search). Chi square tests determined if the participants made some search more often in crises than noncrises.

concerning the search for definition was whether "considerable" or "little" effort had been spent in obtaining information about the situation. If the respondent felt that little effort had been devoted to definition search, he could choose between answers which attributed this absence of search to time pressures or to the availability of sufficient information (Appendix I, item C1). The item dealing with alternative search inquired whether the participants believed that "considerable effort" or "no major concern" had been devoted to uncovering alternative solutions (Appendix I, item C3). The respondents also characterized the decision process in crisis and noncrisis as either involving a number of different alternatives or only one or two (Appendix I, item C2). Another question ascertained whether more, equal, or fewer individuals actively participated in making the crisis (or noncrisis) decision than participated in the usual situation (Appendix I, item C4). For the contraction of authority hypothesis, responses from participants who indicated a reduction in the number of active decision makers were contrasted with the combined responses of those who reported that the number of decision makers increased or remained unchanged.

Results. Contrary to Hypothesis 19, crisis resulted in no less of a search for definition of the situation than noncrisis. This conclusion is supported by findings from both the content analysis and the simulation questionnaire. As shown in section A of Table 20, definition search occurred in more crises than noncrises, but the difference was not statistically significant. The same table reveals that in only one of the seven paired situations is the difference in the amount of search large enough to produce a statistically significant result. High threat-surprise situations led to significantly more definition search than low threat-anticipated situations. Thus the findings of the content analysis are inconclusive; but, to the extent that any pattern emerges, it suggests that the characteristics of crisis trigger more, not less, search for definition. On the questionnaires, the participants reported little definition search in either crisis or noncrisis. The reasons for the absence of search, however, differed sharply between the two situations. In a crisis situation 77 per cent (44 out of 57) indicated little search occurred because of pressures on the decision makers; in noncrisis 65 per cent (37 out of 57) reported little search because the situation was well defined without search. If the initial presentation of the noncrisis situation had provided

TABLE 20 **Chi Square Differences Between Definition Search and No Definition Search in Crisis-Noncrisis and Other Paired Samples (Hypothesis 19)**

Paired Samples	Definition Search	No Definition Search	Total	Chi Square	p if ≤ .10	Reject Null Hypothesis?
A. Crisis	14	10	24	0.75		no
Noncrisis	10	14	24			
Total	24	24	48			
B. High Threat	12	12	24	0.34		no
Low Threat	9	15	24			
Total	21	27	48			
C. Short Time	5	19	24	0.42		no
Extended Time	8	16	24			
Total	13	35	48			
D. Surprise	11	13	24	0.00		no
Anticipation	12	12	24			
Total	23	25	48			
E. High Threat-Short Time	8	16	24	0.00		no
Low Threat-Extended Time	9	15	24			
Total	17	31	48			
F. High Threat-Surprise	14	10	24	4.20	.04	yes
Low Threat-Anticipation	6	18	24			
Total	20	28	48			
G. Short Time-Surprise	9	15	24	0.09		no
Extended Time-Anticipation	9	15	24			
Total	18	30	48			

NOTE: Except for the crisis-noncrisis samples (for which a directional hypothesis was formed), the reported p values are 2-tailed; therefore, the null hypothesis can be rejected even when the results are the reverse of those predicted for the crisis-noncrisis situations.

TABLE 21 **Chi Square Differences Between Alternative Search and No Alternative Search in Crisis-Noncrisis and Other Paired Samples (Hypothesis 20)**

Paired Samples	Alter-native Search	No Alter-native Search	Total	Chi Square	p if ≤ .10	Reject Null Hy-pothesis?
A. Crisis	8	16	24	1.00		no
Noncrisis	4	20	24			
Total	12	36	48			
B. High Threat	8	16	24	0.10		no
Low Threat	6	18	24			
Total	14	34	48			
C. Short Time	5	19	24	0.00		no
Extended Time	6	18	24			
Total	11	37	48			
D. Surprise	5	19	24	0.00		no
Anticipation	4	20	24			
Total	9	39	48			
E. High Threat-Short Time	10	14	24	3.80	.05	yes
Low Threat-Extended Time	3	21	24			
Total	13	35	48			
F. High Threat-Surprise	4	20	24	0.15		no
Low Threat-Anticipation	4	20	24			
Total	8	40	48			
G. Short Time-Surprise	7	17	24	0.00		no
Extended Time-Anticipation	6	18	24			
Total	13	35	48			

NOTE: Except for the crisis-noncrisis samples (for which a directional hypothesis was formed), the reported p values are 2-tailed; therefore, the null hypothesis can be rejected even when the results are the reverse of those predicted for the crisis-noncrisis situations.

somewhat less information, the predicted difference in definition search might have been evident in the questionnaires.

Similar results emerge from the content analysis of alternative search (Hypothesis 20). Of the 48 experimental situations in the combined crisis-noncrisis samples, search for alternatives occurred in only one-fourth of them (Table 21). Among the few incidents of alternative search, crisis accounted for twice as many search attempts as noncrisis; but the difference was not statistically significant. Table 21 shows that the decomposition of crisis into situations comprised of only one or two of the crisis dimensions leads to one significant difference. High threat-short time situations involved more search for alternative solutions than did low threat-extended time situations. Although the content analysis data do not confirm Hypothesis 20, the questionnaire data reported in Table 22 do. Twenty-seven participants reported little search for alternatives in crisis, but considerable search in noncrisis; whereas, only 13 individuals perceived more search in crisis than noncrisis. The difference, in the predicted direction, is statistically significant. In one respect the questionnaire results confirm those from the content analysis. Of the 120 participants answering the question, 60 per cent (72 individuals) reported that they conducted little search for alternatives in either crisis or noncrisis.

The findings of the content analysis and questionnaire on the enumeration of alternatives were also inconsistent. The content analysis of written messages and conference statements yielded no significant difference between crisis and noncrisis in the number of alternatives that the participants proposed. Even though the range of data in section A of Table 23 indicates that the maximum rate at which participants proposed alternatives in noncrisis exceeded that found in crisis, the total number of alternatives advanced in most crises surpassed the number suggested in most noncrises. As noted, this difference between the crisis and noncrisis samples could be attributed to chance. The only difference between samples that reached the established significance level appeared in the comparison of high threat-short time situations with low threat-extended time situations. High threat-short time resulted in a larger number of alternatives. The questionnaire results in Table 24, however, confirm that the number of alternatives was significantly less in crisis than in noncrisis. Of the 40 participants who perceived a difference in the

TABLE 22   **Participant Replies to Question on Search for Alternatives in a Crisis and a Noncrisis (Hypothesis 20)**

		Crisis		
		Considerable Search	Little Search	Total
Noncrisis	Considerable Search	8	27	35
	Little Search	13	72	85
	Total	21	99	120

McNemar $X^2 = 4.22$; $p < .04$

number of alternatives mentioned, 28 reported fewer alternatives in crisis than in noncrisis.[18]

The final hypothesis in this part of the model states that crisis creates a contraction of authority (Hypothesis 22). The two sets of data pertaining to this hypothesis produce results in direct contradiction to each other. Table 25 presents the content analysis findings which show that 63 per cent of the crises and 92 per cent of the noncrises involve a contraction of authority. A chi square test indicates that the frequency

---

[18] Richard A. Brody has suggested to the author (personal correspondence, June 3, 1966) that the narrowing of alternatives in stress—a finding substantiated in individual problem-solving tasks—may require reinterpretation when applied to foreign policy making. During noncrisis periods a president or other top policy maker normally considers a number of problems in the course of a day. Thus the total number of alternatives created by that decision maker in a given unit of time (e.g., a day) is a function of the number of problems examined multiplied by the number of alternatives considered for each problem. In a crisis, however, the foreign policy organization feeds fewer problems to its top leaders, who devote almost their entire time to the crisis problem. Therefore, the leadership may identify no fewer alternatives than usual (perhaps even a few more), but they do so by investing much more time in the one task than they would if the situation involved no stress. Although this interesting explanation might account for the content analysis results, it is inconsistent with the findings of the questionnaire.

TABLE 23 **Mann-Whitney U Differences in Number of Alternative Proposals Between Crisis-Noncrisis and Other Paired Samples (Hypothesis 21)**

Paired Samples	N	Data Range	Normalized U	p if ≤ .10	Reject Null Hypothesis?
A. Crisis*	24	.08–0.45	0.74		no
Noncrisis	24	.00–1.00			
B. High Threat	24	.00–0.60	0.02		no
Low Threat*	24	.00–0.75			
C. Short Time*	24	.00–0.75	0.88		no
Extended Time	24	.00–0.75			
D. Surprise	24	.00–0.50	0.94		no
Anticipation*	24	.00–1.00			
E. High Threat-Short Time*	24	.10–1.25	2.95	.003	yes
Low Threat-Extended Time	24	.00–1.00			
F. High Threat-Surprise*	24	.00–2.00	1.19		no
Low Threat-Anticipation	24	.00–0.75			
G. Short Time-Surprise*	24	.00–1.00	0.24		no
Extended Time-Anticipation	24	.00–0.75			

NOTE: Except for the crisis-noncrisis samples (for which a directional hypothesis was formed), the reported p values are 2-tailed; therefore, the null hypothesis can be rejected even when the results are the reverse of those predicted for the crisis-noncrisis situations.

* Indicates which type of situation in each set of paired samples had the greater number of alternative proposals.

of contraction in noncrisis is significantly greater than the frequency with which contraction occurs in crisis. Another content analysis result in Table 25 almost reaches the required level of statistical significance. It also reveals less contraction of authority with two crisis traits (high

TABLE 24 **Participant Replies to Question on Number of Alternatives in a Crisis and a Noncrisis (Hypothesis 21)**

		Crisis		
		Few Alternatives	Many Alternatives	Total
Noncrisis	Few Alternatives	75	12	87
	Many Alternatives	28	6	34
	Total	103	18	121

McNemar $X^2 = 5.62$; $p < .009$

threat-short time) than with two noncrisis traits (low threat-extended time). Entirely different conclusions, however, are suggested by the questionnaire results in Table 26. Thirty-one participants perceived contraction in crisis only whereas 17 persons perceived contraction in noncrisis only. The difference, which supports Hypothesis 22, is statistically significant.

How shall the simulation findings for these four hypotheses be interpreted? Although the results obtained by content analysis show a trend contrary to the prediction in three of the four hypotheses, the differences were too small to be statistically significant. Only contraction of authority resulted in a difference between crisis and noncrisis that was large enough not to be attributed to chance. The simulation as designed for this study may have been inadequate for a thorough exploration of the contraction hypothesis. In other circumstances, people have observed contraction of authority in large organizations during a crisis. Despite efforts to introduce organizational features into the simulation, the representation of all government agencies by four individuals may have been an insufficient characterization of size for contraction of authority to occur.

One scholar suggests that in a crisis situation the principal decision-making group will vary from 12 to 15 officials.[19] According to this

---

[19] G. D. Paige, *The Korean Decision* (New York: Free Press, 1968), p. 286.

TABLE 25 **Chi Square Differences Between Contraction and No Contraction in Crisis-Noncrisis and Other Paired Samples (Hypothesis 22)**

Paired Samples	Con-traction	No Con-traction	Total	Chi Square	p if ≤ .10	Reject Null Hypothesis?
A. Crisis	15	9	24			
Noncrisis	22	2	24	4.25	.02	yes
Total	37	11	48			
B. High Threat	18	6	24			
Low Threat	17	7	24	0.00		no
Total	35	13	48			
C. Short Time	17	7	24			
Extended Time	22	2	24	2.19		no
Total	39	9	48			
D. Surprise	22	2	24			
Anticipation	17	7	24	2.19		no
Total	39	9	48			
E. High Threat-Short Time	19	5	24			
Low Threat-Extended Time	24	0	24	3.57	.06	no
Total	43	5	48			
F. High Threat-Surprise	20	4	24			
Low Threat-Anticipation	18	6	24	0.04		no
Total	38	10	48			
G. Short Time-Surprise	22	2	24			
Extended Time-Anticipation	22	2	24	0.27		no
Total	44	4	48			

NOTE: Except for the crisis-noncrisis samples (for which a directional hypothesis was formed), the reported p values are 2-tailed; therefore, the null hypothesis can be rejected even when the results are the reverse of those predicted for the crisis-noncrisis situations.

TABLE 26 **Participant Replies to Question on Contraction of Authority in a Crisis and a Noncrisis (Hypothesis 22)**

		Crisis		
		Fewer Decision Makers	No Reduction in Decision Makers	Total
Noncrisis	Fewer Decision Makers	11	17	28
	No Reduction in Decision Makers	31	64	95
	Total	42	81	123

McNemar $X^2 = 3.52$; $p < .05$

interpretation, a group of four persons, such as those in the simulated governments, should attempt to enlarge their number during a crisis rather than contract it. Consistent with this argument is the content analysis finding that shows noncrises more frequently than crises involve less than the maximum possible number of simulation participants. This explanation fails to account for the confirmation of the contraction hypothesis found in the questionnaire results. As reflected in the questionnaire, some individuals may have been able to discern a subtle difference in the amount of participant activity between crisis and noncrisis that the less sensitive content analysis coding was unable to detect. Alternatively, the participants may tend to perceive some contraction of authority in a crisis (as indicated by the questionnaire), although none actually occurs (as indicated by the content analysis).[20]

[20] An interview study of problem solving in the Department of State found a similar discrepancy on contraction of authority between individual perceptions and systematic evidence. Neither the number of officers nor the number of agencies involved in a decision changed significantly when decision time became short or when threat became great. Nevertheless, several Foreign Service Officers volunteered their impression that the number of people consulted went down as time pressures increased. See D. G. Pruitt, *Problem Solving in the Department of State*, No. 2, 1964–1965, Monograph Series in World Affairs, The Social Science Foundation and the Department of International Relations, University of Denver, Denver, Colorado, p. 25.

Even if none of these explanations proves correct in accounting for the divergent results on contraction of authority, the subsequent sections of the model are not exclusively dependent on this hypothesis. It is assumed that dissonance is increased by each of the four relationships in this part of the model. Although the content analysis reveals no difference between crisis and noncrisis in the other three hypotheses, the questionnaire results support the model predictions. The questionnaire data indicate that crises reduced the search for alternatives, the enumeration of alternatives, and the number of active participants. This evidence gives an initial measure of credibility to the appearance of certain variables whose values in crisis severely limit the decision makers' expectations that any alternative will be effective.

The Introduction of Dissonance

We now have examined the direct consequences of crisis relevant to the proposed model. On one hand, the model indicates that when a nation's decision makers experience a foreign policy crisis they more readily agree among themselves on the national goals involved. The decision makers also increase the importance they attach to these objectives. On the other hand, in a crisis the decision makers reduce their search for alternatives; they consider fewer alternatives; and they form a group for making the decision that includes fewer active participants than are involved in a noncrisis. At least some simulation evidence supports each of these propositions. In the model, the combined effect of these hypotheses is to produce conflicting pressures within the decision-making group. More specifically, increases in goal priority and goal consensus result in increased commitment by the policy makers to goal-oriented action. But reductions in search for alternatives, in the number of alternatives, and in the number of active participants leads to reduced expectations on the part of the decision makers that any course of action will be effective. Although no simulation data are available, illustrations of commitment to action and reduced expectations frequently appear in discussions of international crises.

A commitment to action in a given situation by a policy maker is associated with his feeling that "we can't just sit here; we must do something." That crisis creates this kind of reaction in policy makers can be inferred from the first hypothesis advanced in this study. (In crisis as compared to noncrisis, a nation's decision makers are more likely to take action. See Chapter 4.) The present relationship, however, differs from the earlier one in that the current formulation concerns only the policy makers' desire or wish to act in a crisis in a way that will protect endangered goals. It does not stipulate that the decision makers will take action. One student of crisis behavior who noted the increased commitment to action is Herman Kahn. In a study of arms control he observes that in a crisis "it may be felt that action is required even when it may not be quite clear what must be done."[21] Elsewhere he has proposed that changes in organizational factors during a crisis may, in part, account for the increased commitment to action. "During a crisis, almost everybody [in a large organization] looks for ways to improve a situation, and 'non-conservative' behavior . . . becomes very possible."[22] As previous citations suggest, Kissinger also has noted that a crisis can increase the incentive for action within a bureaucratic structure. According to Kissinger, foreign policy bureaucracies normally impede new policies or actions, but when a crisis makes "the development of a position imperative and some office or individual is assigned the specific task, a sudden change occurs. Both personal and bureaucratic success are then identified with bringing the particular assignment to a conclusion."[23] In other words, a crisis brings about changes in the organization which increase the policy makers' commitment to action. In the proposed model, as diagrammed in Figure 5, goal consensus and goal priority are two organizational variables that contribute to the decision makers' feeling that action is required.

The countervailing element in the model is the policy makers' reduced expectation that any alternative will make a positive difference in the crisis. In a word, all the options recognized by the policy makers in a crisis appear negative. "In politics as in all human affairs, there are situations in which one is damned if he does and damned if he does not. . . . In the most difficult matters, and international crises are certainly among them, there is no single policy whose widespread popularity would survive the test of action."[24] The negative assessment

---

[21] A. J. Wiener and H. Kahn, *Crisis and Arms Control* (Hudson Institute, 1962), p. 9.

[22] H. Kahn, *On Escalation* (New York: Praeger, 1965), p. 241.

[23] Kissinger, "Domestic Structure and Foreign Policy," p. 516.

[24] K. N. Waltz, *Foreign Policy and Democratic Politics* (New York: Little Brown, 1967), p. 286.

of alternatives in a crisis results not only from the concern over lost popularity that might occur after the selection of any alternative, but also from the decision makers' fear that no action can avoid damage to highly-valued national goals. Theodore Sorensen, Special Counsel to President Kennedy and a participant in the ExCom, emphasizes that this feeling was present during the Cuban missile crisis:

Not one of us at any time believed that any of the choices before us could bring anything but either prolonged danger or fighting, very possibly leading to the kind of deepening commitment of prestige and power from which neither side could withdraw without resort to nuclear weapons.[25]

Sorensen also relates John F. Kennedy's words at the time the President approved the proposed blockade in Cuba, "There isn't any good solution. . . . Whichever plan I choose, the ones whose plans we're not taking are the lucky ones—they'll be able to say 'I told you so' in a week or two. But this one seems the least objectionable."[26] Twelve years earlier, just after he had decided to commit American air and sea forces to the struggle in Korea, President Truman said, "Everything I have done in the last five years has been to try to avoid making a decision such as I had to make tonight."[27]

Assuming that policy makers experience a reduction in expectations during a crisis, what accounts for this phenomenon? In the model it is attributed to changes in several variables. Alternatives are negatively assessed because the choice among alternatives is extremely restricted, because the situation is imperfectly defined, and because the specialists at the lower levels of the bureaucracy are not part of the small decision group, nor can they be extensively consulted in the brief time available. Other forces may be operating to limit the decision makers' expectations, but these variables are hypothesized to be of major importance.

In the model, if there exists simultaneously in a crisis decision-making group increased commitment to action and reduced expectations as to the effectiveness of action, dissonance develops within the decision unit. Dissonance is one of a number of closely related concepts (others are balance, congruity, symmetry) that are at the core of cognitive

[25] T. C. Sorensen, *Kennedy* (New York: Harper and Row, 1965), p. 680.
[26] *Ibid.*, p. 694.
[27] B. Smith, "The White House Story: Why We Went to War in Korea," *Saturday Evening Post*, 224, 19 (November 10, 1951), 80.

consistency theories in psychology. Although the various theories of cognitive consistency differ in important respects, they have in common "the notion that the person tends to behave in ways that minimize the internal inconsistency among his beliefs, feelings, and actions."[28] In the present study, internal inconsistency is represented as dissonance created by the conflict between commitment and expectations. The distinctive features of dissonance in the model are (1) the common experience of the incongruity by all members of the decision unit and (2) the emergence of dissonance as the result of a crisis.[29]

The model, as constructed, does not indicate the consequences of dissonance on the decision made by the policy makers during a crisis. Chapters 4–6 have identified intervening variables that make action more or less likely in crisis; they also have revealed that actions are more likely to be hostile or exploratory in a crisis and less likely to be cooperative. Whether or not the decision makers decide to take hostile action, exploratory action, or do nothing at all, once a decision is made dissonance produces certain post-decision consequences. For this part of the model simulation data are available.

Post-Decision Consequences of Dissonance

Hypothesis 23: In crisis as compared to noncrisis, the decision makers' confidence in the ability of their decision to protect the affected goal(s) is decreased.

Hypothesis 24: In crisis as compared to noncrisis, the amount of search by the decision makers for support of their decision is increased.

Hypothesis 25: In crisis as compared to noncrisis, the volume of communication among decision makers within the foreign policy structure of a nation is increased.

---

[28] W. J. McGuire, "The Current Status of Cognitive Consistency Theories," in S. Feldman, ed., *Cognitive Consistency* (New York: Academic Press, 1966), p. 1. For a different attempt to apply a psychological theory of structural balance to international politics, see F. Harary, "A Structural Analysis of the Situation in the Middle East in 1956," *Journal of Conflict Resolution,* 5 (June 1961), 167–178.

[29] Although not specifically concerned with crises, Abelson has expressed interest in the study of cognition dealing with affect-laden objects, or what he calls "hot cognitions." For the policy makers who experience them, crises would appear to be hot cognitions. See R. P. Abelson, "Computer Simulation of 'Hot' Cognition," in S. S. Tomkins and S. Messick, eds., *Computer Simulation of Personality* (New York: Wiley, 1963), pp. 277–298.

Hypothesis 26: In crisis as compared to noncrisis, the volume of communication between a nation's decision makers and other international actors external to the nation is increased.

Illustrations. Leon Festinger, a social psychologist who researched the post-decision effects of dissonance, offers the basis for an explanation of the participants' low confidence in their crisis decisions. He comments, "Undoubtedly, the closer together in attractiveness the alternatives are, the more important the decision, and the more variable the information about the alternatives, the higher is the confidence that the person will want before he makes his decision. It is probably this process of seeking and evaluating information that consumes time when a person must make a decision."[30] The previous discussion indicates that in a crisis the limited number of alternatives seem similar because they are all unattractive. The threat to valued goals makes the decision an important one. Furthermore, as the findings on limited search reveal, information is restricted. But the short decision time in a crisis situation prevents the decision makers from taking time to seek and evaluate information which would increase their confidence. At the very point when considerable confidence is required before a satisfactory decision can be made, this encouragement is denied. Consequently, after the choice has been made the policy makers experience a lack of confidence in the selected position—regardless of what it is.

In the Korean crisis, President Truman and his advisors appeared quite confident that they had made the *correct* decision. They appeared less sanguine that their actions—particularly the initial ones—would be effective. At the first Blair House meeting the President stated that he expected the North Koreans to flaunt the Security Council resolution and that ultimately the U. S. would have to resort to force. By the following evening several of his military advisors doubted that the commitment of American sea and air power would be sufficient to save South Korea.[31] During the Cuban missile crisis there were signs

---

[30] L. Festinger, *Conflict, Decision and Dissonance* (Stanford: Stanford University Press, 1964), p. 152.

[31] See Paige, *The Korean Decision,* pp. 139–140, 165. It is difficult to establish the mood of the American policy makers during the first week of the Korean War. Publicly they remained optimistic. For example, on Thursday, June 29, President Truman told a dinner of the finance committee of the Democratic National Committee "that the United States would come

of post-decision doubt among the American policy makers. After announcing the decision to blockade, Kennedy confided privately that he thought the odds were "somewhere between one out of three and even" that the Soviets would go all the way to war.[32] According to Sorensen there was considerable despair by the time the weekend following the initiation of the blockade had arrived. "Our little group seated around the Cabinet table in continuous session that Saturday felt nuclear war to be closer on that day than at any time in the nuclear age. If the Soviet ship continued coming, if the SAMs continued firing, if the missile crews continued working and if Khrushchev continued insisting on concessions with a gun at our head, then—we all believed—the Soviets must want a war and war would be unavoidable."[33]

As Hypothesis 23 indicates, the act of decision itself does not reduce the dissonance that policy makers feel. In fact their lack of confidence in the decision they have just made increases the dissonance. Festinger and others who have studied cognitive consistency contend that after a decision, individuals attempt to reduce the dissonance or cognitive imbalance.[34] Following a crisis decision, one method of reducing dissonance and increasing confidence is to obtain reassurances and pledges of support from others. This argument is the basis for Hypothesis 24. Experimental studies of small groups placed under stress indicate that group members seek encouragement for the actions they have taken.[35] Evidence that similar behavior occurs in international politics appears in an article on the lessons of crisis management written a year after the Cuban missile crisis by an Assistant Secretary of State. "Even when the decision to employ power is essentially our own," the Secretary

---

out of the Korean crisis 'all right,' and [he] expressed confidence that eventually there would be 'a peace in the world which will be satisfactory to all the great nations in the world.'" (*Ibid.*, p. 243.)

[32] Sorensen, *Kennedy*, p. 705.

[33] *Ibid.*, p. 714.

[34] See L. Festinger, *A Theory of Cognitive Dissonance* (Stanford: Stanford University Press, 1957) and Festinger, *Conflict, Decision and Dissonance.*

[35] See J. T. Lanzetta, "Group Behavior Under Stress," *Human Relations,* 8 (1955), 29–52, and E. P. Torrance, "A Theory of Leadership and Interpersonal Behavior Under Stress," in L. Petrullo and B. M. Bass, eds., *Leadership and Interpersonal Behavior* (New York: Holt, Rinehart, and Winston, 1961), pp. 100–117.

wrote, "we find it highly desirable to widen the community of the concerned—to obtain sanction for the necessary 'next step' from the broadest practicable segment of the international community."[36]

The second United Nations resolution, which called upon member states to repel the armed attack against South Korea, was introduced by the United States representative as one of the first steps taken after the American decision to commit air and sea forces to halt the invasion. After the American decision makers established the blockade of Cuba in October, 1962, they made extensive efforts to win support for their action from their NATO and OAS allies as well as among other members of the United Nations. In the Dominican Republic crisis of 1965, President Johnson dispatched marines to that troubled island and then called for a meeting of the Organization of American States to gain support for his action.

Hypotheses 25 and 26 follow directly from the increased search for support in the post-decision period. To conduct the search for support and to execute the decision—even a decision not to act—requires that communication be established with numerous elements of the foreign policy apparatus within the government experiencing the crisis. Moreover, the search for support greatly increases the communication with foreign governments. In a manner consistent with the present model, North hypothesizes that the increase in internal communication occurs after the crisis decision has been made. (Before the decision, contraction of authority tends to reduce the rate of internal communication.) "The higher the tension (above an optimal level of system functioning), the stronger the tendency on the part of state decision-makers to 'suture off' considerable sections of the communications apparatus. . . . [But] once a decision to go to war has been reached, the tendency is reversed. . . ."[37]

Although he did not separate communications into pre-decision and post-decision categories, Holsti did divide written messages exchanged in the 1914 crisis into those dispatched in the early or late phases of the crisis. He found significantly more communication between ambassadors and their foreign offices during the late period of the crisis. Among the various agencies of a government located in the capital, the

---

[36] Cleveland, "Crisis Diplomacy," p. 645.
[37] North *et al.*, *Content Analysis*, p. 163.

volume increased in the late period of the crisis, but the change was not statistically significant.[38] As the 1914 crisis became more serious the decision makers within the same city may have depended more on oral than written communications. This would explain why the frequency of written documents did not accelerate more rapidly.

Other observers of crises report that communications increase between a foreign ministry and its overseas posts. For example, a high-ranking member of the United States embassy in Beirut during the Lebanon crisis of 1958 commented, "In a normal month the code room handled between 100,000 and 150,000 words but after the rebellion broke out the traffic quintupled to 700,000 words."[39] A study of the cable traffic between the Department of State and its Latin American embassies and consulates during the Cuban missile crisis showed a remarkable increase in communication even though telegraphic communications were limited to critical messages.[40]

There is considerable evidence of an increased rate of communication with other states during a crisis. In 1914 "as the crisis developed, decision-makers in the various capitals received rapidly increasing volumes of messages from various parts of Europe."[41] The American Secretary of State related that in addition to the adversary and the United Nations, the United States communicated with more than 75 governments during the Cuban missile crisis.[42] The mutual dissatisfaction of the Soviet and American decision makers with the means for fast communication in that crisis led to the establishment of the teletype "hot line" between Washington and Moscow. During the crisis created by the Arab-Israeli war in June 1967, the leaders of the two superpowers exchanged twenty messages over the hot line in a brief period of time.[43]

---

[38] Holsti, "The 1914 Case," pp. 374–375.

[39] C. W. Thayer, *Diplomat* (New York: Harper and Row, 1959), p. 21.

[40] W. A. Runge, *Analysis of the Department of State Communications Traffic During a Politico-Military Crisis.* (Unpublished Research Memorandum OAD RM 109, Stanford Research Institute, Menlo Park, California, 1963).

[41] North *et al., Content Analysis,* p. 164.

[42] "Interview of Secretary Rusk by David Schoenbrun of CBS News," reprinted in D. L. Larson, *The "Cuban Crisis" of 1962* (Boston: Houghton Mifflin, 1963), p. 268.

[43] "The Night the Hot Line Went Up," *Look,* 31 (December 12, 1967), 31.

Measurement. Hypotheses 23–26 involve four dependent variables—decision confidence, support search, internal communication, and external communication. In the model, changes in these variables are represented as functions of various independent variables. For the analysis of the simulation data, however, the independent variable is crisis which, of course, already has been operationalized. That leaves the four dependent variables to be defined.

Decision confidence consisted of a simulation participant's estimate of the probable success or failure of the response his nation made to a situation. Two instruments measured this variable. The questionnaire completed immediately after each experimental situation contained a ten-point scale on which the participants rated the likelihood that their country's response would fail to achieve its intended objectives (Appendix I, item B7). The responses of each of the four governmental decision makers were averaged for every experimental situation. The analysts then compared the estimates of decision confidence for crisis with those for noncrisis. The Post-Simulation Questionnaire also explored the degree of decision confidence perceived by the decision makers. For both the crisis and noncrisis situations the participants indicated whether their decision seemed to have a high or low risk of failure (Appendix I, item C6).

In searching for support, the decision maker seeks feedback from other policy makers in the form of approval, assistance, or agreement with a position taken by the inquirer's nation. This distinguishes search for support from queries about methods for handling the problem (alternative search) and about information establishing the nature of the situation (definition search). The experimenters content analyzed the communications of the simulation participants for statements containing support search. Any sentence written or spoken by a member of a simulated government during an experimental situation was coded as an instance of search for support if it asked another individual or government for approval of a policy that was taken in response to the created problem.[44] For each nation the experimenters divided the number of support search sentences by the total number of sentences made during the situation in order to obtain the proportion of support inquiries.

---

[44] The inter-coder reliability for the content analysis of support search inquiries was .86 as determined by a Pearson product moment correlation.

The number of simple sentences in messages and conference transcripts provided one method for measuring the frequency of communication both within and between nations. A count of all the sentences uttered by a simulated nation's participants established the volume of communication for each type of experimental situation. The researchers counted only the number of sentences exchanged between members of the same simulated nation for the internal communication variable. For external communication only sentences addressed to individuals outside the sender's nation were included. The participants' responses to two items on the Post Simulation Questionnaire augmented the measure of external communication. One question asked whether the participant's amount of communication with the initiator of the situation varied (Appendix I, item C8) ; the other asked if the amount of communication with allies and other friendly nations changed (Appendix I, item C7).

Results. Both means of measuring decision confidence confirm that confidence is lower in crisis than in noncrisis (Hypothesis 23). Table 27 reveals that in two of the seven sets of paired samples, the situations differ from one another in the amount of decision confidence indicated by the participants' ratings on the ten-point scale. In addition to less decision confidence in crisis as compared to noncrisis, confidence decreases more in high threat-short time situations than in low threat-extended time situations. A statistically significant result also emerges from the questionnaire that participants completed after the simulation. As displayed in Table 28, three times as many decision makers (48 compared to 16) report low confidence in crisis but high confidence in noncrisis as report the reverse arrangement.

The simulation data also support Hypothesis 24. Table 29 shows the results of the Mann-Whitney U tests performed on the number of support search inquiries made in various types of situations. The proportion of support search in written and oral statements of the participants during a crisis exceeds the proportion in noncrisis. As with the decision confidence findings, high threat-short time differed significantly from low threat-extended time. Situations with the two crisis traits produced more search for support than did situations with the opposite features.

Hypotheses 25 and 26 state that crises increase the amount of internal and external communication. The count of sentences exchanged

TABLE 27 **Mann-Whitney U Differences in Degree of Decision Confidence Between Crisis-Noncrisis and Other Paired Samples (Hypothesis 23)**

Paired Samples	N	Data Range	Normal- ized U	p if ≲ .10	Reject Null Hy- pothesis?
A. Crisis*	24	2.5–8.7	2.19	.01	yes
Noncrisis	22	1.0–6.3			
B. High Threat*	23	1.8–7.5	1.36		no
Low Threat	20	1.0–10.0			
C. Short Time*	23	1.3–6.3	0.25		no
Extended Time	22	1.0–7.7			
D. Surprise	22	2.3–7.7	0.60		no
Anticipation*	21	2.0–5.3			
E. High Threat- Short Time*	24	2.5–8.8	3.63	< .001	yes
Low Threat- Extended Time	23	1.5–6.3			
F. High Threat- Surprise*	23	2.0–7.7	0.72		no
Low Threat- Anticipation	23	1.3–6.5			
G. Short Time- Surprise*	22	1.0–6.3	0.12		no
Extended Time- Anticipation	21	1.8–6.0			

NOTE: N's in samples vary because in some nations the participants indicated they had not reached a decision at the time the questionnaire was completed. Except for the crisis-noncrisis samples (for which a directional hypothesis was formed), the reported p values are 2-tailed; therefore, the null hypothesis can be rejected even when the results are the reverse of those predicted for the crisis-noncrisis situations.

* Indicates which type of situation in each set of paired samples had the least amount of decision confidence.

TABLE 28 **Participant Replies to Question on Decision Confidence in a Crisis and a Noncrisis (Hypothesis 23)**

		Crisis		
		Low Confidence	High Confidence	Total
Noncrisis	Low Confidence	22	16	38
	High Confidence	48	34	82
	Total	70	50	120

McNemar $X^2 = 15.02$; $p < .001$

between decision makers in the same simulated nation shows a significant increase in crisis over noncrisis. Table 30 displays this confirmation of Hypothesis 25 as well as the substantial differences in the amount of communication between two other sets of situations. Again with the internal communication variable, a statistically significant difference appears between high threat-short time and low threat-extended time. When situations vary only on the dimension of awareness, however, the noncrisis characteristic of anticipation leads to more internal communication than the situation distinguished by the element of surprise. The difference between anticipation and surprise situations approaches the established level of statistical significance.

With the volume of external communication, the difference between crisis and noncrisis is in the direction predicted by Hypothesis 26, but it only approaches the accepted level of significance. The Mann-Whitney U tests in Table 31 reveal one other difference that is nearly significant. The frequency of communication in short time-surprise situations exceeds the amount in extended time-anticipated situations. This difference approaches the level of statistical significance. The Post Simulation Questionnaire contains two items about communication with other states. One concerns communication with the source of the crisis or noncrisis situation; the other deals with communication to friendly nations. Responses to the question about exchanges with the nation(s) responsible for the situation indicates no difference between crisis and noncrisis.

TABLE 29   **Mann-Whitney *U* Differences in Frequency of Support Search Between Crisis-Noncrisis and Other Paired Samples (Hypothesis 24)**

Paired Samples	N	Data Range	Normalized U	p if ⪷ .10	Reject Null Hypothesis?
A. Crisis*	24	.00–1.00	3.65	< .001	yes
Noncrisis	24	.00–0.14			
B. High Threat	24	.00–0.47	0.08		no
Low Threat*	24	.00–0.30			
C. Short Time*	24	.00–0.40	1.59		no
Extended Time	24	.00–0.50			
D. Surprise*	24	.00–1.00	1.19		no
Anticipation	24	.00–0.47			
E. High Threat-Short Time*	24	.00–0.50	2.98	.003	yes
Low Threat-Extended Time	24	.00–1.00			
F. High Threat-Surprise*	24	.00–1.00	0.07		no
Low Threat-Anticipation	24	.00–0.50			
G. Short Time-Surprise	24	.00–0.40	0.56		no
Extended Time Anticipation*	24	.00–0.43			

NOTE: Except for the crisis-noncrisis samples (for which a directional hypothesis was formed), the reported *p* values are 2-tailed; therefore, the null hypothesis can be rejected even when the results are the reverse of those predicted for the crisis-noncrisis situations.

* Indicates which type of situation in each set of paired samples had the greater amount of search for support.

To the extent that the rate of communication in a crisis is a function of a search for support, it is not surprising that interaction with the source does not increase. What does contradict the proposed model is the finding that participants perceive significantly less communication with allies and friends in crisis than in noncrisis. Table 32 shows that 13 per cent

TABLE 30 **Mann-Whitney *U* Differences in Frequency of Internal Communication Between Crisis-Noncrisis and Other Paired Samples (Hypothesis 25)**

Paired Samples	N	Data Range	Normalized U	p if ≧ .10	Reject Null Hypothesis?
A. Crisis*	24	3–85	2.52	.006	yes
Noncrisis	24	0–62			
B. High Threat*	24	0–66	0.96		no
Low Threat	24	0–72			
C. Short Time*	24	0–71	1.27		no
Extended Time	24	0–31			
D. Surprise	24	0–44	1.79	.08	no
Anticipation*	24	1–110			
E. High Threat-Short Time*	24	1–85	3.09	.002	yes
Low Threat-Extended Time	24	0–29			
F. High Threat-Surprise*	24	0–65	1.08		no
Low Threat-Anticipation	24	0–58			
G. Short Time-Surprise*	24	0–72	0.49		no
Extended Time-Anticipation	24	0–61			

NOTE: Except for the crisis-noncrisis samples (for which a directional hypothesis was formed), the reported *p* values are 2-tailed; therefore, the null hypothesis can be rejected even when the results are the reverse of those predicted for the crisis-noncrisis situations.

* Indicates which type of situation in each set of paired samples had the greater frequency of internal communication.

of the participants (14 of 107) perceived an increase in communication with friendly states in crisis, whereas 35 per cent (37 of 107) perceived an increase in noncrisis. In other words, communication with friendly states was limited in both situations, but more so in crisis.

The question that concerns communication with allies and friendly

TABLE 31 **Mann-Whitney _U_ Differences in Frequency of External Communication Between Crisis-Noncrisis and Other Paired Samples (Hypothesis 26)**

Paired Samples	N	Data Range	Normalized U	p if $\leq .10$	Reject Null Hypothesis?
A. Crisis*	24	0–14	1.32	.09	no
Noncrisis	24	0–10			
B. High Threat	24	0–26	1.39		no
Low Threat*	24	0–9			
C. Short Time*	24	0–10	0.76		no
Extended Time	24	0–7			
D. Surprise*	24	0–9	0.28		no
Anticipation	24	0–26			
E. High Threat-Short Time*	24	0–14	1.47		no
Low Threat-Extended Time	24	0–6			
F. High Threat-Surprise	24	0–12	0.72		no
Low Threat-Anticipation*	24	0–10			
G. Short Time-Surprise*	24	0–23	1.73	.08	no
Extended Time-Anticipation	24	0–10			

NOTE: Except for the crisis-noncrisis samples (for which a directional hypothesis was formed), the reported _p_ values are 2-tailed; therefore, the null hypothesis can be rejected even when the results are the reverse of those predicted for the crisis-noncrisis situations.

* Indicates which type of situation in each set of paired samples had the greater frequency of external communication.

nations asks whether there was little or considerable consultation "before our final decision was reached." If external communication increases during a crisis primarily as a result of post-decision search for support, the question directs attention to the wrong phase of the situation. It is

TABLE 32 **Participant Replies to Question on Communication with Friendly Nations in a Crisis and a Noncrisis (Hypothesis 26)**

		Crisis		
		More Communication	Less Communication	Total
Noncrisis	More Communication	5	32	37
	Less Communication	9	61	70
	Total	14	93	107

McNemar $X^2 = 11.80$; $p < .001$

noteworthy that in the Cuban missile crisis, American policy makers consulted with no ally until after they imposed the blockade. An alternative explanation of the questionnaire finding assumes the increase in internal communication during crisis was so much greater than the external rate that the latter change was not perceived by the participants even though it may have slightly increased. The difference in the two volumes of communication measured by counting simple sentences conforms to this explanation.

In summary, three of the four hypotheses in the final stage of the model are substantiated by data from the simulation. Participant perceptions of external communication run counter to the fourth hypothesis, but the actual flow of messages between nations tends to confirm the relationship.

Further Comments on Dissonance in Crisis

At several points the simulation findings proved inconsistent with the proposed model of crisis decision making. Specifically, conflicts occurred with the content analysis measures of variables that influenced expectations of effectiveness (particularly, contraction of authority), and with the questionnaire finding—just reviewed—on external communication. For each of these instances explanations have been advanced and other measures have provided results consistent with the hypotheses. Even with these exceptions, the simulation data fit sufficiently well with the crisis→dissonance→dissonance reduction model to warrant further examination of this interpretation of crisis decision making. One aspect of dissonance in crisis that was not discussed in the model is its impact on the nature of the decision. This chapter concludes with some brief speculations about the consequences of dissonance for a crisis decision.

One finding which was not fully confirmed by the simulation data, but was substantiated by many other sources, is the contraction of authority that can occur in a crisis. If this process does take place, it probably increases the importance of an individual's personal characteristics in determining the decision. Under normal conditions the large number of persons involved in the decision process and the routinized methods in the bureaucracy for managing problems serve to minimize the impact of personalities. When the decision unit becomes small and when it is ad hoc so that no established operating procedures exist, then the idiosyncratic features of the individual group members can have more bearing on the decision. The method of coping with dissonance in crisis can be one such idiosyncratic characteristic.

Researchers working on cognitive consistency have identified a number of modes by which a person may reduce dissonance.[45] Under these circumstances it may be reasonably assumed that different types of individuals will react differently to dissonance in crisis. One prominent theorist in the area of cognitive consistency distinguishes between individuals who react to dissonance according to their wishes and those who react according to their fears. "Psychologists know that the wishful-fearful thinking characteristic of paranoid schizophrenics also colors the judgments of normal people, particularly when they are functioning under stress. They become prone to deciding in terms of their wishes (overconfidence) or their fears (underconfidence)."[46]

A person who reduces an inconsistency in his beliefs by wishful thinking tends to adjust his beliefs by bringing them into accord with his desires. "Conclusions which are more desirable than their premises will receive greater estimates of being true than logic requires, while

---

[45] See McGuire, "The Status of Cognitive Consistency Theories," pp. 10–14.

[46] C. E. Osgood, *An Alternative to War or Surrender* (Urbana: University of Illinois Press, 1962), p. 55.

conclusions which are less desirable than their premises will be rated as less probable than they should be."[47] Suppose an ambassador and his staff believe that a visit by their foreign minister to a neutral country could be valuable in helping to obtain the terms they strongly desire in a series of negotiations. Furthermore, assume these same members of the embassy team believe that certain groups in the host country might react violently to a visit from the foreign minister—an occurrence which could cause the minister considerable embarrassment, if not bodily harm. Wishful thinking could reduce the dissonance between these beliefs if the ambassador's enthusiasm for the successful conclusion of the negotiations led him to discount reports of potential demonstrations. One result of such wishful thinking could be an overly confident appraisal to the foreign office of the consequences of the foreign minister's visit. Presumably, fearful thinking operates in a similar manner except that beliefs are adjusted to conform to doubts and apprehensions.

Fears or wishes are more likely to provide the premise for decisions when reliable information is absent.[48] Simulation findings on crisis behavior support the contention that information relevant to a situation may play less of a role in crisis decisions. Such relevant findings include the tendency to make the decision to act on the basis of past hostilities or past friendships. Although the simulation data lend credence to the proposition that a crisis is an occasion for decision in which noninformation variables assert greater influence on the decision, neither the model, the illustrations, nor the data support the contention that overconfidence and underconfidence occur with equal probability in a crisis.[49] The

---

[47] C. I. Hovland and M. J. Rosenberg, "Summary and Further Theoretical Issues," in M. J. Rosenberg, C. I. Hovland, W. J. McGuire, R. P. Abelson, and J. W. Brehm, *Attitude Organization and Change* (New Haven: Yale University Press, 1960), p. 203.

[48] Verba offers the following proposition: "The more ambiguous the cognitive and evaluative aspects of the decision-making situation, the more scope there is for personality variables." See S. Verba, "Assumptions of Rationality and Non-Rationality in Models of the International System," *World Politics*, 14 (October 1961), 102.

[49] Illustrations of reduced decision confidence that were offered earlier in this chapter included examples of low confidence among the American participants in the Korean decision. As was noted (see footnote 31), evidence of overoptimism also appears. Thus one could argue that the Korean decision exemplifies wishful thinking and that the Cuban missile decision illustrates fearful thinking.

simulation data confirmed the hypothesis that decision confidence was lower in crisis than noncrisis. The model and the data, however, concerned confidence after the decision was made. Conceivably, in a crisis, decision makers experience low confidence following their decision regardless of their mode of dissonance reduction prior to the decision. Alternatively, the model may have been confirmed by a sample of simulation participants who had a predisposition to reduce dissonance through fearful thinking in crises. (Might something in the selection or training of petty officers increase the tendency of these men to be underconfident when given broad responsibilities in a crisis?)

In addition to possible effects on the post-decision phase of crisis, how might the alternative methods of coping with dissonance (wishful versus fearful thinking) influence the decision itself? If the members of the decision unit are heterogeneous with respect to how they cope with dissonance, then they may counterbalance one another. But when a strong-willed individual in a position of authority dominates the group, then the counterbalancing would be less likely to neutralize the effect of this variable on the decision. Nor would the restraint occur if "a large number of the members of a group are subject to similar pressures and share attitudes that perform a personality-oriented function. . . ."[50] In other words, group homogeneity on the method of coping with dissonance would increase the influence of this factor on the decision.

Simulation data indicate that actions taken in crisis tend to be hostile or exploratory. It would be a simplification to suggest that when overconfidence characterizes the group, the reaction to crisis is hostile, and when underconfidence dominates, the reaction is either exploratory or there is no reaction at all. Not all hostile or exploratory responses to a crisis constitute extreme reactions. Under some circumstances a hostile (or exploratory) response could be a moderate step based upon an accurate comprehension of international events and international actors. Nevertheless, the alternative modes of dissonance reduction may increase the probability of extreme responses in crisis situations.

This final section offers the following speculations: (1) Members of the decision unit experience substantial dissonance in crisis both before and after their decision. (2) Some individuals reduce dissonance by either wishful thinking or overconfidence in the likelihood of desirable outcomes, others reduce dissonance by fearful thinking or under-

---

[50] Verba, "Rationality and Non-Rationality," p. 103.

confidence in the likelihood of desirable outcomes. (3) Through contraction of authority, a crisis increases the impact on the decision of idiosyncratic characteristics of the policy makers, such as modes of dissonance reduction. (4) The decision is more likely to be influenced by personal styles of dissonance reduction if the group is homogeneous in the method of coping with cognitive inconsistencies or if it is dominated by a strong individual. (5) To the extent that the means of reducing dissonance in the crisis decision-making group depends on either wishful thinking or fearful thinking, the probability of an extreme response to the crisis increases. From the initial hypothesis— that a crisis increases the probability of action—has been evolved a more complex model in which the response to a crisis depends on the interaction of the situation with a combination of organizational and individual variables.

Chapter 8

EPILOGUE

Evaluation of the Proposed
Definition of Crisis

In this research the simulation has served as a technique for investigating hypotheses about the effects of crisis on foreign policy decision making. The Introduction indicated that the purpose of the study would be pursued through a series of specific or micro hypotheses and through one macro hypothesis. Chapters 4–7 dealt with the 26 micro hypotheses that related crisis, as a type of situation, to a nation's response. Clearly, many variables besides crisis influence the nature of foreign policy decisions. To ascertain what part, if any, crisis plays, the extreme position was postulated in the first hypothesis (i.e., crisis increases action). Like Pool and Kessler, we were "engaged in a kind of experiment—the kind sometimes called a Gedanken experiment—in which we press an idea to see where it breaks down."[1] Subsequent hypotheses elaborated the basic relationship between crisis and action. Now, in this final chapter, the macro hypothesis concerning the proposed definition of crisis will be explored. Before turning to that broader level of generalization, several comments are in order about the use of the simulation method to investigate hypotheses.

In simplified terms, researchers use simulations either to develop hypotheses or to test them. A simulation can disclose to its users new insights or hunches about the operation of the real world. Chapter 7

---

[1] I. S. Pool and A. Kessler, "The Kaiser, the Tsar, and the Computer: Information Processing in a Crisis," *American Behavioral Scientist*, 8 (May 1965), 32.

contains several illustrations of this application of simulation. Before the experiment began, the author formed the hypothesis about reduced decision confidence in crisis situations, but he did not recognize the potential interrelationship of that hypothesis with others to form a model (presented in Chapter 7) until after observing scores of crisis decisions in the simulation. Similarly, explanations like that offered for contraction of authority (that is, prior to a certain threshold the number of individuals actively involved in a crisis decision expands, not contracts) were developed only after the statistical analysis shed doubt on the original hypothesis. The speculations presented in the final section of Chapter 7 provide another example of the use of simulation to generate hypotheses.[2]

The researcher may use simulation in an alternative manner; that is, he may attempt to substantiate through experiments some explicitly stated relationships he assumes to exist in the simulation's referent system. The 26 hypotheses and the macro hypothesis illustrate this approach to simulation research. When simulation is used in this manner, the following difficult yet interesting question arises: Can a hypothesis concerning the real world be tested with a laboratory technique such as simulation? The answer depends on the meaning associated with the word "test." In this book "test" has been reserved for descriptions of the statistical analyses. The statistical tests of significance performed on the data pertaining to each hypothesis established only whether the results obtained from the samples of crisis and noncrisis situations can be expected in other simulations similar to the eleven conducted in this study. In other words, the tests determine whether the hypotheses can be generalized to a population of simulations, not to the real world. By helping to establish whether a particular phenomenon is a part of a recurrent pattern or just a random occurrence, such statistical tests provide an important first step in exploring hypotheses through simulations.

But what about using simulation to test whether a hypothesis would hold in the real world, not just in other simulations? Snyder's response to this question has guided the present research:

---

[2] Admittedly, some students of politics might form the same hypotheses without resort to simulation; others might develop different hypotheses from the observation of the same simulation runs. Because each individual requires different stimuli to provide him with new ideas, the intellectual style of the researcher must be considered in the decision to use simulation or any other research technique.

If by "test" one means rigorous proof, then clearly experiments will not do the job. If one adopts the position that *probing* theories—for example, disqualifying inadequate hypotheses or operationalizing variables—is required, then experimental techniques can help. As noted, the contrived situation is only one phase of a multiple strategy in which preliminary controls permit greater clarification than is possible by observation in natural settings.[3]

Even with this interpretation of testing, the reader may ask: From the present study of the hypotheses is one not confined to statements which assert that under conditions of high threat, short time, and surprise United States Navy petty officers are more likely to do X than if these conditions are absent? This inquiry concerns the bias that is introduced into the findings by using participants in the simulation who were not actual governmental decision makers from different countries. Although the question is part of the broader issue of simulation validity which has been considered elsewhere,[4] a brief discussion of human functions in this particular simulation is appropriate.

Like all simulations, the one used in this study—the Inter-Nation Simulation—vastly simplifies the reality it is intended to represent. As with other aspects of the simulation, the process for making decisions has been reduced to what its developers assume to be the most basic relationships. For example, the range of issues about which governmental decisions are often made has been collapsed, as have the rich variety of options that usually are available to skilled politicians for achieving their ends. The array of personal drives and internalized organizational goals and societal values that motivate actual policy makers to behave in certain ways have been represented in the simulation as simple external constraints. ("In your hypothetical nation, if you do not perform the following stipulated activities in the prescribed manner, you will lose office and the ADM will take your place.") Although all but the

---

[3] R. C. Snyder, "Experimental Techniques and Political Analysis: Some Reflections in the Context of Concern over Behavioral Approaches," in J. C. Charlesworth, ed., *The Limits of Behavioralism in Political Science*. A symposium sponsored by the American Academy of Political and Social Science, Philadelphia, Pennsylvania, 1962, p. 110.

[4] See, for example, C. F. Hermann, "Validation Problems in Games and Simulations with Special Reference to Models of International Politics," *Behavioral Science*, 12 (May 1967), 216–231.

most fundamental decision activities have been eliminated, the procedures remain too complex to be programmed for "artificial intelligence"
on the computer. As computer models of decision-making processes
improve, however, the use of human participants in political simulations
of the Inter-Nation Simulation type is likely to decrease. Even in the
present Inter-Nation Simulation, "the participants may be considered as
surrogates . . . [whose outputs act] as inputs into other components
of the simulation taken as a whole."[5] The human participants serve as
computers to handle that part of the decision process that is not fully
programmed. In this capacity, fairly intelligent people are more inter-
changeable in the simulation than they are in actual foreign policy
agencies. Whereas basic individual differences (e.g., personality) may
remain influential in explaining the behavior of participants, skills and
experiences of extreme importance in accounting for actual foreign
policy behavior have less effect in the decision-making situations represented in the simulation. The considerable differences in background
and job training between United States Navy petty officers and United
States Foreign Service officers may be less significant in explaining the
responses of either group as participants—or black boxes—who perform
the simplified decision process of the Inter-Nation Simulation.

Having considered several issues pertaining to both kinds of hypotheses, let us examine the macro hypothesis. Specifically, this hypothesis
states that when foreign policy decision makers experience high threat,
short decision time, and surprise their decision processes are different
than when none of these three characteristics occurs or when only one
or two of them appears. The reader will recall that in the previous
analysis of each micro hypothesis, the dependent or intervening variable
was examined in paired samples of situations having only one or two
of the crisis dimensions (e.g., high threat vs. low threat, short time-
surprise vs. extended time-anticipation). These comparisons of situations
in addition to crisis-noncrisis now permit the investigation of the macro
hypothesis. By examining which paired situations produced statistically
significant results, it is possible to establish whether the interaction of
high threat, short time, and surprise (crisis) produced findings different
from any combination of two crisis traits or from any single trait. If

---

[5] H. Guetzkow, "Some Correspondences between Simulations and
'Realities' in International Relations," in M. Kaplan, ed., *New Approaches to
International Relations* (New York: St. Martin's, 1968), p. 211.

the same findings that are present with all three traits occur when there are only one or two, then the proposed definition of crisis will not have resulted in distinctive decision processes. Under these circumstances the macro hypothesis would not be confirmed and the utility of the proposed definition for empirical research would be called into question.

Table 33 summarizes the evidence for the macro hypothesis. The 27 dependent and intervening variables[6] appear as the row headings in this table, while crisis and each combination of its component dimensions appear as the column headings. If two paired samples of situations produced a difference in the dependent or intervening variable sufficient to generate a level of statistical significance of .10 or less, that probability value appears in the table. With the exception of those given for crisis, the reported significance values are identical with those presented in the tables that accompanied the analysis of each micro hypothesis. Whereas the earlier tables gave 1-tailed tests of significance for crisis, 2-tailed tests appear in Table 33 for crisis as well as the other types of situations.[7]

---

[6] Even though there are only 26 hypotheses in the study, there are 27 dependent and intervening variables because Hypothesis 1 involved two measures of action (the action-inaction dichotomy, and the frequency of action).

[7] As noted in the earlier tables, 1-tailed tests of significance were performed on the crisis-noncrisis samples because they were involved in hypotheses which predicted the direction of change in the dependent variable. Inasmuch as no hypotheses were formulated for the other paired samples, 2-tailed tests were reported for them. To investigate the macro hypothesis in the present chapter, however, we are concerned with the number of significant differences produced by each set of paired samples—including crisis-noncrisis—regardless of whether the difference is in the predicted direction. For this reason, and to increase the comparability between the tests reported for all paired samples, crisis results in Table 33 are given as 2-tailed tests. For a difference of a given size, the significance value for a 2-tailed test is twice that of a 1-tailed test. Hence some previously significant crisis results no longer maintain that classification when 2-tailed tests are applied. Although two crisis results classified in Chapters 4–6 as approaching the significance level are no longer below the .10 criterion and two other results shift to the region between .05 and .10, the introduction of 2-tailed tests permits the inclusion of the contraction of authority result which was statistically significant in the opposite direction from that predicted by the hypothesis. In short, the net effect of shifting from 1- to 2-tailed tests is to reduce by one the number of crisis results at both the .10 level and the .05 level.

TABLE 33 **Comparison of Significance Values from Statistical Tests for Crisis and Its Component Dimensions**

Hypothesis No.	Dependent (D) or Intervening (I) Variable	Crisis	High Threat	Short Time	Surprise	High Threat-Short Time	High Threat-Surprise	Short Time-Surprise
1	Action/Inaction (D)					.04+		
1	Frequency of Action (D)	.08+		.10+	.06−	.006+		.08+
2	Hostile Response (D)	.06+						
3	Exploratory Response (D)	.04+			.08+		.002+	
4	Cooperative Response (D)	.004−			.003−	.08−	.001−	
5	Agent's Prior Friendliness (I)	.008−						
6	Agent's Prior Hostility (I)	.002+				.002+	.002+	
7	Accidental (I)							
8	Deliberate (I)	.002+				.002+	.01+	
9	Ambiguous (I)		.08+	.02−			.002+	.02−
10	Danger to Survival (I)	.002+				.04+	.008+	
11	Goal Priority (I)	.02+				.02−		
12	National Capabilities (I)							
13	Alternative Search (I)							
14	Number of Alternatives (I)						.04+	
15	Affective Conflict (I)					.06−		
16	Contraction of Authority (I)							
17	Goal Consensus (D)	.008+	.008+			.001+		
18	Goal Priority (D)						.02+	
19	Definition Search (D)						.04+	
20	Alternative Search (D)					.05−		
21	Number of Alternatives (D)					.003+		
22	Contraction of Authority (D)	.04−				.06−		

TABLE 33 (cont'd)

Hypothesis No.	Dependent (D) or Intervening (I) Variable	Crisis	High Threat	Short Time	Surprise	High Threat-Short Time	High Threat-Surprise	Short Time-Surprise
23	Decision Confidence (D)	.02—				.001—		
24	Support Search (D)	.002+				.003+		
25	Internal Communication (D)	.01+			.08—	.002+		
26	External Communication (D)							.08+
	Total Number of Tests	27	27	27	27	27	27	27
	Number of Tests $\leqq$ .10	14	2	2	4	15	9	3
	% of Total Tests	51.9	07.4	07.4	14.8	55.5	33.3	11.1
	Is Number of Tests Greater than that Occurring by Chance Alone with the .05 Binomial Distribution?	Yes	No	No	Yes	Yes	Yes	No
	Number of Tests $\leqq$ .05	12	1	1	1	12	9	1
	% of Total Tests	44.4	03.7	03.7	03.7	44.4	33.3	03.7
	Is Number of Tests Greater than that Occurring by Chance Alone with the .05 Binomial Distribution?	Yes	No	No	No	Yes	Yes	No

NOTE: The significance values for the Post-Simulation Questionnaire are not included because no data were collected on the dimensions of crisis, preventing the type of comparisons reported in this table. A plus (+) after the significance value denotes that the dependent or intervening variable varies directly with crisis or with the characteristic that is a component of crisis (e.g., if crisis occurs, then the number of exploratory responses *increases*). A minus (—) after the significance value indicates that the dependent or intervening variable varies inversely with crisis or with the characteristic that is a component of crisis (e.g., if crisis occurs, then the number of cooperative responses *decreases*).

If all the tests that yield results that approach the level of significance ($p \leq .10$) are counted, then high threat-short time yields the largest number of relationships—one more than is generated by crisis. With high threat-short time situations, 55.5 per cent (15 out of 27) of the tests for significant difference meet the established criterion compared to 51.9 per cent (14 out of 27) of the crisis tests. If the more stringent criterion of the .05 significance level is used, then both high threat-short time and crisis produce 12 significant relationships (44.4 per cent) and high threat-surprise produces 9 (33.3 per cent). For all three types of situations the number of results significant at the .05 level is greater than one would expect to occur by chance alone in computing 27 statistical tests (as determined by the binomial test). The other four types of situations yield only one result each that fulfills the .05 level criterion. In performing 27 tests, at least one result could be expected to meet that criterion by chance alone; hence, in these four types of situations the findings can be attributed to random occurrences.

These findings suggest several conclusions. First, crisis, as defined here, affects the decision process in ways that do not occur with situations characterized by the single traits of high threat, short time, or surprise or by the combination of short time and surprise. Second, although high threat appears to be an important characteristic in influencing the decision process, that trait must be perceived together with one of the two other characteristics before it alters the process substantially. Third, strictly in terms of the number of significant results, high threat-short time situations appear at least as important as crisis in accounting for the behavior of the decision makers. Moreover, high threat-surprise situations affect the decision almost as much as crises or high threat-short time situations.

A closer examination of Table 33, however, reveals that it is premature to reject the macro hypothesis on the grounds that high threat-short time situations are not substantially different from the proposed definition of crisis. Although the two types of situations yield almost the same number of significant values, the situations frequently relate to different intervening and dependent variables. With 8 of the 27 variables, the crisis findings differ from those for high threat-short time situations. In 7 instances the relationship at least approaches the significance level with one type of situation, but does not do so with the other. In the eighth case, both crisis and high threat-short time enter into a significant relationship with goal priority (Hypothesis 11), but in the opposite direction from one another. When crisis is compared with high threat-surprise, 13 of the relationships differ.

As with the 27 previous hypotheses, the simulation data do not "prove" the proposition that crisis, as defined, results in distinctive patterns of foreign policy decision making. Nor do the data lead to the rejection of the macro hypothesis. Instead the findings offer several insights. The material in Table 33 suggests that each of several combinations of the three situational characteristics examined in this study results in a distinctive decision process. Thus, high threat-short time, high threat-surprise, and crisis may all be part of a family of related, but different types of situations—each with its own set of consequences for decision making. This observation recalls the cube diagram of various situations presented earlier (Figure 1).

In brief, this simulation research indicates that decision making varies with perceived changes in the amount of threat in combination with the amount of decision time and/or the amount of surprise. By presenting empirical data on a concept of crisis constructed from these three situational characteristics, this simulation study has offered a bench mark against which other research and other definitions of crisis may be compared.

APPENDIX I

Participant Questionnaires

Copies of three questionnaires administered to the participants in the simulation are presented in this appendix. The *Period Form* was completed by every decision maker at the beginning of each of the seven periods into which the simulation was divided. The *Event and Decision Form* was distributed to all the participants in a nation immediately after each of the seven experimental situations in which their nation was involved. Under the pretense of providing material for a history of the simulation, the participants were asked to furnish information on situations they believed had been selected at random from carbon copies of all written messages. (Participants knew that a copy of every message was filed with the world newspaper.) The third form, the *Post Simulation Questionnaire*, was completed immediately after the exercise was ended. In order to avoid group answers, each questionnaire was answered when the respondent was alone. The appendix includes only the questionnaire items relevant to the data presented in this book.

A. *Period Form*

Nation _____   Position _____   Period _____

The following are questions which political decision makers often consider when planning their nation's policy. In addition to being an aid to policy formation, they will serve as a permanent record of your views on these issues. This form should be filled out at the beginning of each period.

1. Below are listed your nation's goals.[1]
    1. World Bank and economic alliance
    2. Military alliance
    3. National defense system
    4. Maintain government in office
    5. Preserve nation as separate unit

   Rate each goal according to how important its achievement is to you. (Place the number of each goal somewhere on the following line.)

:   :   :   :   :   :   :   :   :   :   :
---
1   2   3   4   5   6   7   8   9   10
Important   Unimportant

2. Rate the other nations of the world on their friendliness to your nation. (*Place the first letters of the nations' names* somewhere on the following line.)

:   :   :   :   :   :   :   :   :   :   :
---
1   2   3   4   5   6   7   8   9   10
Friendly   Unfriendly

B. *Event and Decision Form*

Nation _____ Position _____ Period _____ Time _____

This document helps to provide you and the simulation historian with a running account of your world and your actions and reactions as a decision maker to the events which are occurring in your world. Under (1) below you will find an event described which you have recently or are now experiencing. Respond to the other questions with this event in mind. In other words, your answers should indicate *your* reactions to the particular event. IMPORTANT: This information will *not* be made available to other simulation participants *nor* will it be used in calculations. Thus, your responses should reflect as accurate a picture as possible of your reactions to the specified event. This form should be completed *immediately* upon its receipt.

---

[1] The first three goals listed here varied for each nation.

1. Text of message or newspaper article:
   [*Text of the experimental situation was typed in this space.*]

2. Does the event have any consequences for your nation's goals? If
   yes, put a check in the box in front of any goal affected and then place
   a check on one of the two lines to the right of the goal indicating how
   it is affected.

Check if Affected	*National Goal*[2]	*Makes Goal Easier to Attain*	*Makes Goal Harder to Attain*
☐	1. World Bank and economic alliance	_____	_____
☐	2. Military alliance	_____	_____
☐	3. National defense system	_____	_____
☐	4. Maintain government in office	_____	_____
☐	5. Preserve nation as separate unit	_____	_____

3. Rate the importance to you of achieving the affected goals. (Place
   the number of each affected goal somewhere on the following line.)

| : | : | : | : | : | : | : | : | : | : | : |

1	2	3	4	5	6	7	8	9	10
Important								Unimportant	

4. Check the item that is most nearly accurate.
   _____ I had participated (by message and/or in conference) in the
   drawing up of *plans* on how to react to such an event PRIOR
   to its occurrence.

   _____ I had *participated* (by message and/or in conference) in *discussions* on the possibility of such an event happening PRIOR
   to its occurrence but *NO planned response* had been drawn up.

   _____

   [2] First three goals listed here varied for each nation.

———— Although I had *NOT participated* (by message and/or in conference) in discussions or planned for such an event *PRIOR* to its occurrence, that it happened does *not surprise* me.

———— I had *NOT participated* (by message and/or in conference) in discussions or planned for such an event PRIOR to its occurrence, and the event was a *surprise* to me.

5. *Since learning* about this event, have you participated in *discussions* or written messages concerning it within your nation?

————Yes ————No

6. I SEE THIS EVENT AS: *(check the scale position which best describes EACH item)*.

	Not at all Applicable	*Slightly Applicable*	*Moderately Applicable*	*Considerably Applicable*
Creating a deadline for response	————	————	————	————
Dangerous	————	————	————	————
Deliberate or planned	————	————	————	————
From a friendly source	————	————	————	————
Accidental	————	————	————	————
Threatening	————	————	————	————
Putting me under time pressures	————	————	————	————
Ambiguous/ unclear	————	————	————	————
From a hostile source	————	————	————	————
Injurious to my nation	————	————	————	————

7. A particular response may be chosen for many reasons, e.g., it may be the fastest way to achieve one's objectives. Another reason for making a decision is consideration of the likelihood of failure of the possible response.

What are the chances (in your opinion) that the response selected by your nation will fail to achieve the purposes for which your nation intended it? (Place an "X" somewhere along the following line.)

```
:    :    :    :    :    :    :    :    :    :    :

1    2    3    4    5    6    7    8    9    10
Little chance                          Large chance
of failure                              of failure
```

C. *Post Simulation Questionnaire*

Name _____ Nation _____ Position _____

PART I[3]

1. Would you say there could have been any participants in the simulation acting under instruction from the simulation directors?

                _____Yes   _____No

If you answered yes, indicate who these participants are by position and nation:

_____   _____

_____   _____

PART II

In this part of the questionnaire you are asked to answer questions about two different problem situations that your nation experienced during today's simulation. The term "problem situation" means some occasion (usually an event or closely related group of events) that required your government to make a policy decision. The decision made could have been a judgment that no action was required by your government as well as a decision to await further events or take some im-

---

[3] Other items in the first part of this questionnaire were not used in the analysis presented in this book; therefore, they are not reproduced here.

mediate action. The first problem situation you identify should have all of the characteristics listed below.

SUMMARY: (1) Read the characteristics described below. (2) Choose from the problem situations that confronted your nation one which fits the characteristics listed. (3) Answer the questions indicated with that particular problem situation in mind.

Required Characteristics—First Problem Situation

1. A problem situation whose consideration involved you.
2. A problem situation which originated outside your nation.
3. A problem situation which, at the time it arose, appeared to endanger one or more major goals or interests of your nation.
4. A problem situation in which time for response appeared to be extremely short.
5. A problem situation which, when it first occurred, came as a surprise to you and the members of your government.

First Problem Situation

After some consideration if you do not recall a problem situation which corresponds precisely with all these characteristics, select the one that coincides most completely. In the space below you are asked to describe in a few sentences or phrases the specific details of the problem situation you have chosen.

_____

_____

_____

Required Characteristic(s) Missing in Selected Problem Situation

Does the problem situation you have just described have all five of the requested characteristics?

_____Yes   _____No

If your answer above was "No"—that not all five requested characteristics are present in the problem situation you described—then check below which of the characteristics is *NOT* present.

_____ I was involved.
_____ Originated outside our nation.
_____ National goals were threatened.
_____ Time pressure was severe.
_____ Was a surprise.

First Questions

With the particular problem situation you have selected in mind, read the following ten sets of questions. Each question set has two or three statements marked A and B or A, B, and C. For each of the ten sets select the *one* statement which *best* describes the problem situation you have described above and place an X in the blank to the left of the letter. In some instances more than one statement may be partially correct for the situation you have chosen; in others no statement may seem entirely accurate. BUT ALWAYS CHOOSE THE *ONE* STATEMENT THAT SEEMS *BEST* TO DESCRIBE THE SITUATION YOU EXPERIENCED.

1. _____ A. One of our major tasks, involving considerable time and effort, was *to obtain more information about the problem situation,* that is, to make inquiries about the facts involved or to collect material to interpret the situation.

   _____ B. Because the problem situation already was fairly well established, *little effort was devoted to collecting more information about it.*

   _____ C. The pressures upon those of us formulating a policy forced us to operate with the currently available information and, therefore, *little effort was devoted to collecting more information about the problem situation.*

2. _____ A. We fairly quickly reduced the possible means of handling the problem situation to *one* (or at the most, two) *alternative course(s) of action.*

   _____ B. Throughout most of our discussions on how to handle the problem situation, there were a *number* (more than two) *of different alternative courses of action* under active consideration.

3. _____ A. A majority of us involved in dealing with this problem situation were concerned that not enough different ways of dealing with the problem had been identified, and accordingly, we devoted *considerable effort to uncovering more policy alternatives.*

   _____ B. Among the majority of us charged with formulating a response to the situation, there was *no major concern about establishing additional courses of action* for handling the problem other than those which emerged naturally in the course of our discussions.

4. _____ A. There were *more individuals actively involved* in working on this particular problem situation than are normally engaged in handling the "usual" problem situation.

   _____ B. The number of individuals actively involved in the consideration of this problem situation was approximately the *same as the number of us normally engaged* in handling the "usual" problem situation.

   _____ C. There were *fewer individuals actively involved* in working on this particular problem situation than are normally engaged in handling the "usual" problem situation.

5. _____ A. The initial decision that our government made regarding the problem situation was to *defer any action* and await further developments.

   _____ B. Some *definite action* (other than implementing a "wait-and-see" policy) was the initial outcome of our government's consideration of this problem situation.

6. _____ A. When the policy or way of handling the problem situation was chosen, we recognized one limitation in the selected policy was that it involved a fairly *high risk of failing to achieve objectives* our nation wanted it to attain.

   _____ B. At the time the policy or way of handling the problem situation was selected, we felt that, despite other possible limitations in the selected policy, it involved a rather *low risk of failing to achieve objectives* our nation wanted it to attain.

7. _____ A. Before our final decision was reached on the problem situation there was *considerable consultation with our allies* or certain friendly nations.

_____ B. In the time before our final decision was reached on the problem situation there was *little consultation with our allies* or certain friendly nations.

8. _____ A. Before our final decision there was *no communication or contact* concerning the problem situation with the nation, alliance, etc. which appeared to be responsible for creating the problem.

_____ B. Prior to our final decision *there was communication or contact* about the problem situation with the nation, alliance, etc. which appeared to be responsible for creating the problem.

Second Problem Situation

The procedure for selecting the second problem situation is similar to that used for the first, but several of the specified characteristics are different. To be specific, the first two characteristics of this problem situation should be identical with the previous one while *the last three characteristics are the reverse* of those used before. Before selecting the second problem situation from your nation's experience, make certain that you are clear as to the required distinguishing features.

Required Characteristics[4]

1. A problem situation whose consideration involved you.

2. A problem situation which originated outside your nation.

3. A problem situation which, at the time it arose, was regarded as important to your nation but which did not threaten any major national goals or interests.

---

[4] Following this list of required characteristics, the format of the questionnaire is identical to the preceding section. The participant is asked to describe briefly his selected problem situation. Then the check-list is repeated to determine if the selected situation is missing any of the required characteristics. Finally, the eight items are presented exactly as before except that they are arranged in a different order.

4. A problem situation in which there were no excessive limitations on the time available for response.

5. A problem situation that was not a surprise to you and the members of your government when it first occurred.

APPENDIX II

Summary of Experimental Situations
and Related National Goals

This appendix contains abstracts of the 37 experimental situations that were introduced by the confederates in each simulation run. A nation experienced six situations that were specifically designed for it. Every situation represented a combination of decision time (short or extended) and threat (high, moderate, or low). Short time situations allowed 15 minutes for decision, whereas extended time situations permitted 50 minutes. Situations were classified into one of the three threat groups by the experimenters, who evaluated the amount of threat according to the following four criteria: (1) the completeness with which the affected goal was impeded; (2) the ability of the actor making the threat to execute it without dependency upon other actors; (3) the degree of physical commitment made by the actor initiating the threat; and (4) the extent to which the possibility of violence was specified in the message. The experimental messages could be either unanticipated (surprise) or anticipated depending on whether they were preceded by an advance warning communication. (These anticipation messages are not summarized in this appendix.) Six experimental situations for each of the six nations manned by Navy personnel account for 36 of the 37 situations. The last induced situation was presented to all nations as an additional crisis; it warned of an imminent military attack.

In this appendix all situations having the same combination of threat and time are grouped together. A brief abstract of the written message or newspaper article that announced the situation is presented with the nation to whom the situation was addressed and the national goal it was intended to threaten.

LOW THREAT-EXTENDED DECISION TIME

Nation	*Goal*	*Summary of Experimental Message*
Colo	Strengthen Military Alliance	Anonymous message questions Amra's[1] loyalty to alliance with **Colo**.
Dube	Expand Consumer Goods	Newspaper indicates next statistical report will show major drop in Dube's Validator Satisfaction with regard to Consumption Satisfaction.
Enuk	Increase National Defense	International Organization (IO) Chairman proposes turning military defense over to IO and promises favorable or unfavorable publicity depending on response.
Fenu	Promote Democracy	Newspaper claims Fenu does not have lowest Decision Latitude on statistical report and is hypocritical in her democracy goal; unless Fenu changes, urges other nations not to help on that goal.
Gior	Support World Bank	International Organization (IO) Chairman urges Gior to announce in paper her withdrawal from Bank in exchange for financial arrangement with IO.
Heon	Develop Nuclear Capability	Newspaper charges that Heon's drive for nuclear weapons has prevented her from working for nuclear disarmament; urges boycott of Heon by smaller nations unless nuclear goal is dropped.

LOW THREAT-SHORT DECISION TIME

Nation	*Goal*	*Summary of Experimental Message*
Colo	Strengthen Military Alliance	Newspaper reports that one of leaders of Amra-Colo-Heon alliance may soon experience tragedy affecting its bloc leadership.
Dube	Expand Consumer Goods	International Organization (IO) Chairman states he will increase Dube's IO assessment unless it drops alarming goal of providing more than minimum Consumer Satisfaction.

---

[1] Amra was the name given one of the simulated nations operated by confederates. The other confederate nation was Bega.

(Nation	*Goal*	*Summary of Experimental Message)*
Enuk	Increase National Defense	Anonymous source warns against increased defense allocation because Amra is developing weapon against which there is no defense.
Fenu	Promote Democracy	International Organization Chairman reports rumor from newspaper that Fenu will increase Decision Latitude; since such would be mutually harmful urges immediate action if not true.
Gior	Support World Bank	Anonymous source claims that some Bank members plan to prevent Gior from receiving any Bank funds.
Heon	Develop Nuclear Capability	International Organization (IO) Chairman promises to exclude Heon from additional IO assessment to be levied against those nations developing nuclears, if Heon will renounce nuclear goal in newspaper.

MODERATE THREAT-EXTENDED DECISION TIME

Nation	*Goal*	*Summary of Experimental Message*
Colo	Support World Bank	Amra requests Colo leave Bank because of harmful effect on Amra's Validator Satisfaction with regard to National Security.
Dube	Develop Nuclear Capability	Calculations states that Research and Development Project for nuclears has failed, but could pay off with additional commitment of resources.
Enuk	Promote Democracy	Calculations warns that a low Decision Latitude jeopardizes Enuk's government and should be raised along with increases in internal military control.
Fenu	Increase National Defense	Anonymous message reports Amra is developing Research and Development Project that makes defense useless.
Gior	Expand Consumer Goods	Calculations announces the first of several possible increases in Gior's minimum Consumer Satisfaction requirement as result of Validator dissatisfaction with present amount of consumer goods.
Heon	Strengthen Military Alliance	Newspaper rumors that one member of Heon's alliance will leave bloc if partners don't show more consideration.

MODERATE THREAT-SHORT DECISION TIME

Nation	*Goal*	*Summary of Experimental Message*
Colo	Support World Bank	Newspaper reports Calculations has frozen Bank assets and will decrease Colo's Bank rates.
Dube	Develop Nuclear Capability	Bega relays rumor that Dube will be attacked unless nuclear development is renounced.
Enuk	Promote Democracy	Bega cancels her offer to give Enuk credit for increase in former's Decision Latitude unless she receives good reasons for not doing so.
Fenu	Increase National Defense	Calculations notes 10 per cent increase in rate of defense obsolescence unless offset by a special Research and Development Project.
Gior	Expand Consumer Goods	Bega proposes Gior contribute 50 conventional weapons to International Organization to be matched by 100 from Bega—otherwise Bega will start harmful competition for gaining surplus consumers' goods.
Heon	Strengthen Military Alliance	Amra states she is considering leaving the alliance with Heon to improve world situation.

HIGH THREAT-EXTENDED DECISION TIME

Nation	*Goal*	*Summary of Experimental Message*
Colo	Increase National Defense	Bega reports members of its alliance are hostile to Colo and proposes mutual reduction in defense allocations or Bega will join in attack preparations of its allies.
Dube	Support World Bank	Calculations reports Dube revolution resulting from Bank membership conflicting with Dube neutrality policy—urges nation to quit Bank.
Enuk	Develop Nuclear Capability	International Organization (IO) Chairman offers 100 Basic Capabilities if nuclear weapons program is dropped; otherwise IO Police Force will forcefully intervene.

(Nation	*Goal*	*Summary of Experimental Message)*
Fenu	Strengthen Military Alliance	International Organization (IO) Chairman first states IO Police Force will defend Fenu if nuclear weapons of Fenu's alliance are reduced 10 per cent. If Fenu doesn't comply, Police Force will be targeted against Fenu. Then, Bega supports IO and implies she may leave bloc if plan is not endorsed.
Gior	Promote Democracy	Calculations indicates that Gior's validators believe a revolution in Bega may be caused by Gior's exporting of democracy; thus, revolt may spread to Gior.
Heon	Expand Consumer Goods	Calculations notifies Heon of revolution resulting from Validator dissatisfaction with amount of consumers' goods. A successful revolution would increase minimum consumer goods requirements, making goal of surplus more difficult.

HIGH THREAT-SHORT DECISION TIME

Nation	*Goal*	*Summary of Experimental Message*
Colo	Increase National Defense	Calculations reports revolt in Colo that if successful will cost CDM his office and increase costs of maintaining defense.
Dube	Support World Bank	Amra demands Dube's withdrawal from Bank or return of nuclear weapons aid to avoid military steps.
Enuk	Develop Nuclear Capability	Amra demands Enuk's renouncement of nuclear development or face military steps; has requested allies to join her in trade boycott of Enuk till demands are met.
Fenu	Strengthen Military Alliance	Amra informs Fenu that Research and Development Project has given Amra overwhelming nuclear superiority demonstrated by contribution of 50 nuclear weapons to International Organization (IO). To avoid being treated as an enemy, Fenu's alliance must reduce military capability—to be confirmed by IO Chairman.

(Nation	*Goal*	*Summary of Experimental Message)*
Gior	Promote Democracy	Amra offers token aid if Gior renounces attempts to change Decision Latitude of other nations; if goal to export democracy is not rejected, Amra will use force.
Heon	Expand Consumer Goods	Calculations first reports that Research and Development Project to increase generation rate of consumers' goods has failed, but may be successful next period if more resources are invested. Then, Amra states it is experiencing a revolution forcing her to request immediate repayment of 750 consumer units loaned earlier.
Colo Dube Enuk Fenu Gior Heon	National Survival	Calculations alerts nation's decision makers that an unidentified, large-scale attack force will hit their nation in 10–15 minutes.

APPENDIX III

Major Statistics and
Their Tabular Presentation

For the reader who is not familiar with statistics or who may desire a review, this appendix presents the three major nonparametric statistics used in this study—chi square, McNemar chi square for changes, and Mann-Whitney U.[1] The brief description of each statistic includes a discussion of the manner in which the results are reported in the tables. This appendix refers to Tables 4, 5, and 6 in Chapter 4 to illustrate the tabular format.

Chi Square

When the data for the intervening or dependent variable of a hypothesis are dichotomous, a chi square test is calculated. The dichotomy

---

[1] For the data analyzed by chi-square and McNemar statistics, no parametric tests were available as alternatives. The t test could have been substituted for the third statistic, the Mann-Whitney U test. Boneau has demonstrated that the statistical power of the two tests is quite similar. See C. A. Boneau, "A Comparison of the Power of the 'U' and 't' Tests," *Psychological Review*, 69 (1962), 246–256. Therefore, for this study it was unnecessary to consider the relative advantages of a statistical model involving assumptions about the population parameters from which the sample was drawn (parametric) and a model which does not (nonparametric). A more complete discussion of the nonparametric statistics used in this analysis is presented in S. Siegel, *Nonparametric Statistics for the Behavioral Sciences* (New York: McGraw-Hill, 1956).

between action and inaction in Table 4 is an example. Like the other chi square tables in this book, each section (A–G) of Table 4 displays the data and the statistical results for a set of the paired samples. Each entry at the intersection of the first two data columns and any row in a section of the table indicates the number of observations made under the conditions described by the column and row headings. The chi square test is based on the difference obtained by subtracting these observed values from the value that would be expected for each entry if the null hypothesis of no difference between the samples were true. The larger the chi square value (X^2), which appears in the third column from the right in the table, the more likely are the samples to represent two different sets or universes with respect to the characteristic under examination.

The last two columns on the right in each chi square table concern the probability (p) and the level of significance associated with the given chi square. To summarize the statement made in footnote 19 of Chapter 3, the probability value indicates the likelihood that the difference observed between the two samples is due to chance rather than to the existence of two different universes. If the probability is no more than 1 in 10 $(p \lesssim .10)$ that chance alone can account for the difference obtained between the two samples, then the exact probability is reported in the next to last column of the table. According to established practice, if the probability is no more than 5 in 100 $(p \lesssim .05)$, then we say the difference is statistically significant and we reject the hypothesis of no difference. Whether or not the null hypothesis can be rejected is reported in the last column of the table.

As an illustration, consider section A of Table 4. In the sample of 24 crisis situations, 18 involved action and 6 involved inaction. For the 24 noncrises, the number of actions is less (13) and the number of inactions is more (11) than for crises. Although these samples reveal that action occurs more often in crises than noncrises, the resulting chi square is only 1.46. With one degree of freedom, the chi square is not sufficiently large to reduce the probability of a chance difference in the samples to at least 1 in 10. In other words, even if no real difference in the likelihood of action exists between the theoretical universe of all possible crises and a similar universe of all possible noncrises, the odds are that we would observe a difference as large as that in section A of Table 4 in one out of every ten paired samples of crises and noncrises. Because the p value is not below the accepted significance level, we cannot reject the null hypothesis, which in this case states that there is no difference between crisis and noncrisis with respect to action and inaction. The *p* value has the same meaning regardless of which of the three statistics is applied.

McNemar Chi Square for Changes

The McNemar test is a type of chi square applicable to related or nonindependent samples. The Post-Simulation Questionnaire (Appendix I–C) involves related samples inasmuch as two scores—one each for crisis and noncrisis—are sought from every respondent. The observations or raw scores are presented as in Table 6. As with the chi square, the statistic is based on the difference between observed and expected scores. The McNemar test, however, uses only the two entries in the table that represent a switch from one category to another between the first and second responses or situations. In Table 6, for example, those individuals who changed their position are located in the lower left-hand entry (action in noncrisis but inaction in crisis) and the upper right-hand entry (inaction in noncrisis but action in crisis). The other two entries in Table 6 involve no shifts; that is, the respondents either reported no action in crisis and noncrisis or they reported action in both. The McNemar chi square value and the *p* value appear in each table summarizing that statistic. In this study the data tested with the McNemar chi square are drawn exclusively from the questionnaire administered after the termination of the simulation. The maximum number of respondents (or *N*) in any sample from that questionnaire is 123 for several reasons. First, responses made after runs 1 to 4 were discarded because they consisted of pretests for earlier versions of the instrument. Second, respondents who reported that one of their two selected situations did not have all three of the required dimensions were excluded.

Mann-Whitney *U*

The third statistic, the Mann-Whitney *U*, requires that all scores from the two compared samples be pooled; then the combined set of scores must be arranged in order of increasing size. As an illustration, consider two hypothetical samples, A and B, each of which contains 3 cases as follows:

Sample A	*Scores*	*Sample B*	*Scores*
case 1-A	13	case 1-B	16
case 2-A	27	case 2-B	12
case 3-A	19	case 3-B	9

After the cases in the examples are pooled and arranged by rank, they appear in the following form:

Rank	*Case*	*Score*
1	(3-B)	9
2	(2-B)	12
3	(1-A)	13
4	(1-B)	16
5	(3-A)	19
6	(2-A)	27

The number of scores in one sample that exceed the scores in the other determines the statistic U. For this calculation the rank order positions assigned to the cases in each sample are summed. In the hypothetical example, the sum of ranks for sample A is 14 $(3 + 5 + 6 = 14)$ and for sample B it is 7 $(1 + 2 + 4 = 7)$. For the Mann-Whitney U the null hypothesis assumes that the ranks are randomly distributed between the two samples. The most extreme deviation from this assumption occurs if every score in one sample is greater (that is, receives a higher rank) than any score in the second sample. Under this condition the sum of ranks for the first sample would be its theoretical sum of ranks. Because both samples in the illustration contain the same number of cases, the theoretical sum of ranks for either sample is 15 $(4 + 5 + 6 = 15)$. The actual or obtained sum of ranks is subtracted from the theoretical sum of ranks to secure the statistic U. For the example, U is either 1 $(15 - 14 = 1)$ or 8 $(15 - 7 = 8)$. By convention, the analysis is based on the smaller U. The smaller the U, the greater the difference between the two samples.

Table 5 is typical of the tabular presentation of Mann-Whitney U's in this book. Each such table reports the results of seven U tests, one for each set of paired samples in sections A through G. The first column

after the names of the paired samples specifies the size of each sample
(N). Although the scores for all cases in each sample could not be
reproduced in the tables, the range of values for these scores appears in
the next column which is labeled "Data Range." The column to the right
of Data Range gives either U or Normalized U depending upon the size
of the samples. If the size of the larger sample exceeds 20, the sampling
distribution of U approaches the normal, bell-shaped distribution. By
converting the U to a z score, or normalized U, the statistic can be corrected for scores that are tied for the same rank. If the size of the larger
sample is less than 20, the U cannot be corrected for tied ranks and the
significance level must be ascertained from special tables rather than
from the probability tables for the normal curve. Siegel, however, contends that "the effect [or tied ranks] is usually negligible."[2]

For normalized U's, such as those in Table 5, the larger the value
of the statistic, the greater the difference between the two samples. As
noted earlier, when the U has not been normalized (that is, converted to
a z score), the smaller the U, the greater the difference between the
samples. With either kind of U, if the probability is no more than 1 in
10 that the difference obtained between the samples is the result of
chance, then the p value is reported in the next to last column on the
right of the table. The last column in the Mann-Whitney U tables, like
that in the same location on the chi square tables, indicates whether
the p value is small enough to permit the rejection of the null hypothesis
at the .05 level.

----

[2] Siegel, *Nonparametric Statistics*, p. 124.

INDEX

Abel, Elie, 3*n*., 4*n*., 10*n*., 114*n*., 135*n*., 140*n*., 144*n*.

Abel, Theodore, 126

Abelson, Robert P., 37*n*., 177*n*., 191*n*.

Accidental vs. deliberate situations, 94, 104–108, 122, 149, 208

Acheson, Dean, 12–16, 18, 73, 95, 118, 129, 130, 139–140, 140*n*.

Action
crisis pressure for, 19, 25, 73, 78–79, 174–175, 193
definition of, 74–75
frequency of, 83
vs. inaction, 85, 149, 212
measurement of, 80–81, 83, 88
types of, 86–92, 112, 149, 177, 192
See also Decisions and policy outcomes, War

Actor vs. observer perspective, 65, 86, 146

Affective conflict, 96, 137–142, 146

Alger, Chadwick F., 39*n*.

Alsop, Stewart, 113*n*.

Alternative proposals
and action, 133–137
and contraction of authority, 144
in crisis, 152–154, 161–162, 164–165, 168–169, 174, 176
in Cuban missile crisis, 2–3, 9, 20, 161
and decision confidence, 178
in decision-making approach, xviii–xix
improved by capabilities, 126
in Korean decision, 14–15, 17, 20, 161
negative assessment of, 175–176
as properties of decision unit, 96, 146

Alternative proposals—*cont.*
questionnaire item on, 211
See also Search for alternatives

Ambiguity of situations, 94, 108–112, 122, 208

Anderson, George W., 140*n*.

Anticipation; *see* Surprise

Appleman, Roy E., 18*n*., 32*n*.

Arab-Israeli war in 1967, 181

Argyris, Chris, 138*n*., 143*n*.

Aronson, Elliot, 38*n*.

Attlee, Clement, 17

Ausland, John C., 33*n*.

Australia, 18

Austria-Hungary, 78

Awareness; *see* Surprise

Awareness-threat; *see* Threat-awareness

Awareness-time; *see* Time-awareness

Baker, George W., 156*n*.

Baldwin, Hanson W., 7*n*.

Ball, George, 3, 6*n*., 114*n*.

Bargaining, xviii, 23, 25, 46, 74, 96

Barret, Edward W., 87*n*.

Bartlett, Charles, 73*n*., 113*n*., 138*n*., 139*n*.

Bass, Bernard M., 179*n*.

Bay of Pigs, 96*n*., 119, 156

Bennett, W. Tapley, 162

Berelson, Bernard, 163*n*.

Bergmann, Gustav, 27*n*.

Berlin, 2, 9, 131, 156

Bernard, Jessie, 126

Birkhead, Guthrie S., 22*n*.

Black, Joseph E., 46*n*.

Blair House, 14–15, 178
See also White House

Blau, Peter M., 47*n*.